GROWN iN BRiTAiN COOKBOOK

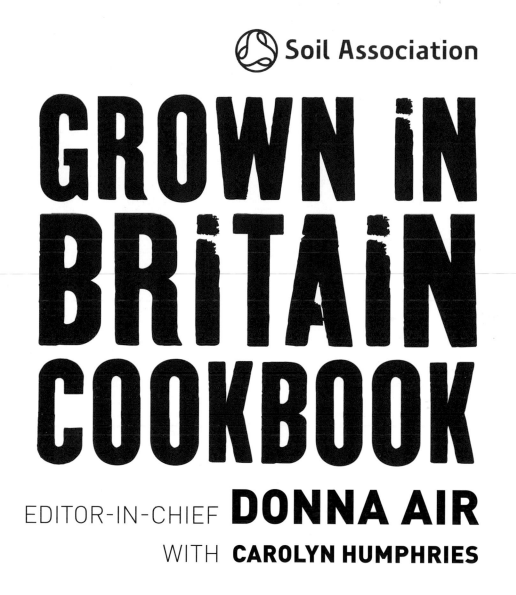

Soil Association

GROWN iN BRITAIN COOKBOOK

EDITOR-IN-CHIEF **DONNA AIR**

WITH **CAROLYN HUMPHRIES**

DK

LONDON, NEW YORK, MELBOURNE,
MUNICH, AND DELHI

Designer: Miranda Harvey
Photographers: Peter Anderson, Roger Dixon,
Cath Harries
Food photography: William Reavell
Editor: Helena Caldon

Project Editor: Laura Nickoll
Senior Art Editor: Elly King
Managing Art Editor: Christine Keilty
Managing Editor: Dawn Henderson
Senior Jacket Creative: Nicola Powling
Senior Production Editor: Jennifer Murray
Senior Production Controller: Mandy Inness
CTS: Sonia Charbonnier

First published in Great Britain in 2009
by Dorling Kindersley Limited
80 Strand, London WC2R 0RL

Penguin Group (UK)

Copyright © 2008 Dorling Kindersley Limited
This paperback edition published 2010
by Dorling Kindersley Limited

2 4 6 8 10 9 7 5 3 1

A CIP catalogue record for this book
is available from the British Library.

ISBN 978 1 4053 5429 5

Printed and bound in Singapore by
Tien Wah Press

Discover more at
www.dk.com

Soil Association
www.soilassociation.org

CONTENTS

FOREWORD BY DONNA AIR **6**

INTRODUCTION BY THE SOIL ASSOCIATION **8**

WHAT'S IN SEASON WHEN 10

VEGETABLES AND HERBS 46
Globe Artichokes 48; Asparagus 50; Aubergines 54; Carrots 58;
Other Roots 64; Cabbages 70; Leafy Greens 76; Flowering Greens 82;
Celery and Fennel 88; Beans 90; Peas 96; Squashes 102;
Onions and Leeks 108; Mushrooms 112; New Potatoes 116;
Maincrop Potatoes 122; Jerusalem Artichokes 128; Sweet Peppers 130;
Chillies 134; Marsh Samphire 138; Sweetcorn 140; Tomatoes 142;
Salad Leaves 148; Cucumbers and Radishes 156; Herbs 158

FRUIT, NUTS, AND HONEY 162
Apples 164; Berries 172; Stone Fruits 180; Currants 188;
Grapes and Figs 192; Pears, Quinces, and Medlars 196; Rhubarb 200;
Nuts 204; Honey 206

FISH AND SEAFOOD 208
Oily Fish 212; Cod Family 220; Flat Fish 226; Speciality Sea Fish 232;
Smoked Fish 238; Crustaceans 242; Molluscs 248

MEAT, POULTRY, AND GAME 254
Beef and Veal 256; Pork 262; Cured Meats and Sausages 270;
Lamb and Goat 276; Chicken 282; Turkey, Duck, and Goose 288;
Game Birds 294; Furred Game 300

CHEESE, DAIRY, AND EGGS 306
Hard Cheeses 310; Soft Cheeses 314; Blue Cheeses 318; Dairy 322;
Eggs 328

GRAIN 334

RESOURCES **344** INDEX **348** ACKNOWLEDGMENTS **352**

FOREWORD BY DONNA AIR

About eight years ago, before I became pregnant with my daughter, I found myself becoming more aware of the type of food I was eating, because I was so passionate about it – for a skinny Geordie lass, eating good food has always been one of my favourite pastimes. I exaggerate not when I say I used to, and still do, get very excited when I find a good goats' cheese, or a delicious olive oil. I began visiting farms and farmers' markets, talking to dedicated producers, and discovered the enormous benefits of introducing seasonal and local ingredients to my diet. This was the start of a journey of thinking about food, and the process it goes through before it hits our plates, in a whole new light.

It was then (pardon the pun) a very "organic" step when I was asked by the Soil Association to help with Organic Fortnight in 2006. As a spokesperson, drawing attention to their tireless campaigns, I have found my relationship with them, and the work they do on the ground, educational as well as truly inspiring. So I was thrilled to be asked to help with this very lovely cookbook.

Who has time to put smiley faces on our child's pizza every day? Or build vegetables into the leaning tower of Pisa? I want simplicity, ease, and goodness when feeding loved ones. My favourite "cheat" is to rely on most of the work being done before I even start cooking – seasonal and organic produce, locally grown, tastes better as well as having higher nutritional benefits. Buying food like this makes my job much easier, as it tends to need a lot less doing to it. I often spend no longer than 10 minutes making our family dinner, grilling some chicken or fish, mashing up some fresh peas and new potatoes to make a tasty vegetable dish, and serving it with a bowl of seasonal leaves. Let's be honest, a great piece of fish or meat will taste wonderful no matter who's cooking!

I also know that I am supporting my local community when I am buying seasonal and local food, and by supporting organic agriculture I'm putting less strain on the planet's energy system. By choosing and cooking food grown locally in harmony with nature and the seasons, I know I am making an important contribution to my family's health, and the health of others.

The *Grown in Britain Cookbook* is an excellent guide to what to buy, and when to buy it, and offers us all simple, friendly ideas on what to do with it. Let's all reconnect with our food, celebrate all things British, and enjoy the simplicity of coming together to share a delicious meal. Home is where the foundations and the very heart of what we do are laid. We all have power to do this; collectively we can make a big difference.

Donna Air is a keen supporter and advocate of the Soil Association. She was the face of Organic Fortnight 2006, and launched the Soil Association's report on nursery food in 2008 (see www.nurseryfood.org).

INTRODUCTION BY THE SOIL ASSOCIATION

Eating and sharing good food is life-enhancing. Cooking at home for friends and family, and feeling the sense of community that eating together brings, is one of the simplest yet most meaningful joys in life. The experience is even richer when a meal is based on food with a story – when you know where it has come from, and how it has been produced. Sourcing locally-grown produce, and getting to know the farmers selling at the local market or supporting your neighbourhood box-scheme can change your relationship with food completely. And eating food that has been produced and grown in balance with nature rather than against it, is not just about avoiding additives and pesticides for your own sake, it's good for the planet too.

That's why the Soil Association is delighted to be part of the *Grown in Britain Cookbook* – helping you source and cook good food in a more sustainable way. Although the Soil Association is perhaps best known in the UK for its certification of organic food, we are also a membership charity campaigning for planet-friendly food and farming. For over 60 years we have been promoting the links between healthy soil, healthy plants, healthy animals, healthy people, and a healthy planet. The diversity and quality of produce available in the UK are incredible. An enormous range of fruit and vegetables grow well here, some of our cheese is as good as it gets, the best of our meat and game is top class, and being an island nation means we're never far from fantastic seafood.

At the forefront of great British food are more than 4,000 Soil Association Certified organic producers. Their care for their land, livestock, and plants not only produces high-quality food; it is key to our future. Producing food with respect for nature through sustainable, organic methods is a practical response to the challenges of climate change and depletion of the earth's diminishing resources. As a consumer, changing the way you think about food — making the connection with local food producers, cooking more from scratch with fresh ingredients, and understanding the benefits of organic production — can help to safeguard the planet. This book shows you how.

Patrick Holden is Director of the Soil Association. To find out more about its work, and help build a food movement for change, go to www.soilassociation.org/joinus.

Patrick Holden

The British food calendar

Each of the following monthly lists tell you what's in season when, and what is at its best. The photographs are a selection of ingredients that are at their best.

The All Year Round list on pp10–11 features British produce you can enjoy throughout the year.

WHAT'S IN SEASON WHEN

ALL YEAR ROUND

These British ingredients can be found at the same quality year round. Others are also available all year but have a specific time when they are at their best, so they are included on the relevant monthly pages. Cheeses don't usually have "bests", but they are a good example of a food you should taste at different times and decide when in the year you prefer them; their flavour can vary according to the diet of the animals, which in turn alters the taste of the milk.

Mushrooms, cultivated p112

Bay leaves p158

Chicken, free-range p282

Pearl barley p338

Spelt p338

Salmon, organically farmed p212

Hard, soft, and blue
cheeses pp308–21

Crayfish p242

Eggs, free-range p328

Beef p256

WHAT'S IN SEASON

VEGETABLES AND SALAD
Cauliflower 82
Lettuce, round
    and curly 148
Mushrooms,
    cultivated 112
Salad cress 148
Spinach 76
Watercress 148

HERBS 158
Bay
Rosemary
Sage
Thyme

GRAINS 338
Barley
Oats
Rye
Spelt
Wheat

FISH AND SEAFOOD
Brown shrimp 242
Freshwater crayfish,
    farmed 242
Halibut, farmed 226
Herring 212
Mussels, farmed 248
Oysters, farmed rock
    (Pacific) 248
River trout: brown,
    rainbow,
    organically farmed
    212

Salmon, organically
    farmed 212
Scallops, king,
    farmed 248
Sea bass, organically
    farmed 232
Sea bream,
    organically farmed
    232
Sea trout, organically
    farmed 212

MEAT, POULTRY, AND GAME
Beef 256
Chicken,
    free-range 282
Duck, free-range 288
Goat 276
Guinea fowl,
    free-range 294
Pork 262
Veal, pink 256
Venison, different
    species wild,
    organically farmed,
    and
    free-range park
    300

CHEESE, DAIRY, AND EGGS
Cheeses 310–19
Eggs, free-range 328

JANUARY

January can feel a little flat after all the Christmas and New Year celebrations. It's the heart of winter: short days and long nights. But it's also the time for glorious British root vegetables, leeks, and celery – perfect for hearty soups and stews. Hare's good in that pot too, and you can still enjoy some fabulous game birds; with partridge making a change from the meaty festive birds. There's also plenty of fresh seafood, including monkfish and scallops, while plenty of apples and pears are available from store. Illustrated here are some of the best that January offers.

Celery p88

Chicory p148

salad cress p148

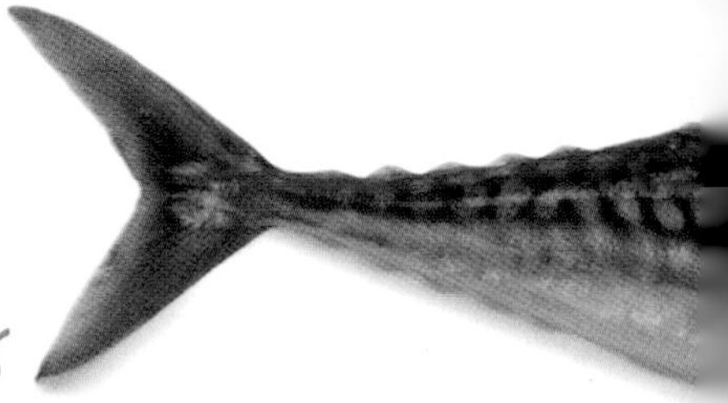

Chanterelle mushrooms p112

Leeks p108

Turnips p64

Scallops p248

Partridge p294

Dab p226

Mackerel p212

Hare p300

WHAT'S IN SEASON

at its best | available

VEGETABLES AND SALAD

Asian greens:
  mustard
  greens, pak choi 76
  mizuna, mibuna
  148
Beetroot 64
Brussels sprouts 70
Cabbages: red, white,
  green, Savoy 70
Carrots, maincrop 58
Cauliflower 82
Cavolo nero 76
Celeriac 64
Celery 88
Chanterelle
  mushrooms 112
Chicory 148
Jerusalem
  artichokes 128
Kale 76
Leeks 108
Lettuce, round 148
Onions 108
Parsnips 64
Potatoes, maincrop
  122
Purple sprouting
  broccoli 82
Radicchio 148
Rocket 148
Salad cress 148
Salsify 64
Shallots 108
Spinach 76
Swede 64
Swiss chard 76
Turnips 64

HERBS 158

Bay
Rosemary
Sage
Thyme

FRUIT AND NUTS

Apples: cooking and
  dessert 164
Pears 196
Walnuts, brown 204

FISH AND SEAFOOD

Brill 226
Clams 248
Cockles 248
Cod 220
Crabs: brown, spider
  242
Dab 226
Dover sole 226
Grey mullet 232
Haddock 220
John Dory 232
Langoustines 242
Lemon sole 226
Lobster 242
Mackerel 212
Monkfish 232
Mussels, wild 248
Oysters, native 248
Prawns, northern
  242
Razor clams 248
Red gurnard 232
Red mullet 232

River trout, wild:
  rainbow 212
Scallops, king 248
Sea bass, wild 232
Sea bream, wild 232
Turbot 226
Whelks 248
Whiting 220
Witch 226

POULTRY AND GAME

Duck, wild (Mallard)
  228
Goose, wild 228
Hare 300
Partridge 294
Pheasant 294
Turkey, free-range
  288
Woodcock 294

FEBRUARY

Apart from all the lovely roots, you can enjoy some
wonderful leafy greens such as cavolo nero, and cabbages and
spring greens. The first luscious pink stalks of forced rhubarb
appear, and an abundance of seafood from langoustines to
John Dory. All these are pictured here, but see the list for still
more to choose from in February.

Red mullet p232

Purple sprouting
broccoli p82

Cabbages: red, white,
green, Savoy p70

Rhubarb,
forced p200

John Dory p232

Cavolo nero p76

Langoustines p242

Spring greens p76

WHAT'S IN SEASON

at its best | available

VEGETABLES AND SALAD
Asian greens:
  mustard greens, pak choi 76
  mizuna, mibuna 148
Beetroot 64
Brussels sprouts 70
Cabbages: red, white, green, Savoy 70
Carrots, maincrop 58
Cavolo nero 76
Celeriac 64
Celery 88
Chicory 148
Jerusalem artichokes 128
Kale 76
Leeks 108
Lettuce, round 148
Onions 108
Parsnips 64
Potatoes, maincrop 122
Purple sprouting broccoli 82
Radicchio 148
Rocket 148
Salad cress 148
Salsify 64
Sea kale 76
Shallots 108
Spinach 76
Spring greens 76
Swede 64
Turnips 64
Watercress 148

HERBS 158
Bay
Rosemary
Sage
Thyme

FRUIT
Apples, cooking and dessert 164
Pears 196
Rhubarb, forced 200

FISH AND SEAFOOD
Brill 226
Clams 248
Cockles 248
Crabs: brown, spider 242
Dab 226
Dover sole 226
Grey mullet 232
Haddock 220
John Dory 232
Langoustines 242
Lemon sole 226
Lobster 242
Mackerel 212
Mussels, wild 248
Oysters, native 248
Prawns, northern 242
Razor clams 248
Red gurnard 232
Red mullet 232
River trout, wild: rainbow 212
Scallops, king 248
Sea bass, wild 232
Sea bream, wild 232
Turbot 226
Whelks 248
Whiting 220
Witch 226

POULTRY AND GAME
Rabbit, wild 300
Turkey, free-range 288
Wood pigeon 294

MARCH

This is the in-between season. Winter is nearly over, but spring hasn't quite sprung. However, there is still plenty to enjoy with sweet, early carrots and purple sprouting broccoli. Look out for tender young lettuces like lollo rosso, and chicory. There's still lots of seafood around, so you can enjoy such treats as turbot, sea bream, or a bowl of steaming mussels. We're showing a pick of the best here.

Green cabbage p70

Chives p158

Lollo rosso p148

Carrots, early p58

Nettles p76

Mussels p248

Crabs: brown, spider p242

Turbot p226

Whelks p248

sea bream, wild p232

WHAT'S IN SEASON

at its best | available

VEGETABLES AND SALAD
Asian greens:
  mustard greens,
  pak choi 76
  mizuna, mibuna 148
Cabbages, green 70
Cabbages: red, white,
  Savoy 70
Carrots, early 58
Cauliflower 82
Cavolo nero 76
Celeriac 64
Chicory 148
Dandelion 148
Jerusalem artichokes
  128
Kale 76
Leeks 108
Lettuce, round 148
Lollo rosso 148
Nettles 76
Onions 108
Parsnips 64
Potatoes, maincrop
  122
**Purple sprouting
  broccoli 82**
Radicchio 148
Rocket 148
Salad cress 148
Shallots 108
Sorrel 76
Spinach 76

Spring greens 76
Spring onions 108
Swede 64
Turnips 64
Watercress 148

HERBS 158
Bay
Chives
Marjoram
Mint
Oregano
Parsley
Rosemary
Sage
Thyme

FRUIT
Apples, cooking 164
Rhubarb, forced 200

FISH AND SEAFOOD
Clams 248
**Crabs: brown, spider
  242**
Dab 226
Dover sole 226
Grey mullet 232
John Dory 232
Langoustines 242
Lemon sole 226
Lobster 248
Mussels, wild 248

Oysters, native 248
**Prawns, northern
  242**
Razor clams 248
Red gurnard 232
Red mullet 232
**River trout, wild:
  rainbow 212**
Scallops, king 248
Sea bream, wild 232
Turbot 226
Whelks 248
Winkles 248

POULTRY AND GAME
Rabbit, wild 300
Turkey, free-range
  288
Wood pigeon 294

APRIL

Spring is just beginning. If you're lucky enough to find
morel mushrooms, make the most of them. Cauliflowers
are blooming, pea shoots, radishes, spring onions, and
dandelion leaves are all ready and waiting to turn into
delicious salads, perhaps with some potted brown
shrimps or a fresh lobster. We're showing
a pick of the best here.

Radishes p156

Pea shoots p96

Cauliflower p82

Dandelion leaves p148

Morel mushrooms p112

Rosemary p158

Thyme p158

Sage p158

Spring onions p108

Native oyster p248

Lobster p242

WHAT'S IN SEASON

at its best | available

VEGETABLES AND SALAD
Asian mustards: mizuna, mibuna 148
Asparagus 50
Cabbages: red, white, green 70
Carrots, early 58
Cauliflower 82
Chicory 148
Dandelion 148
Leeks 108
Lettuces: lollo rosso, oakleaf 148
Lettuces: round, Little Gem 148
Morel mushrooms 112
Nettles 76
Pea shoots 96
Potatoes, maincrop 122
Purple sprouting broccoli 82
Radishes 156
Rocket 148
Salad cress 148
Sorrel 76
Spinach 76
Spring greens 76
Spring onions 108
Turnips 64
Watercress 148

HERBS 158
Bay
Chives
Marjoram
Mint
Oregano
Parsley
Rosemary
Sage
Thyme

FRUIT
Apples, cooking 164
Rhubarb: forced, outdoor 200

FISH AND SEAFOOD
Brown shrimp 242
Clams 248
Grey mullet 232
John Dory 232
Langoustines 242
Lobster 242
Oysters, native 248
Plaice 226
Prawns, northern 242
Razor clams 248
Red gurnard 232
Red mullet 232
River trout, wild: brown, rainbow 212
Sea trout, wild 212
Whelks 248

POULTRY AND GAME
Rabbit, wild 300
Turkey, free-range 288
Wood pigeon 294

MAY

Spring is upon us with succulent asparagus, tender baby broad beans, and the first new potatoes, including majestic Jersey Royals. There's an abundance of fresh herbs and sweet green garlic and the first tender, juicy, delicate, home-reared lamb is available. Plaice would be a good choice for fish, lovely with a seasonal watercress sauce. Outdoor rhubarb is excellent, too. The small selection pictured here should whet your appetite.

Rocket p148

Asparagus p50

Broad beans p90

Borage p158

Watercress p148

New potatoes: first earlies p116

Lovage p158

Rhubarb, outdoor p200

Plaice p226

Mint p158

Lamb p276

WHAT'S IN SEASON

at its best | available

VEGETABLES AND SALAD
Asian mustards: mizuna, mibuna 148
Asparagus 50
Broad beans 90
Cabbages: red, white, green 70
Carrots, early 58
Carrots, maincrop 58
Cauliflower 82
Courgettes 102
Dandelion 148
French beans 90
Lettuces: lollo rosso, oakleaf 148
Lettuce, round 148
Morel mushrooms 112
Nettles 76
New potatoes: first earlies, speciality salad 116
Pea shoots 96
Potatoes, maincrop 122
Purple beans 90
Radishes 156
Rocket 148
Salad cress 148
Sorrel 76

Spinach 76
Spring onions 108
Turnips 64
Watercress 148

HERBS 158
Bay
Borage
Chervil
Chives
Coriander
Dill
Garlic
Lovage
Marjoram
Mint
Oregano
Parsley
Rosemary
Sage
Thyme

FRUIT
Cherries 180
Elderflowers 172
Rhubarb, outdoor 200
Strawberries 172

FISH AND SEAFOOD
Cod 220
Coley 220
Grey mullet 232
Haddock 220
John Dory 232
Langoustines 242
Lobster 242
Plaice 226
Pollack 220
Prawns, northern 242
Red gurnard 232
River trout, wild: brown, rainbow 212
Sea trout, wild 212
Whelks 248
Whiting 248

MEAT, POULTRY, AND GAME
Lamb 276
Rabbit, wild 300
Turkey, free-range 288
Wood pigeon 294

JUNE

Early summer and more and more produce will be available, including deep purple aubergines, nutty baby turnips, and plenty of salad leaves. Speciality salad potatoes are fabulous and strawberries will now be ripe and juicy. Delicate elderflowers will grace the hedgerows – the perfect flavouring for gooseberries (also at their best). Seek out British cherries, too, and squid and crabs will also make great eating. Illustrated here are some of the best June has to offer.

Aubergines p54

River trout, wild: brown, rainbow p212

Spinach p76

Lettuces: Batavia, Cos, frisée, Little Gem, iceberg, lollo rosso, oakleaf p148

Gooseberries p172

Crabs: brown, spider p242

Strawberries p172

Cherries p180

Elderflowers p172

WHAT'S IN SEASON

at its best | available

VEGETABLES AND SALAD
Asian mustards:
   mizuna, mibuna 148
Asparagus 50
Aubergines 54
Beetroot 64
Broad beans 90
Cabbages, white 70
Carrots, early 58
Carrots, maincrop 58
Cauliflower 82
**Chanterelle
   mushrooms 112**
Cucumbers 156
Globe artichokes 48
Lamb's lettuce 148
**Lettuces: Batavia,
   Cos, frisée, Little
   Gem, iceberg, lollo
   rosso, oakleaf 148**
Lettuces: round 148
Nettles 76
**New potatoes: first
   earlies, speciality
   salad 116**
Onions 108
Pea shoots 96
**Peas: garden,
   mangetout, sugar
   snaps 96**
Potatoes,
   maincrop 122
Purple (kidney) beans
   90
Radishes 156

Rocket 148
Salad cress 148
Sorrel 76
Spinach 76
Spring onions 108
Turnips 64
Turnips (baby) 64
Watercress 148
Waxpod (white) beans
   90

HERBS 158
Borage
Chervil
Coriander
Garlic
Marjoram
Mint
Oregano
Parsley
Rosemary
Sage
Tarragon
Thyme
Wild fennel

FRUIT, NUTS, AND HONEY
Cherries 180
Elderflowers 172
Gooseberries 172
Honey 206
**Rhubarb, outdoor
   200**
Strawberries 172
Walnuts, green 204

FISH AND SEAFOOD
Cod 220
Coley 220
**Crabs: brown, spider
   242**
Haddock 220
Langoustines 242
Lobster 242
Plaice 226
Pollack 220
**River trout, wild:
   brown, rainbow 212**
Sea bream, wild 232
Sea trout, wild 212
Squid 248
Whelks 248
Whiting 220

MEAT, POULTRY, AND GAME
Lamb 276
Rabbit, wild 300
Turkey, free-range
   288
Wood pigeon 294

JULY

Now you'll see an abundance of British fare, from regal globe artichokes, fennel, and kohl rabi, to courgettes and their flowers. The currant season is also under way, and blueberries, raspberries, and loganberries come into their own for some mouthwatering desserts. If they need a little sweetening, it's the heart of our honey season, too. Try the seaside specials – whelks and winkles – or grilled Cornish sardines for a summertime treat. Green walnuts will be ready for pickling this month too. These four pages of pictures show only a taster of what's on offer.

French beans p90

Courgette flowers p102

Courgettes (long and ball) p102

Peas: garden, mangetout, sugar snaps p96

Kohl rabi p70

Globe artichokes p48

Haddock *p220*

Cornish sardines *p212*

Whelks *p248*

Winkles *p248*

Redcurrants *p188*

Whitecurrants *p188*

Blackcurrants *p188*

Fennel *p88*

Basil *p158*

Loganberries *p172*

Blueberries *p172*

Blackberries
p172

samphire *p138*

Walnuts, green p204

Apricots p180

Honey p206

Raspberries p172

WHAT'S IN SEASON (JULY)

at its best | available

VEGETABLES AND SALAD
Asian mustards: mizuna, mibuna 148
Aubergines 54
Beetroot 64
Broad beans 90
Calabrese 82
Carrots, early 58
Carrots, maincrop 58
Cauliflower 82
Chanterelle mushrooms 112
Chillies 134
Courgettes (long and ball) 102
Courgette flowers 102
Cucumbers 156
Fennel 88
Flat helda beans 90
French beans 90
Globe artichokes 48
Kohl rabi 70
Lettuces: Batavia, Cos, frisée, Lamb's lettuce Little Gem, iceberg, lollo rosso, oakleaf 148
Lettuce, round 148
New potatoes, speciality salad 116
New potatoes, first earlies 116
Onions 108
Potatoes, maincrop 122
Patty pan squash 102
Peas: garden, mangetout, sugar snaps 96
Pea shoots 96
Purple (kidney) beans 90
Radishes 156
Rocket 148
Runner beans 90
Salad cress 148
Samphire 138
Sorrel 76
Spinach 76
Spring onions 108
Sweet peppers 130

Swiss chard 76
Turnips (baby) 64
Turnips 64
Tomatoes 142
Watercress 150
Waxpod (white) beans 90
Yellow crookneck squash 102

HERBS 158
Basil
Bay
Borage
Chervil
Chives
Coriander
Dill
Garlic
Marjoram
Mint
Oregano
Parsley
Rosemary
Sage
Tarragon
Thyme
Wild fennel

FRUIT, NUTS, AND HONEY
Apricots 180
Blackberries 172
Blackcurrants 188
Blueberries 172
Cherries 180
Gooseberries 172
Honey 206
Loganberries 172
Raspberries 172
Redcurrants 188
Rhubarb, outdoor 200
Strawberries 172
Walnuts, green 204
Whitecurrants 188

FISH AND SEAFOOD
Brown shrimp 242
Cod 220
Coley 220
Cornish sardines 212

Crabs: brown, spider 242
Dab 226
Dover sole 226
Haddock 220
Langoustines 242
Plaice 226
Pollack 220
River trout, wild: brown, rainbow 212
Sea bass, wild 232
Sea bream, wild 232
Sea trout, wild 212
Squid 248
Whelks 248
Whiting 248

MEAT, POULTRY, AND GAME
Lamb 276
Rabbit, wild 300
Turkey, free-range 288
Wood pigeon 294

AUGUST

Now you are spoilt for choice! Deep purple, golden, and stripy chioggia beetroot are still at their best, and all the salad vegetables are in season along with sweetcorn cobs, runner beans, and marrows. There are plenty of fresh fragrant herbs to enhance the more fully-flavoured British lamb that's available now. Look out for gnarled horseradish, too – great to flavour plump mackerel. Grouse appear from 12 August and green cobnuts and early apples are ripening, as are the plum family. Illustrated here are some of the best August has to offer.

Sweetcorn p140

Patty pan squash p102

Marrows p102

Batavia lettuce p148

Beetroot p64

Cucumbers p156

Potatoes, maincrop p122

Tomatoes *p142*

Coriander *p158*

Tarragon *p158*

Runner beans *p90*

Thyme *p158*

Chervil *p158*

Purple beans *p90*

Marjoram *p158*

Garlic *p158*

Grouse p294

Wood pigeon p294

Apples, dessert p164

Langoustines p242

Lamb p276

Rainbow trout p212

Whiting p220

32 WHAT'S IN SEASON WHEN

Plums p180

Damsons p180

Greengages p180

Cobnuts/hazelnuts
(green) p204

WHAT'S IN SEASON (AUGUST)

at its best | available

VEGETABLES AND SALAD
Asian mustards: mizuna, mibuna 148
Aubergine 54
Beetroot 64
Broad beans 90
Cabbages, green 70
Calabrese 82
Carrots, early 58
Carrots, maincrop 58
Chanterelle mushrooms 112
Chillies 134
Courgettes 102
Courgette flowers 102
Cucumbers 156
Fennel 88
Flat (helda) beans 90
French beans 90
Globe artichokes 48
Kohl rabi 70
Lamb's lettuce 148
Lettuces: Batavia, Cos, frisée, Little Gem, iceberg, lollo rosso, oakleaf 148
Lettuce, round 148
Marrows 102
Nettles 76
New potatoes, speciality salad 122
Onions 108
Patty pan squash 102
Pea shoots 96
Peas: garden, mangetout, sugar snaps 96
Peppers 130
Potatoes, maincrop 122
Purple (kidney) beans 90
Radishes 156
Rocket 148
Runner beans 90
Salad cress 148
Samphire 138
Sorrel 76
Spinach 76
Spring onions 108
Sweetcorn 140

Swiss chard 76
Tomatoes 142
Turnips 64
Waxpod (white) beans 90
Watercress 148
Yellow crookneck squash 38

HERBS 158
Basil
Bay
Borage
Chervil
Chives
Coriander
Dill
Garlic
Horseradish
Lovage
Mint
Marjoram
Oregano
Parsley
Rosemary
Sage
Tarragon
Thyme
Wild fennel

FRUIT, NUTS, AND HONEY
Apples, dessert 164
Apricots 180
Bilberries 172
Blackberries 172
Blackcurrants 188
Blueberries 172
Cobnuts/hazelnuts, green 204
Damsons 180
Elderberries 172
Figs 192
Gooseberries 172
Greengages 180
Honey 206
Loganberries 172
Plums 180
Raspberries 172
Redcurrants 188
Rhubarb, outdoors 200
Strawberries 172
Whitecurrants 188

FISH AND SEAFOOD
Cod 220
Coley 220
Crabs: brown, spider 242
Dab 226
Dover sole 226
Haddock 220
Langoustines 242
Mackerel 212
Monkfish 232
Plaice 226
Pollack 220
Red mullet 232
River trout, wild: brown, rainbow 212
Sea bass, wild 232
Sea bream, wild 232
Sea trout, wild 212
Squid 248
Whiting 220
Whelks 248

MEAT, POULTRY, AND GAME
Grouse (from 12th) 294
Hare 300
Lamb 276
Rabbit, wild 300
Turkey, free-range 288
Wood pigeon 294

SEPTEMBER

There are loads of winter squashes still around, Asian greens for salads and stir-fries, calabrese is still excellent, and the stunning romanesco appears. Colourful sweet and chilli peppers are at their best. Figs, grapes, apples, and pears are sweet and juicy, and you'll still be able to pick plump blackberries in the hedgerows, or buy the cultivated varieties, to go with them. You could also enjoy excellent venison, or wild goose by Michaelmas (29th September). We've illustrated a selection of the best of the month, to whet your appetite.

Pak choi p76

Asian greens p76

Swiss chard p76

Romanesco p82

Carrots p58

Calabrese p82

Ball courgette p102

Chillies p134

Oregano p158

Peppers p130

Parsley p158

Shallots p108

WHAT'S IN SEASON WHEN **35**

Duck, wild
(Mallard) p294

Grapes p192

Pears p196

Woodcock
(Scotland only)
p294

Dab p226

Dessert apples p164

Turbot p226

WHAT'S IN SEASON (SEPTEMBER)

at its best | available

VEGETABLES AND SALAD

Acorn, butternut, harlequin, and gem squashes 102
Asian greens: mustard greens, pak choi 76 mizuna, mibuna 148
Aubergines 54
Beetroot 64
Cabbages: green, Savoy 70
Calabrese 82
Carrots: early, maincrop 58
Celery 88
Chanterelle mushrooms 112
Chillies 134
Chinese leaf 148
Courgettes (long and ball) 102
Courgette flowers 102
Cucumbers 156
Fennel 88
French beans 90
Globe artichokes 48
Kale 76
Kohl rabi 70
Lamb's lettuce 148
Leeks 108
Lettuces: lollo rosso, oakleaf 148
Lettuces: Batavia, Cos, frisée, Little Gem, iceberg, round 148
Marrows 102
Nettles 76
New potatoes, speciality salad 116
Onions 108
Patty pan squash 102

Peas: garden, mangetout, sugar snaps 96
Peppers 130
Potatoes, maincrop 122
Pumpkins 102
Purple (kidney) beans 90
Radicchio 148
Radishes 156
Rocket 148
Romanesco 82
Runner beans 90
Salad cress 148
Shallots 108
Sorrel 76
Spinach 76
Spring onions 108
Sweetcorn 140
Swiss chard 76
Tomatoes 142
Turnips 64
Watercress 148
Waxpod (white) beans 90
Wild mushrooms (except morel) 112

HERBS 158

Basil
Borage
Chervil
Chives
Dill
Garlic
Lovage
Marjoram
Mint
Oregano
Parsley
Rosemary
Sage
Tarragon
Thyme
Wild fennel

FRUIT AND NUTS

Apples, dessert 164
Bilberries 172
Blackberries 172
Chestnuts 204
Cobnuts/hazelnuts, brown 204
Damsons 180
Elderberries 172
Figs 192
Grapes 192
Loganberries 172
Pears 196
Plums 180
Raspberries 172
Rhubarb, outdoors 200
Strawberries 172
Walnuts, brown 204

FISH AND SEAFOOD

Brown shrimp 242
Cockles 248
Cod 220
Coley 220
Cornish sardines 212
Crabs: brown, spider 242
Dab 226
Dover sole 226
Grey mullet 232
Haddock 220
John Dory 232
Mackerel 212
Monkfish 232
Mussels 248
Oysters, native 248
Plaice 226
Red mullet 232
River trout, wild: brown, rainbow 212
Sea bass, wild 232
Sea bream, wild 232
Sea trout, wild 212

Squid 248
Turbot 226
Whelks 248
Whiting 220

MEAT, POULTRY, AND GAME

Duck, wild (Mallard) 294
Goose: free-range, wild 288
Grouse 294
Hare 300
Lamb 276
Partridge 294
Rabbit, wild 300
Turkey, free-range 288
Woodcock (Scotland only) 294
Wood pigeon 294

Figs p192

Cod p220

OCTOBER

October's often the best month to go mushrooming in the early-morning dew – as long as you know what you're looking for. You might be lucky enough to find field mushrooms in your farmers' market. It is, of course, also the time for pumpkins and other winter squashes – delicious to eat in a number of ways, not just hollowing out for Halloween. Elderberries and sloes are ripe and ready for picking, and seek out quinces for jelly, cheese, or to add another dimension to the cooking apples available. There's plenty of game and fish, too, like dabs and sea bass. We're showing a pick of the best here.

Chinese leaf p148

Acorn, butternut, harlequin, and gem squashes p102

Kohl rabi p70

Celeriac p64

Rabbit, wild p300

Wood pigeon p294

Pumpkins p102

New potatoes, speciality salad p116

Field mushrooms p112

Turkey p288

Elderberries p172

Quinces p196

Apples, cooking
and dessert p164

Red mullet p232

sloes p180

WHAT'S IN SEASON (OCTOBER)

at its best | available

Walnuts, brown p204

Cobnuts/hazelnuts, brown p204

VEGETABLES AND SALAD

Acorn, butternut, harlequin, and gem squashes 102
Asian greens: mustard greens, pak choi 76 mizuna, mibuna 148
Aubergines 54
Beans: French, purple, runner 90
Beetroot 64
Cabbages: green, Savoy 70
Calabrese 82
Carrots, maincrop 58
Cavolo nero 76
Celeriac 64
Celery 88
Chanterelle mushrooms 112
Chicory 148
Chillies 134
Chinese leaf 148
Courgettes 102
Cucumbers 156
Fennel 88
Flat (helda) beans 90
Globe artichokes 48
Jerusalem artichokes 128
Kale 76
Kohl rabi 70
Lamb's lettuce 148
Leeks 108
Lettuce, round 148
Marrows 102
Nettles 76
New potatoes, speciality salad 116
Onions 108
Parsnips 64

Peas: garden, mangetout, sugar snaps 96
Peppers 130
Potatoes, maincrop 122
Pumpkins 102
Radicchio 148
Radishes 156
Rocket 148
Romanesco 82
Salad cress 148
Shallots 108
Sorrel 76
Spinach 76
Swede 64
Swiss chard 76
Tomatoes 142
Turnips 64
Watercress 148
Waxpod (white) beans 90
Wild mushrooms (except morel) 112

HERBS 158

Bay
Chervil
Chives
Coriander
Horseradish
Marjoram
Mint
Oregano
Parsley
Tarragon

FRUIT AND NUTS

Apples, cooking and dessert 164
Blackberries 172
Chestnuts 204

Cobnuts/hazelnuts, brown 204
Elderberries 172
Figs 192
Grapes 192
Pears 196
Quinces 196
Raspberries 172
Sloes 180
Walnuts, brown 204

FISH AND SEAFOOD

Brill 226
Clams 248
Cockles 248
Cod 220
Coley 220
Cornish sardines 212
Crabs: brown, spider 242
Dab 226
Dover sole 226
Grey mullet 232
Haddock 220
John Dory 232
Lemon sole 226
Lobster 242
Mackerel 212
Monkfish 232
Mussels 248
Oysters, native 248
Plaice 226
Pollack 220
Razor clams 248
Red gurnard 232
Red mullet 232
Scallops, king 248
Sea bass, wild 232
Sea bream 232
Sea trout, wild 212

Squid 248
Turbot 226
Whiting 220
Winkles 248

POULTRY AND GAME

Duck, wild (Mallard) 294
Goose: free-range, wild 288
Grouse 294
Hare 300
Partridge 294
Pheasant 294
Rabbit, wild 300
Turkey, free-range 288
Woodcock 294
Wood pigeon 294

sea bass, wild p232

NOVEMBER

We are into winter now. Celeriac and parsnips are plentiful;
try them, instead of potatoes, as chips – delicious teamed
with some fresh pollack in a crispy batter (a great alternative
to cod). You will love the sweet, tender Brussels tops and
the more robust kale. Oyster-flavoured salsify is great too.
There's lots of game, including wild duck (Mallard), and
you can treat yourself to loads of seafood. Northern prawns
are particularly good now. Pictured is just a small selection
of what November has to offer.

Mizuna p148

Jerusalem
artichokes p128

Cavolo nero p76

Kale p76

Parsnips p64

salsify p64

Brill p226

Prawns, northern p242

Pollack p220

Medlars p196

WHAT'S IN SEASON

at its best | available

VEGETABLES AND SALAD

Acorn, butternut, harlequin, and gem squashes 102
Asian greens: mustard greens, pak choi 76 mizuna, mibuna 148
Beetroot 64
Brussels sprouts 70
Brussels tops 70
Cabbages: red, white, green, Savoy 70
Calabrese 82
Cauliflower 82
Carrots, maincrop 58
Cavolo nero 76
Celeriac 64
Celery 88
Chanterelle mushrooms 112
Chicory 148
Chillies 134
Chinese leaf 148
Jerusalem artichokes 128
Kale 76
Kohl rabi 70
Lamb's lettuce 148
Leeks 108
Lettuce, round 148
Onions 108
Parsnips 64
Potatoes, maincrop 122
Pumpkins 102
Radicchio 148
Radishes 156
Rocket 148
Romanesco 82
Salad cress 148

Salsify 64
Shallots 108
Sorrel 76
Spinach 76
Swede 64
Swiss chard 76
Turnips 64
Watercress 148
Waxpod (white) beans 90
Wild mushrooms (except morel) 112

HERBS 158

Bay
Horseradish

FRUIT AND NUTS

Apples, cooking and dessert 164
Chestnuts 204
Medlars 196
Pears 196
Quinces 196
Sloes 180
Walnuts, brown 204

FISH AND SEAFOOD

Brill 226
Clams 248
Cockles 248
Cod 220
Coley 220
Cornish sardines 212
Crabs: brown, spider 242
Dab 226
Dover sole 226
Grey mullet 232
Haddock 220
John Dory 232
Lemon sole 226
Lobster 242
Mackerel 212
Monkfish 232
Mussels, wild 248

Oysters, native 248
Plaice 226
Pollack 220
Prawns, northern 242
Razor clams 248
Red gurnard 232
Red mullet 232
Scallops, king 248
Sea bass, wild 232
Sea bream, wild 232
Squid 248
Turbot 226
Whiting 220
Witch 226

POULTRY AND GAME

Duck, wild (Mallard) 294
Goose: free-range, wild 288
Grouse 294
Hare 300
Partridge 294
Pheasant 294
Rabbit, wild 300
Turkey, free-range 288
Woodcock 294
Wood pigeon 294

DECEMBER

It's the month for chestnuts roasting on the fire, baby Brussels sprouts, and puréed Jerusalem artichokes with a brace of pheasant. Turkeys and geese have been fattened for the festivities and there's plenty of seafood to enjoy, including indulgent native oysters, or a selection of fish for a seafood stew, such as red gurnard, clams, and coley. Pictured is a pick of the best.

Red cabbage p70

Brussels sprouts p70

Red gurnard p232

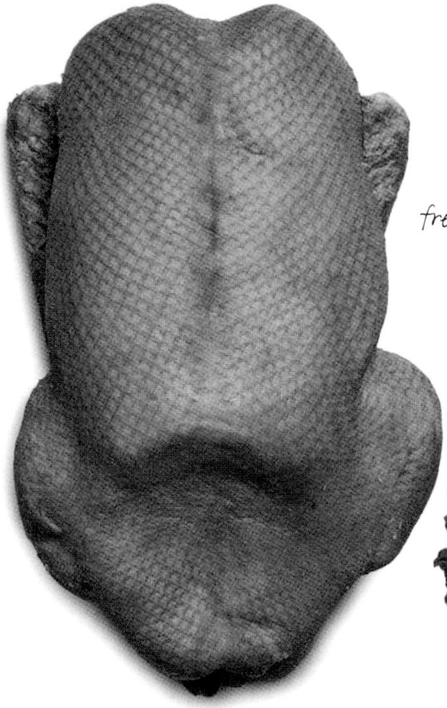

Goose, free-range p288

Savoy cabbage p70

Chestnuts p204

Pheasant p294

Oysters, native p248

WHAT'S IN SEASON

at its best | available

VEGETABLES AND SALAD

Acorn, butternut, harlequin, and gem squashes 102

Asian greens: mustard greens, pak choi 76 mizuna, mibuna 148

Beetroot 64

Brussels sprouts 70

Brussels tops 70

Cabbages: red, white, green, Savoy 70

Carrots, maincrop 58

Cauliflower 82

Cavolo nero 76

Celeriac 64

Celery 88

Chanterelle mushrooms 112

Chicory 148

Chinese leaf 148

Jerusalem artichokes 128

Kale 76

Leeks 108

Lettuce, round 148

Parsnips 64

Potatoes, maincrop 122

Radicchio 148

Radishes 156

Rocket 148

Salad cress 148

Salsify 64

Shallots 108

Spinach 76

Swede 64

Turnips 64

Watercress 148

HERBS 158

Bay

Horseradish

FRUIT AND NUTS

Apples, cooking and dessert 164

Chestnuts 204

Pears 196

Walnuts, brown 204

FISH AND SEAFOOD

Brill 226

Clams 248

Cockles 248

Cod 220

Coley 220

Crabs: brown, spider 242

Dab 226

Dover sole 226

Grey mullet 232

Haddock 220

John Dory 232

Langoustines 242

Lemon sole 226

Lobster 242

Mackerel 212

Monkfish 232

Mussels, wild 248

Oysters, native 248

Plaice 226

Pollack 220

Prawns, northern 242

Razor clams 248

Red gurnard 232

Red mullet 232

Scallops, king 248

Sea bass, wild 232

Sea bream 232

Turbot 226

Whiting 220

Witch 226

POULTRY AND GAME

Duck, wild (Mallard) 294

Goose: free-range, wild 288

Grouse (to 10 Dec, not NI) 294

Hare 300

Partridge 294

Pheasant 294

Rabbit, wild 300

Turkey, free-range 288

Woodcock 294

sea bream p232

VEGETABLES & HERBS

GLOBE ARTICHOKES

Globe artichokes are a type of thistle that came from North Africa, but varieties are now grown in many parts of the world, including the UK. Here, they are mostly cultivated in the south west. After cooking, the dusky green or purple flower buds have a succulent, fleshy base to each leaf, which when pulled off reveals a sweet, nutty-flavoured, tender heart. They are a labour of love, being fiddly to prepare and eat, but take your time over it and enjoy.

Don't cook in aluminium, copper, or iron pans or the artichokes will discolour.

Globe artichokes The fleshy-based leaves are pulled off to reveal the prize — a tender, creamy, slightly smoky-flavoured heart.

WHAT WHEN AND HOW

WHAT TYPES
Globe artichokes: The main flower head is at the top of the plant. They are popular with organic growers. Seek them out in farmers' markets and among small local sellers.
Baby artichokes: They are fully mature but picked from lower down the plant where they don't develop as much.
We aren't featuring cardoons here as they are a rarity. If you are lucky enough to find them, they look like huge heads of celery with spiky leaves but have the sweet, nutty flavour of artichoke. The growing stalks are blanched by being covered to exclude the light for about a month before harvesting. This tenderizes them and prevents bitterness. Best served boiled or braised.

WHEN IN SEASON
June–October (best July–September)

HOW TO CHOOSE AND STORE
Choose firm, tight heads that feel heavy and still have a short stalk attached. Avoid those that are opening or appear dried out, or have discoloured leaves. The larger the flower head, the larger the highly prized heart. Store in the chiller box in the fridge or in a cool, dark place for up to 5 days, but best eaten fresh.

Baby artichokes Can be quartered and eaten raw, or cooked. Brush with lemon juice, when cut, to prevent discolouration.

PERFECT PAIRINGS

MELTED BUTTER or **FRENCH DRESSING** as a dip for the succulent leaves and the fleshy heart.
FRESH PRAWNS, **CRAB**, or **LOBSTER** with artichoke hearts: prepare the artichokes as for eating (below), then cut the hearts in quarters and toss with French dressing and the seafood of your choice. Roast or chargrill the hearts in **OLIVE OIL**, then serve as part of an Italian antipasti or as a topping for pizza.

SIMPLE WAYS TO ENJOY

TO PREPARE

GLOBE ARTICHOKES
Twist off the stalk (the strings will come away with it). Pull off any damaged outer leaves at the base. Trim the base, if necessary, so it stands upright. Trim the tips off the leaves with scissors. Gently open up the leaves at the top. Pull off a cluster of tiny pale leaves inside (they should come away in one clump), scoop out the feathery choke underneath with a spoon, exposing the heart. If not cooking straight away, place upside down in a bowl of acidulated water (water with a tablespoon of lemon juice added) to prevent discolouration.

BABY ARTICHOKES
Cut off the stalk and about 1cm (½in) off the top. Halve, quarter, or slice. Put in acidulated water if not using immediately.

TO EAT GLOBE ARTICHOKES

Pull off one leaf at a time, dip the fleshy part into the butter, dressing, or sauce, then draw it between your teeth. Discard the leaf. When all the big leaves are eaten, trim off any hard base, then eat the heart with a knife and fork.

GLOBE ARTICHOKES WITH CHILLI AND PEPPER SALSA
Prepare and cook large artichokes. Drain well. Mix some chopped, skinned red pepper (see page 131) with a few chopped black olives, chopped capers, and some skinned, seeded, and chopped tomatoes. Flavour with fresh or crushed dried chilli and moisten with olive oil and lime juice. Season and add a pinch of sugar. Spoon into the cavities left by the chokes.

GRILLED BABY ARTICHOKES WITH GARLIC AND LEMON OLIVE OIL
Whisk some olive oil with a little lemon juice and finely grated zest, and a little crushed garlic. Season. Trim and quarter a few baby artichokes. Toss in some of the dressing. Place on foil on the grill rack. Grill, turning once or twice, until golden and tender. Serve drizzled with the remaining dressing.

ARTICHOKE HEARTS AND MUSHROOMS WITH SMOKED SALMON
Mix quartered, cooked artichoke hearts with some baby button mushrooms. Drizzle with olive oil, a good squeeze of lemon juice, some chopped thyme and seasoning to taste. Toss gently. Marinate for at least 30 minutes. Cut thin smoked salmon slices into strips. Wrap a strip round each piece of artichoke and mushroom. Secure with cocktail sticks. Serve with a bowl of mayonnaise to dip into. Also good made using canned artichoke hearts.

ASPARAGUS

British asparagus is among the finest in the world. The subtle flavour of its succulent stems is reminiscent of fragrant, freshly-cut grass. It is a true taste of summer and is in a class of its own. An expensive vegetable to buy because each spear is harvested by hand, it is well worth the indulgence. Asparagus thrives in rich, well-drained soil, and keeping the beds weeded organically is a labour of love. Some is grown in polytunnels to extend the short season, but connoisseurs say it isn't as good. Open buds mean spears have been forced to grow too quickly.

WHAT WHEN AND HOW

WHAT TYPES
Green asparagus: The main British crop with green stalks and purple heads. Look out for sprue – the thinning of the early crops – which is slim and tender and often cheaper.
White asparagus: Not so widely available in the UK. Grown in deep trenches under mulch to keep it in the dark and stop it from turning green, then cut when just the tips appear above ground.

WHEN IN SEASON
Late April/May–June (polytunnel crop in early April)

HOW TO CHOOSE AND STORE
Buy spears with plump, firm stems and tight buds. The stalks should snap crisply. Avoid if rubbery, shrivelled, or with woody, dirty stems, or if the buds are opening. It is often sold in bunches but is sometimes available loose, which is usually a cheaper way to buy it. Best eaten very fresh, but can be stored in the chiller box of the fridge for up to 3 days.

Green asparagus The spears are succulent almost right to the base. Thick stems may need a little trimming (see to prepare, opposite). Steam or boil, but particularly good roasted or griddled.

The stalks should be almost pure white.

White asparagus It is highly prized by some for its slightly sweeter, creamier flavour and texture. Best steamed or boiled and served cold.

PERFECT PAIRINGS

MELTED BUTTER, **OLIVE OIL**, **FRENCH DRESSING**, or **HOLLANDAISE SAUCE** (see page 330) can be drizzled over hot or cold spears. **EGGS**, soft-cooked and split so they gently trickle on to the cooked spears, or chopped hard-boiled, sprinkled over. Serve in omelettes and quiches too. **SMOKED SALMON** or **SMOKED HAM** or **BACON** (grilled), laid alongside or wrapped around small clusters of cooked spears. **LAMB** or **CHICKEN** served with the spears as a sauce, accompaniment, or stuffing,

SIMPLE WAYS TO ENJOY

TO PREPARE

Trim about 2.5cm (1in) off the base of the stems if they seem at all woody. The spears can be tied in bundles, if liked, then boiled upright in a deep pan. Cover it with a lid, or, if it's not deep enough to do this, make a loose tent with foil over the top to cover but not damage the tips (the traditional way of cooking, to help prevent the heads falling off). Thick stalks can be pared with a potato peeler, but it is usually not necessary.

Allow about 6 thick or 10 thin stems per person as a starter, 6–8 small tips or 3 heaped tablespoons of cut spears as an accompaniment.

ASPARAGUS WITH SOFT-COOKED QUAIL'S EGGS

Steam or boil green asparagus. Don't overcook or the tips will fall off. Drain, if necessary. Lightly boil 2 or 3 quail's eggs per person for 1 minute. Plunge in cold water. Carefully remove the shells. Lay the cooked asparagus on warm plates. Drizzle with melted butter. Put the eggs on top and gently split open so the yolk trickles out. Add a good grinding of black pepper.

COOL ASPARAGUS WITH GARLIC AND HERB MAYONNAISE

Steam or boil white or thick green asparagus. Flavour some mayonnaise with crushed garlic and chopped parsley and tarragon. Season to taste. Use as a dip.

GRIDDLED ASPARAGUS WITH OLIVE OIL AND SHEEP'S CHEESE

Cook oiled green spears in an even layer either in a preheated, electric griddle, or in a griddle pan, turning once, until tender and bright green. Arrange on plates. Drizzle with olive oil and balsamic vinegar or balsamic glaze. Sprinkle with a few grains of coarse sea salt and scatter flakes of freshly shaved hard sheep's cheese (or Parmesan) over.

ROAST ASPARAGUS AND TOMATOES

Cut the spears into short lengths. Toss with some whole cherry tomatoes and spring onions in olive oil in a roasting tin. Roast in a hot oven for about 20 minutes. Sprinkle with toasted sesame seeds and some seasoning. Drizzle with more olive oil, and serve with lemon wedges.

ASPARAGUS CREAM CHEESE QUICHE

SERVES 4–6 **PREPARATION TIME** 20 minutes, plus chilling **COOKING TIME** 45 minutes **VARIATION** Use the same weight of aubergines, peppers, or courgettes, to replace the asparagus. Try spinach; wilt it lightly first and squeeze out all the excess moisture. (You'll need about 350g/12oz fresh leaf spinach.)

1 Sift the flour and salt into a bowl. Add the fat and rub in with the fingertips until the mixture resembles fine breadcrumbs. Mix with 2 tbsp cold water to form a firm dough. Knead gently on a lightly floured surface. Roll out and use to line a 20cm (8in) flan ring set on a baking sheet. Chill for 30 minutes.

2 Preheat the oven to 200°C (400°F/Gas 6). Fill the pastry-lined flan ring with crumpled foil, or line with greaseproof paper and fill with baking beans. Bake for 10 minutes. Remove the foil, or paper and baking beans, and bake for a further 5 minutes to dry out. Remove from the oven. Lower the oven temperature to 180°C (350°F/Gas 4).

3 Toss the asparagus in a little olive oil. Cook on a hot griddle pan for 2 minutes each side until bright green and just tender.

4 Spread the cream cheese over the bottom of the pastry case. Sprinkle with the thyme, some pepper, and the Cheddar. Trim the asparagus spears to fit the flan, as necessary. Scatter the asparagus trimmings over the cheese and lay the whole spears attractively on top. Beat the eggs and cream together with a little salt and pepper. Pour into the flan. Bake in the oven until golden and set, about 30 minutes. Serve warm or cold.

INGREDIENTS
FOR THE PASTRY
175g (6oz) plain flour
A pinch of salt
45g (1½oz) cold lard, diced
45g (1½oz) cold butter, diced

FOR THE FILLING
175g (6oz) green asparagus
  spears
A little olive oil
115g (4oz) cream cheese
2 tsp chopped fresh thyme
Freshly ground black pepper
85g (3oz) mature Cheddar
  cheese, grated
2 eggs
150ml (5fl oz) single cream

AUBERGINES

Also known as eggplant (because one particular strain is the same size and creamy colour of a large, white hen's egg). The plants need warmth, so are grown in polytunnels or glasshouses in the UK. Centuries ago it was thought you would go mad if you ate aubergines, but, thankfully, Italian cooks in the Middle Ages decided they were a real treat worth eating, and so their fame grew. They are highly prized around the world and, when cooked, have a delicious, subtle, smoky flavour and a soft and creamy texture.

The flesh should be firm and shiny with no blemishes.

Aubergines The flesh acts like a sponge, soaking up any moisture and flavours mixed with it. Good fried, grilled, stuffed, or puréed.

WHAT WHEN AND HOW

WHAT TYPES
Worldwide there are many different varieties, from creamy white ovoids to pink stripy ones, and round types, all with a similar flavour. Here you will mostly find home-grown, large, purple ones and baby versions of the same.

WHEN IN SEASON
June–October

HOW TO CHOOSE AND STORE
Choose firm, shiny specimens that feel heavy for their size. The skin should spring back at once when pressed. Avoid any that feel soft, are wrinkled, or have brown patches – they will be bitter. The stalks should be fresh and green. Store in the chiller box in the fridge for up to 5 days.

Baby aubergines Perfect for using in curries and South-East Asian dishes. They have thinner skins than their larger relative, and a sweet, delicate flavour.

PERFECT PAIRINGS

Use **OLIVE OIL** when frying; they can be simmered with **TOMATOES**, **GARLIC**, and **ONIONS**, or use these as a filling for them. **SWEET SPICES** such as **CINNAMON**, **PAPRIKA**, **CUMIN**, and **CORIANDER** enhance their smoky flavour, but so does hot **CHILLI**. **LAMB** pairs really well, minced as a stuffing or layered for a moussaka, or grilled and served with aubergine chips (see below).

SIMPLE WAYS TO ENJOY

TO PREPARE

With most modern varieties it is not necessary to salt them to remove the bitter juices. Simply cut off the green stalk and calyx and slice or dice, or halve, scoop out the seeds, and stuff.

AUBERGINE WITH TOMATOES, BASIL, AND MELTED CHEESE

Brush a sliced aubergine with oil. Cook on a hot griddle pan until ribbed brown and soft on both sides. Place in individual gratin dishes. Cover each with a dollop of passata and torn fresh basil leaves. Season. Sprinkle with grated mild Cheddar. Grill until golden and the passata is heated through.

AUBERGINE CHIPS WITH MINTED YOGURT

Mix some thick plain yogurt with plenty of finely chopped fresh mint. Season. Chill. Cut aubergines into finger-width chips. Toss in a little plain flour, seasoned with salt, pepper, and a good pinch of ground cinnamon. Deep-fry until golden. Drain on kitchen paper. Serve hot with the yogurt.

AUBERGINE PÂTÉ

Boil a whole trimmed aubergine in a pan of water for 10 minutes until tender. Drain, then peel off the purple skin. Purée the flesh with the chopped white part of a couple of spring onions, and a few spoonfuls of fresh soft cheese to form a pâté. Flavour with a splash of lemon juice and olive oil. Season well. Finely chop the green part of the spring onions and stir in. Spoon into small pots. Chill. Serve with hot toast.

BABY AUBERGINE CURRY

Split some baby aubergines not quite right through. Fry a few black mustard seeds in oil until they pop. Add a chopped onion and chopped garlic clove, and fry to soften. Add some Madras curry paste, a can of chopped tomatoes, a seeded and chopped thin green chilli, and the aubergines. Cover. Simmer for 10 minutes. Remove the lid, then simmer until the aubergines are tender and oil floats on the top. Season. Stir in some chopped coriander.

GRIDDLED AUBERGINE AND BEAN SALAD WITH PESTO DRESSING

SERVES 4 **PREPARATION TIME** 20 minutes, plus soaking **COOKING TIME** 55 minutes **VARIATION** Use coriander in the pesto instead of the basil, or a bought organic red pesto, and if you haven't got time to soak and cook dried beans, use a can of rinsed organic beans. **SERVE WITH** crusty bread.

1 Drain the beans. Put in a pan with plenty of water, bring to the boil and boil rapidly for 10 minutes.

2 Reduce the heat, part-cover, and simmer gently for about 40 minutes or until tender.

3 Meanwhile, about 10–15 minutes before the beans are cooked, trim the aubergines and cut into 5mm (¼in) slices lengthways. Brush with olive oil. Cook on a hot griddle for 2–3 minutes each side until tender and striped. You may need to do this in batches.

4 Drain the beans and return to the pan. Drizzle with 2 tbsp olive oil, and add the garlic, some seasoning, and a little of the lemon juice, to taste. Add the tomatoes and spring onions and toss over a gentle heat for a couple of minutes to heat through.

5 Blend the pesto with 3 tbsp olive oil. Taste, and add a dash of lemon juice, if liked.

6 Mix the aubergine slices with the bean mixture. Spoon into bowls. Drizzle the pesto dressing over and scatter with the olives.

INGREDIENTS
115g (4oz) dried flageolet or
  pinto beans, soaked in
  cold water overnight
2 fairly small aubergines
Olive oil
1 garlic clove, crushed
Salt and freshly ground black
  pepper
1–2 tbsp lemon juice
115g (4oz) baby plum tomatoes,
  halved
2 spring onions, finely chopped
3 tbsp basil pesto (p161 or
  use bought)
A few black olives

CARROTS

Carrots thrive in open ground, covered with straw in winter to protect them from the frost. They've been eaten since time immemorial, but in the past they were thin, bitter, purple or red roots. It is said that Dutch growers cultivated the sweeter orange variety in honour of William of Orange, their king, in the 16th century. Now there are many different shapes and sizes, from freshly pulled, organic, new baby carrots, as crisp as apples and as sweet as honey, to large, mature, versatile maincrop ones. All of these varieties can be enjoyed in many different savoury and sweet dishes.

WHAT WHEN AND HOW

WHAT TYPES
Early: New young carrots through spring and summer. Look out for little finger ones and longer new-season ones (loose or bunched with green tops) and the short, baby, bullet-shaped chantenay (large ones are grown most of the year). You may even find some little round Parisian ones.
Maincrop: Larger, mature carrots pulled fresh in summer and autumn, but then stored for use throughout the winter. Purple and white (yellow) varieties are making a comeback; they look stunning, but they taste much like any other carrot.

WHEN IN SEASON
Early: March–September
Maincrop: September–February

HOW TO CHOOSE AND STORE
Choose dry, fresh-smelling carrots, preferably still with a bit of mud on them. Avoid any that are green at the stalk end (they aren't fully mature), or any that have been washed and left wet (or are wet from being over-chilled), or are split. If bunched, leaves should be a fresh, bright green – avoid if wilted or brown. Keep unwashed or bunched carrots (with the tops twisted off to stop them going limp) for up to 2 weeks in a bag in a cool, dark place. If they are washed, refrigerate for up to a week.

The more orange the colour, the sweeter they'll be.

Finger carrots Tiny new carrots with exceptional flavour. Scrub and eat raw, whole, with dips or lightly cook.

Chantenay Originated in France. Very sweet baby and large ones can be washed and cooked whole, but you may prefer to quarter large ones lengthways.

Recognizable cone shape.

Leaves should be bright green and fresh.

White (yellow) carrots
These are very sweet and juicy, but not widely available.

Bunched carrots Delicious, sweet, fragrant carrots for scrubbing and grating raw, or for lightly cooking.

Maincrop Large carrots in a variety of shapes with an excellent flavour, eaten fresh in summer, or stored.

Purple Use as other carrots; cook these with them for an unusual colour combination.

Purple outside, orange in centre.

PERFECT PAIRINGS

SWEET SPICES like cumin, coriander, nutmeg, cinnamon, ginger, and mixed spice enhance purées, soups, and cakes. **CORIANDER**, **PARSLEY**, or **CHIVES** sprinkled over cooked or grated carrots. **SWEDE**, **BEETROOT**, and **PARSNIP** grated, roasted or puréed with them. **ORANGE JUICE** and zest added when sautéing, or to soup. **HONEY** to add extra sweetness and a sticky glaze.

SIMPLE WAYS TO ENJOY

TO PREPARE

Organic carrots are not subjected to chemical pesticides, so just wash (or scrub if muddy) early varieties thoroughly. Peeling or scraping is necessary only for stored carrots that may have slightly bitter skins. Cut off green tops if bunched. Top and tail. Leave small carrots whole, cut large ones in chunks, matchsticks, or slices before cooking.

WARM CARROT AND MUSTARD SEED SALAD

Grate some carrots into a salad bowl. Heat enough olive oil to cover the base of a small frying pan. Add a shake of black mustard seeds. Fry until they pop. Add a squeeze of lemon juice. Stir, pour over salad, season, toss, and serve.

HONEY-GLAZED CARROTS

Boil or steam whole baby carrots until almost tender. Melt some butter in a frying pan. Add the carrots; toss for a few minutes. Drizzle with clear honey; toss until stickily glazed. Season. Garnish with chopped parsley.

ROASTED SPICED CARROTS

Cut some large carrots into fingers. Place in a roasting tin. Drizzle with olive oil, the zest and juice of an orange and a good pinch each of ground cumin, nutmeg, and ginger. Season. Toss well. Dot with tiny flakes of butter. Cover with foil. Roast at 190°C (375°F/Gas 5) until tender. Serve with a spoonful of thick plain yogurt on top and plenty of chopped coriander.

CARROT AND CUMIN SOUP

Soften some sliced carrots, a chopped onion, and chopped potato in a knob of butter, stirring. Add a little ground cumin, stir for 30 seconds. Cover well with vegetable stock. Add a bay leaf and a whole dried chilli (optional). Season and simmer until really tender. Discard the chilli. Purée. Thin with milk. Reheat. Garnish with snipped chives and chopped walnuts.

BABY CARROTS AND CUCUMBER WITH LENTIL AND OLIVE DIP

Boil some red lentils until pulpy. Drain, if necessary. Beat in a little tahini (sesame paste), crushed garlic, some plain yogurt, and chopped black olives. Season. Sharpen with lemon juice. Garnish with torn coriander leaves. Serve with scrubbed baby carrots and sticks of cucumber.

CARROT CAKE WITH SOFT CHEESE FROSTING

SERVES 12–14 **PREPARATION TIME** 30 minutes **COOKING TIME** 35–40 minutes **VARIATION** Try this with half carrots and half parsnips for an interesting twist. You can add a handful of chopped walnuts or some raisins to the mix for extra texture and flavour, too. It's also good plain, without the frosting.

1 Preheat the oven to 180°C (350°F/Gas 4). Grease two 20cm (8in), deep sandwich tins and line the bases with baking parchment.

2 Thinly pare the zest of half the orange, cut into thin strips and boil in water for 2 minutes. Drain and set aside. Finely grate the remaining zest and squeeze the juice.

3 Cream the butter and sugar together until light and fluffy. Add the eggs and the zest and juice of the orange and whisk in thoroughly. Add the remaining cake ingredients, except the carrots, and beat well with a wooden spoon. Fold in the carrots.

4 Spoon the mixture into the prepared tins and level the surface. Bake in the oven for about 35–40 minutes until risen, golden, and just firm to the touch. Cool slightly, then turn out on to a wire rack, remove the paper and leave to cool.

5 To make the frosting, mix the cheese with the orange zest and icing sugar. Add enough orange juice so the frosting forms soft peaks. Sandwich the cake together with half the frosting and spread the remainder over the top. Decorate with the reserved strips of orange zest.

INGREDIENTS
FOR THE CAKE
1 large orange
225g (8oz) butter, softened
225g (8oz) light soft brown sugar
4 large eggs
115g (4oz) wholemeal flour
85g (3oz) self-raising flour
2 tsp baking powder
1 tsp ground mixed spice
60g (2oz) ground almonds
2 large carrots, grated, about
  300g (10oz)

FOR THE FROSTING
225g (8oz) cream cheese
Grated zest and juice of ½ orange
75g (2½oz) icing sugar, sifted

CARROT AND BEETROOT SALAD WITH TOASTED SEEDS

ELISABETH WINKLER

Elisabeth is contributing editor of *Living Earth*, the Soil Association magazine, and blogs at realfoodlover. wordpress.com

SERVES 4–6 **PREPARATION TIME** 30 minutes **COOKING TIME** 3–4 minutes

This vividly-coloured salad is more than pretty; it's packed with antioxidants, too. Both carrots and beetroot have long UK seasons, but choose them hard and fresh for a salad.

1 Scrub the carrots and beetroot, and trim the tops and tails. Keep the carrots whole for easy grating. Peel the beetroot and cut in half.

2 Coarsely grate the raw vegetables and combine in a large bowl. Cover and store in the fridge for up to 24 hours, if not serving immediately, then remove and dress 1 hour before needed, to bring to room temperature.

3 For the vinaigrette, put the oil, vinegar, and garlic, if using, in a screw-top jar, put the lid on tightly and shake vigorously.

4 Gently heat the remaining teaspoon of olive oil in a small frying pan and toast the seeds for 3–4 minutes over a moderate heat, stirring frequently to prevent sticking. Add the soy sauce at the end of the cooking, if using. Most of the sauce will evaporate, leaving a salty taste and extra browning for the seeds. Store the toasted seeds in a jar with a lid if preparing the day before.

5 When ready to serve, add the chopped parsley or snipped cress to the grated carrot and beetroot. Shake the vinaigrette again, pour over the vegetables, then season to taste. Toss the salad gently until everything glistens. Scatter the toasted seeds over and serve.

INGREDIENTS
FOR THE SALAD
600g (1lb 5oz) carrots
1 bunch raw beetroot, about
  600g (1lb 5oz)
Small bunch of fresh parsley,
  when in season, chopped,
  or snipped salad cress

FOR THE VINAIGRETTE
6 tbsp olive oil, plus 1 tsp for
  toasting the seeds
50ml (2fl oz) balsamic vinegar
1 garlic clove, crushed (optional)
50g (1¾oz) sunflower or pumpkin
  seeds
1 tsp soy sauce (optional)
Salt and freshly ground
  black pepper

OTHER ROOTS

Here we celebrate the delicious swollen bases of plants – the casserole kings. They aren't, technically, all roots; some are stems or corms, but they all grow underground. Most of these are organically produced along the east coast and each has its own unmistakable, honeyed, earthy flavour. Baby turnips have a translucent flesh and a hint of mustard; salsify is reminiscent of oysters; creamy celeriac tastes more strongly of celery than celery stalks themselves. Local variation can be key: certain Cornish swedes, for example, are famed for their flavour, obtained from the area's soil.

Parsnip A creamy-textured root with cream-coloured flesh and a strong, sweet aroma and flavour. Particularly good roasted.

WHAT WHEN AND HOW

WHAT TYPES

Beetroot: Round roots with firm skin and red, golden, or pink-and-white-striped flesh.
Celeriac: Related to celery. The edible part is the swollen, gnarled corm of the plant.
Parsnip: Cream-coloured, carrot-shaped vegetable whose flavour improves with a touch of frost. Cook baby ones whole.
Salsify: Long root with white skin and flesh. Look out for the rarer scorzonera – similar, but with a brownish-black skin.
Swede: Traditional hardy winter vegetable with rough skin and orange flesh – known as "neeps" in Scotland.
Turnip: Sweet baby earlies and larger, winter ones with white and purple skins.

WHEN IN SEASON

Beetroot: June–February; **Celeriac:** September–March; **Parsnip:** October–March; **Salsify:** November–February; **Swede:** October–March; **Turnip:** Winter crop, all year; baby, June–July

HOW TO CHOOSE AND STORE

Choose roots that are heavy for their size but not too large: small means sweet. They should be firm and unblemished (celeriac looks gnarled where it has been trimmed but should not have damp brown patches). Avoid any shrivelled roots. Leaves should be fresh, not wilted. Store in a cool, dark place for up to a week.

Turnip Baby ones have a delicate flavour. Thinly peel and grate, or cook whole. Larger ones have a sweet, mustardy kick. Best used in small quantities in soups, stews, or casseroles, or mashed with carrots or potatoes.

Distinctive white and pinky-purple skin.

Swede A heavy vegetable with thick outer skin and sweet orangey-gold flesh. Delicious roasted, mashed, or in soups, stews, and casseroles.

Tough outer skin that needs peeling thickly.

Burpee's golden beetroot The flesh is a rich orangey-yellow and won't stain your fingers as much as the red. Use as red beetroot.

Red beetroot The richest flavour of all the beets. Enjoy grated raw, or cooked and served hot or cold. Also delicious pickled.

salsify Also known as oyster plant, as it is said to taste like oysters when cooked. Good in soups or grated in salads. Add a tablespoon of flour to the cooking water to retain its white colour.

Chioggia beetroot Looks prettiest raw in salads; it loses its stripes and goes white or pink when cooked.

Celeriac Tender, creamy-white flesh with a flavour of celery. It is delicious shredded raw, and when cooked it becomes soft and creamy-textured.

PERFECT PAIRINGS

BEETROOT The aniseed flavours of **DILL** or **CARAWAY**, sprinkled over cooked beets. **CELERIAC**, **SALSIFY**, **SWEDE** **BUTTER** and **BLACK PEPPER** in mashed roots. **PARSNIP** **BEEF** roasted with them, or slow-cooked in a casserole. **FOR ALL** **MAYONNAISE** thinned with a little sunflower oil and lemon juice for a dressed grated salad; **WALNUTS** chopped and scattered over cooked roots, or added to a salad.

SIMPLE WAYS TO ENJOY

TO PREPARE

BEETROOT
For red beetroot, wear rubber gloves. Scrub gently. If using raw, peel and grate. If cooking, cut off the leaves but don't cut through the skin. Leave the root intact or the beets will "bleed" into the cooking water and lose colour and flavour. Remove the skins after cooking. If roasting red beets with other roots, squashes, or potatoes, peel first but try to keep them separate from the rest in the tin whilst cooking or all may be stained red. The other two beetroots don't stain so much, but are still best prepared as above and cooked in their skins.

CELERIAC AND SALSIFY
Cut a slice off the top and root end. Peel thickly, cut into pieces, or grate for a salad, and plunge immediately into water with 1 tbsp lemon juice, to prevent browning.

SWEDE AND WINTER TURNIPS
Cut off the top and root end. Peel thickly; cut into chunks.

PARSNIPS AND BABY TURNIPS
Cut off the top and root end. Peel thinly. Cut large parsnips into thick wedges for roasting or slice or dice. Leave baby parsnips and turnips whole.

BEETROOT, TURNIP, AND CELERIAC SOUP
Peel and coarsely grate 1 or 2 beetroots, a turnip and ½ small celeriac. Place in a saucepan with a small grated onion. Cover with chicken or vegetable stock and a splash of red wine vinegar. Season. Simmer until tender. Taste and reseason. Serve hot or chilled, topped with a spoonful of soured cream or thick yogurt and a few caraway seeds.

PARSNIP OR SALSIFY CREAM
Peel and slice parsnips or salsify. Drop immediately into boiling water with 1 tsp lemon juice added and cook for 4 minutes until almost tender. Drain and place in a buttered ovenproof dish. Season well and add a good grating of nutmeg. Cover with single cream. Top with foil. Bake at 190°C (375°F/Gas 5) until tender. Remove the foil to brown the surface.

SWEDE, PARSNIP, AND CARROT SATAY
Part-cook some diced swede, parsnip, and carrot in boiling salted water for a few minutes. Drain. Thread on to soaked wooden skewers. Put on foil on a grill rack. Brush with melted butter, honey, and a little paprika. Grill until golden, turning and rebrushing once. Heat a few spoonfuls of whole-nut peanut butter with milk to form a thick dipping sauce. Flavour with chilli powder and chopped coriander. Serve with the satay sticks.

ROOT CHIPS OR CRISPS
Peel and cut into fingers or slice on a mandolin. Dry thoroughly. Deep-fry in hot oil until golden. Don't burn. Drain on kitchen paper. Season with salt.

CELERIAC AND SMOKED BACON SOUFFLÉ PIE

SERVES 4 **PREPARATION TIME** 40 minutes, plus chilling **COOKING TIME** 50 minutes **VARIATION** You can experiment with other roots, too: try parsnips or Jerusalem artichokes instead of celeriac, or substitute chopped walnuts for the bacon. A mixture of carrots and swede, or turnips, would be equally tasty. **SERVE WITH** a lightly dressed green salad.

1 Mix the flour and salt in a bowl. Add the caraway seeds. Rub in the butter until the mixture resembles breadcrumbs. Stir in the cheese. Mix 3 tbsp cold water with the egg yolk and stir into the flour mixture to form a firm dough, adding more water if necessary. Knead gently on a lightly floured surface, then wrap and chill for at least 30 minutes. Reserve the egg white for the filling.

2 Meanwhile, cook the celeriac in boiling, lightly salted water until tender. Drain and return to the pan. Dry out briefly over a gently heat. Mash with the butter and milk. Dry-fry the bacon until cooked but not crisp. Add to the celeriac with any fat in the pan. Beat in the egg yolks and snipped chives. Season well.

3 Preheat the oven to 200°C (400°F/Gas 6). Roll out the pastry and use to line a 20cm (8in) flan tin. Fill with crumpled foil or line with greaseproof paper and fill with baking beans. Bake in the oven for 10 minutes. Remove the foil or paper and beans and cook for a further 5 minutes to dry out. Remove from the oven.

4 Whisk all three egg whites until stiff. Add 1 tbsp of the whites to the celeriac mixture to slacken slightly. Fold in the remainder with a metal spoon. Spoon into the pastry case. Bake in the oven for about 25 minutes until risen, just set and golden. Serve hot.

INGREDIENTS
FOR THE PASTRY
175g (6oz) wholemeal or
    spelt flour
A good pinch of salt
1 tbsp caraway seeds
75g (2½oz) cold butter, diced
85g (3oz) farmhouse Cheddar
    cheese, grated
1 egg, separated

FOR THE FILLING
1 celeriac, about 450g (1lb),
    peeled and cut into chunks
60g (2oz) butter
4 tbsp milk
4 streaky bacon rashers, diced
2 eggs, separated
2 tbsp snipped fresh chives
Freshly ground black pepper

MIXED ROOT TEMPURA WITH DIPPING SAUCE

SERVES 4–6 **PREPARATION TIME** 25 minutes **COOKING TIME** 12–18 minutes **VARIATION** Use any mixture of root vegetables you like. We've added a few chunks of leek for colour, flavour, and texture. **SERVE WITH** garlic-flavoured mayonnaise, or sweet chilli dipping sauce, instead of the soy-ginger sauce.

1 Mix the dipping sauce ingredients together in a small saucepan. Heat gently, stirring, until the honey dissolves, then bring to the boil. Pour into a small bowl and leave to cool.

2 Blanch all the prepared vegetables in boiling water for 2 minutes. Drain and dry well on kitchen paper. Put in a large bowl. Sprinkle with the cornflour and toss to coat.

3 Whisk the batter ingredients together in a bowl until smooth (the mixture will be quite runny). Heat the oil for deep-frying until a cube of day-old bread browns in 30 seconds when dropped in. Dip about a sixth of the vegetables into the batter. Drain off any excess from each piece as you drop it into the oil – it should have only a thin coating. Fry for 2–3 minutes until tender, crisp, and golden, turning over as necessary. Drain on kitchen paper on a large baking sheet and keep warm whilst frying the remaining batches. Skim off any floating little pieces of batter between batches. Serve with the dipping sauce.

INGREDIENTS
FOR THE DIPPING SAUCE
3 tbsp clear honey
3 tbsp balsamic vinegar
1 tsp grated fresh root ginger
1 garlic clove, finely chopped
¼–½ tsp dried chilli flakes
3 tbsp soy sauce

FOR THE VEGETABLES
1 parsnip, cut into short fingers
½ small swede
½ small celeriac, cut into
  small chunks
1 large carrot, cut into
  short fingers
1 large leek, trimmed and
  cut into thick slices
2 tbsp cornflour
Oil, for deep-frying

FOR THE BATTER
85g (3oz) self-raising flour
85g (3oz) cornflour
200ml (7fl oz) sparkling
  mineral water
2 tsp sunflower oil
½ tsp salt
¾ tsp cumin seeds

CABBAGES

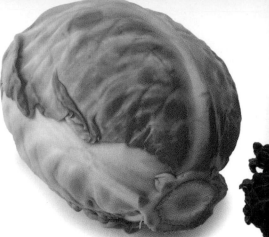

The image of soggy school-dinner cabbage has gone. Modern cabbage is fabulous, whether served simply cooked or as part of numerous dishes from soups to salads, main courses to pickles. Here we've stuck to the tight-headed varieties with firm hearts grown throughout the UK, plus kohl rabi – the cabbage turnip – and sweet, nutty Brussels sprouts and their tops. We've put other varieties elsewhere in this book: cavolo nero (black cabbage) is in Leafy Greens, and Chinese cabbage is with Salad Leaves. Apart from being brassicas, cabbages are known as cruciferous vegetables, because their flowers are shaped like a cross.

White Mild, sweet flavour and crunchy texture. It is delicious cooked, pickled, or in salads.

WHAT WHEN AND HOW

WHAT TYPES
Red: Hearty, deep purple, sold without outer leaves.
White: Tight, creamy–pale green. Sold trimmed.
Green: Winter varieties like bluey-green January King, bright green spring ones, like pointed hispi, (grown year-round and to fill the late spring gap) and round summer and autumn ones, like primo.
Savoy: Familiar crinkly-leaved ones, like Ormskirk.
Kohl rabi: The swollen, green (called white) and purple stem is the choicest part.
Brussels sprouts: Tight buds from the size of a thumbnail to a golf ball. They improve with frost – that's why they're good at Christmas!
Brussels tops: Small-leafed heads of the Brussels plant, an excellent second crop.

WHEN IN SEASON
Red: November–May (best December–February); **White:** November–June (best December–February); **Green:** August–May (best December–March); **Savoy:** September–February (best December–February); **Kohl rabi:** July–November; **Brussels sprouts:** November–March; **Brussels tops:** November–December

HOW TO CHOOSE AND STORE
All should feel firm and smell sweet. Avoid any with discoloured or wilting outer leaves. Choose kohl rabi no bigger than a cricket ball. Remove the leaves before storing. Store whole in a biodegradable plastic bag in the chiller box in the fridge: whole 2–3 weeks, sprouts 4–5 days, sprout tops 2 days.

Outer leaves should be fresh and firm.

Round green There are numerous varieties grown through the seasons. Good all-rounders.

Sold with or without the leaves.

Brussels sprouts Lightly steam or boil whole, or slice and stir-fry. Good for soup, too.

The smaller the sprout, the sweeter the taste.

The large
outer leaves
can be stuffed.

Savoy Familiar crinkly
leaves; good lightly
steamed, boiled,
or stir-fried.

Red Usually braised, pickled,
or marinated as a salad.
Turns bright red when
subjected to an acid like
vinegar, lemon juice, or wine.

If the outer leaves are
there, they should
have a good bloom.

Hispi Pointed green
cabbage with excellent
sweet flavour. Good
stir-fried or just
lightly steamed.

Purple kohl rabi
Purple variety of
green kohl rabi. Use
in the same way.

Green (white) kohl rabi The green, swollen
stem tastes like a cross between white
cabbage and turnip. Use as turnip in soups,
stews, or served in parsley or white sauce.

CABBAGES **71**

PERFECT PAIRINGS

RED and **WHITE** **APPLES** and **PEARS**, raw or cooked; **CARAWAY** and **FENNEL SEEDS** cooked with or to garnish; **RAISINS**, **SULTANAS**, or **CHOPPED APRICOTS** in salads and braises. **GREEN**, **SAVOY**, **SPROUTS**, **SPROUT TOPS**, and **KOHL RABI** **MELTED BUTTER**, or **OLIVE OIL**, and **FRESHLY GROUND BLACK PEPPER** to dress; **WALNUTS**, **HAZELNUTS**, or cooked **CHESTNUTS**, tossed in butter; **CELERY** braised with them in stock; **CURRY PASTE** stirred in when cooked. **FOR ALL** **PORK**, **BACON**, and **SAUSAGES** to accompany, or in soups and casseroles.

SIMPLE WAYS TO ENJOY

TO PREPARE

For how to cook cabbage perfectly as a plain vegetable, see Leafy Greens, p78.

RED, WHITE, GREEN, AND SAVOY CABBAGES
Remove any damaged outer leaves. Cut in half or quarters. Discard any thick central core and shred or cut into chunks.

BRUSSELS SPROUTS
Remove any damaged outer leaves, and trim the stalk end. If large, cut a cross in the base so they cook quickly and evenly.

BRUSSELS TOPS
Remove any thick stalks. No need to cut up.

KOHL RABI
Remove the leaves if necessary (you can cook them separately). Peel and cut into chunks.

BRUSSELS SPROUTS WITH VENISON SAUSAGE AND CHESTNUTS →

Boil or steam some Brussels sprouts until bright green and just tender. Drain, if necessary. Meanwhile, dry-fry pieces of venison sausages, turning until brown and cooked through. Remove from the pan. Add a good knob of butter and some cooked chestnuts (fresh or frozen). Toss until hot. Add to the sprouts with the sausages. Season. Toss. Garnish with chopped parsley. Serve on their own, or with Christmas turkey.

COLESLAW

Combine shredded red or white cabbage, a little grated onion and some grated carrot. Moisten with mayonnaise thinned with a little oil and vinegar. Mix again. Season with salt, pepper, and a pinch of sugar.

CABBAGE WITH CELERY

Chop some celery sticks, discarding any strings. Simmer in a little chicken or vegetable stock with a bay leaf until softened. Add some shredded cabbage or Brussels tops. Bring back to the boil, recover and cook until just tender but still with some "bite". Drain off any remaining liquid, discard the bay leaf. Season well with black pepper.

KOHL RABI WITH PEAS AND CAMEMBERT

Cook some diced kohl rabi (or turnips) in a little chicken or vegetable stock with a crushed garlic clove and some shelled peas. Cover and simmer until just tender. Drain if necessary. Add a good knob of butter, some chopped mint and a diced good wedge of Camembert. Stir gently until the cheese starts to melt, then serve straight away.

CRUNCHY VEGETABLE CRUMBLE

JEANETTE ORREY

Jeanette is School Meals Policy Advisor to the Soil Association, and author of *The Dinner Lady*. She won the *Observer* Food Award in 2003 for "Person who has done most for the food and drink industry".

SERVES 6 **PREPARATION TIME** 30 minutes **COOKING TIME** 45–50 minutes
With this recipe you can ring the changes by using whatever vegetables are in season, and the children will love helping you cook.

1 Preheat the oven to 200°C (400°F/Gas 6). Prepare the seasonal vegetables as appropriate, and cut into largish pieces. Put any root vegetables, including the onions and garlic, into a roasting tin, and mix with the oil. Roast for 15 minutes.

2 If using vegetables such as broccoli or cauliflower, blanch them in boiling water for a few minutes. Drain and set aside.

3 For the topping, put the flour into a large mixing bowl. Add the butter and rub in with the fingertips until the mixture resembles breadcrumbs. Add the oats and cheese, and combine.

4 To make the sauce, melt the butter in a pan, then add the flour and cook over a gentle heat until the mixture turns sandy in colour and texture. Gradually add the milk, beating all the time, and cook until the mixture thickens. Continue to cook for a further 5 minutes over a low heat, stirring occasionally.

5 Place all the vegetables on the bottom of a large, square, deep dish, then pour over the sauce. Finally, sprinkle over the topping. Cover with foil, and bake in the oven for about 15 minutes. Uncover, and bake for another 15–20 minutes or until the cheese topping is bubbling and golden.

INGREDIENTS
FOR THE FILLING
900g (2lb) seasonal vegetables
225g (8oz) onions, roughly
 chopped
1 garlic clove, crushed
1 tbsp olive oil

FOR THE TOPPING
60g (2oz) plain flour
30g (1oz) butter, diced
30g (1oz) rolled oats
60g (2oz) Cheddar
 cheese, grated

FOR THE WHITE SAUCE
45g (1½oz) butter
45g (1½oz) plain flour
750ml (1¼ pints) milk

WINTER CABBAGE SALAD

INGREDIENTS
FOR THE SALAD
½ small red cabbage,
  finely shredded
2 celery sticks, chopped
1 red and 1 green dessert
  apple, cored and diced
1 good handful of sultanas
1 good handful of walnut halves,
  roughly chopped
6 radishes, sliced

FOR THE DRESSING
½ tsp English mustard
Salt and freshly ground
  black pepper
6 tbsp double cream,
  lightly whipped
2 tbsp white wine vinegar
2 tsp light soft brown sugar

SERVES 6 **PREPARATION TIME** 15 minutes **VARIATION** The dressing can also be made with mayonnaise or crème fraîche instead of whipped cream. **TO SERVE** at a party, gently peel off a few outside leaves before you cut the cabbage in half and use them to line the serving bowl. They will look like petals around the edge.

1 Mix all the salad ingredients together in a bowl.

2 In another bowl, add the mustard and a little salt and pepper to the cream. Whisk in the vinegar to form a thick pouring consistency. Sweeten with the sugar.

3 Pour the dressing over the salad and toss. Pile into a serving bowl.

LEAFY GREENS

Some are indigenous, such as sorrel and kale, others have been brought here from abroad, such as Asian greens or Italian cavolo nero. They are widely cultivated organically except nettles, which grow everywhere. All have a sweetish flavour with varying hints of bitterness. Cook them quickly, in as little water as possible, to retain their goodness and colour.

WHAT WHEN AND HOW

WHAT TYPES
Asian greens: Green and red mustards, various pak choi – hybrid joi choi, bred for the UK climate; tat soi. (See Salad Leaves, p148.)
Cavolo nero: Tuscan black cabbage with greenish-black, coarse leaves.
Swiss chard: Also called seakale beet or silver beet. Shiny, green leaves; white, orange, or red stalks.
Spring greens: Fresh green cluster of "squeaky" leaves.
Kale: Coarse purple or green leaves with thickish, pale mid ribs.
Sorrel: Spear-shaped green leaves.
Spinach: True spinach, spinach beet, and New Zealand spinach.
Nettles: Young tips of the familiar weed.

WHEN IN SEASON
Asian greens, cavolo nero, and kale: September–March; **Swiss chard:** July–November; **Spring greens:** February–April; **Sorrel:** March–November; **Spinach:** All year; **Nettles:** March–October (best March–May)

HOW TO CHOOSE AND STORE
Choose firm stalks and fresh, green leaves. Avoid if yellowing or wilting. Tender leaves, like pak choi, bruise easily. Pick young nettle tips only. All are best eaten fresh. Kale becomes bitter if stored too long. If necessary, store greens unwashed in a biodegradable plastic bag in the chiller box in the fridge for 2–3 days.

small leaves are good in salads.

Yellow or orange swiss chard Good chopped in stir-fries. Like red chard, baby leaves are good in salads.

Red swiss chard sometimes called rhubarb chard, this tastes milder than white chard. Treat the same way.

White swiss chard Most common variety. The leaves and stalks can be cooked separately or chopped whole and cooked like greens. Thicker stalks are good cut in strips and steamed with melted butter.

use these leaves instead of spinach.

Spinach There are different types that ensure a year-round supply. They shrink a great deal when cooked, so use lots.

Sorrel Green, lemony-flavoured leaves that are treated like spinach. Throw small leaves in salads.

Mustard green-in-snow These leaves have a peppery flavour that gets hotter as they mature.

Cavolo nero The dark green, almost black, cabbage leaves have a rich, strong flavour.

Kale The tight curly leaves have an intense flavour.

Pak choi (bok choi) Fleshy, pale green, or white-stemmed plant; good raw, steamed, or stir-fried.

Spring greens Sweet, tender, and mild-tasting leaves.

Nettles Cook like spinach. They make an excellent tisane as well as a vegetable.

PERFECT PAIRINGS

ASIAN MUSTARD GREENS, **KALE**, **SPRING GREENS**, **CAVOLO NERO**, or **SWISS CHARD**
GARLIC and **SOY SAUCE** or **GINGER**, **CHILLIES**, and **CREAM** tossed through; thinly shredded and stir-fried with grilled **MEAT**, **CHICKEN**, or **FISH**; **BACON**, crisped and crumbled as a garnish, or boiled, with the greens thrown in towards the end of cooking. **SWISS CHARD**, **SORREL**, **NETTLES**, or **SPINACH** **POACHED EGGS**, or poached or grilled **SMOKED** or **OILY FISH**; **FOR ALL** **OLIVE OIL** or **MELTED BUTTER** with **TOASTED ALMONDS** or **PINE NUTS**.

SIMPLE WAYS TO ENJOY

TO PREPARE

Wash thoroughly to remove grit.

PAK CHOI
Trim the root end, then leave whole, if small, or shred.

MUSTARDS, CAVOLO NERO, KALE, SPRING GREENS, SWISS CHARD, SPINACH
Cut out the tough central stalks, then shred or cut the leaves into chunks, or leave whole.

NETTLES
Wear rubber gloves. Discard any tough stalks. Wash well. When cooked, they lose their sting.

HOW TO COOK PERFECT GREENS

ASIAN GREENS, KALE, SPRING GREENS, SWISS CHARD STALKS, CAVOLO NERO
Cook in a pan with 2.5cm (1in) boiling water, until just tender, pushing down well. Drain. Or steam for 3–8 minutes.

SWISS CHARD LEAVES, SORREL, NETTLES, SPINACH
Shake off water. Cook gently in a dry pan for 2–3 minutes, tossing the leaves, until just cooked. Drain, pressing the leaves to remove excess water.

WILTED GREENS WITH TOASTED SESAME SEEDS
Finely shred Asian greens, cavolo nero, kale, or spring greens. Put in a pan. Cover with boiling water. Bring back to the boil and cook for 1 minute. Drain. Drizzle with a little toasted sesame oil, and a little olive oil. Toss and add some toasted sesame seeds.

HOT OR CHILLED CREAMY GREEN SOUP
Gently fry a chopped onion and a large peeled and diced potato in a good knob of butter for 2 minutes without browning. Fill the pan with chard, sorrel (or half sorrel and half lettuce), nettles, or spinach. Add chicken or vegetable stock and some chopped fresh thyme. Part-cover and simmer until soft. Purée. Thin with milk and a little cream. Season to taste and add a pinch of grated nutmeg. Reheat or chill before serving.

SPINACH OR NETTLE AND GOAT'S CHEESE FRITTATA
Wilt some nettles or spinach. Drain thoroughly. Chop. Soften some chopped spring onions in a little olive oil in a large frying pan. Add the spinach or nettles. Toss. Add a chunk of soft goat's cheese, cut into small pieces, and a few torn basil leaves. Season. Pour over some beaten eggs. Cook gently until the base is set and golden, lifting and stirring the mixture gently. Brown the top under a hot grill. Serve cut into wedges with crusty bread.

CRISPY SEAWEED
Roll up any greens and very finely shred. Deep-fry in small batches in hot oil for 30 seconds until bright green and crispy. Drain on kitchen paper. Reheat the oil between each batch. Sprinkle with salt and a little Chinese five-spice powder. Toss.

WILD NETTLES AND SCRAMBLED EGG

PATRICK HOLDEN

Patrick is an organic farmer, and Director of the Soil Association.

SERVES 1 **PREPARATION TIME** 2 minutes **COOKING TIME** 5–6 minutes

Nettles are amazing. They are a classic wild food and grow somewhere near all of us. In nature they are a healing plant, and they heal us in the most delicious way, too, with their high iron and mineral content. Remember to wear gloves when picking nettles.

1 Place the washed nettle tips in a saucepan with a drop of water and the butter. Stir and cook for 1–2 minutes until the nettles have wilted. Simmer for another couple of minutes until they are soft and there is just a small amount of juice left.

2 Meanwhile, break the eggs into a pan and whisk in a splash of milk. Heat gently, stirring all the time, until they begin to scramble.

3 Just as the eggs start to solidify, take the pan off the heat. Mix in the cooked nettles, season to taste, and serve either on, or with, buttered wholegrain toast. This is ideal as a healthy breakfast or a light snack.

INGREDIENTS
About 20g (¾oz) nettle tips (to loosely fill 1 small colander)
Large knob of butter
2 eggs
A splash of milk
Salt and freshly ground black pepper

SPINACH, FRESH TOMATO, AND BLUE CHEESE PIZZA

SERVES 2–4 **PREPARATION TIME** 20 minutes, plus rising **COOKING TIME** 20 minutes **VARIATION** You can buy British mozzarella. Try using goat's cheese instead of blue, and try baking the pizza with a couple of eggs on top for the last 10 minutes. The sage gives a lovely warm flavour, but you could use some fresh basil scattered over at the last minute instead.

1 Mix the flour, salt, sugar, and yeast in a bowl. Mix with the water to form a soft but not sticky dough. Knead gently on a lightly floured surface for at least 5 minutes until smooth and elastic (or make in a processor or mixer with the dough hook). Cover and leave in a warm place until doubled in size, about 1 hour.

2 Meanwhile, put the tomatoes in a bowl and cover with boiling water. Leave for 30 seconds, drain, plunge in cold water, then remove the skins and chop the flesh. Mix with the tomato purée, sugar, and some salt and pepper. Shake the excess water from the spinach. Cook the spinach in a pan with no extra water for 3 minutes, stirring until wilted. Drain thoroughly. Leave to cool, then squeeze out the excess liquid.

3 Preheat the oven to 220°C (425°F/Gas 7). Put a large pizza pan or baking sheet in the oven to heat.

4 Knock back the dough. Reknead and roll out to a large round, about 30–35cm (12–14in) in diameter. Oil the hot pan or baking sheet and put the dough on it.

5 Spread the tomato mixture over the dough, not quite to the edges. Scatter the spinach and cheeses over. Sprinkle with the chopped sage. Drizzle with a little more olive oil. Season with freshly ground black pepper. Bake for about 20 minutes, until the dough is golden brown.

INGREDIENTS
FOR THE PIZZA DOUGH
225g (8oz) strong plain flour
½ tsp salt
¼ tsp caster sugar
1 tsp easy-blend dried yeast
150ml (5fl oz) warm water
1 tbsp olive oil, plus extra for
  greasing and drizzling

FOR THE TOPPING
4 ripe tomatoes
3 tbsp tomato purée
½ tsp caster sugar
Salt and freshly ground
  black pepper
225g (8oz) fresh spinach,
  well washed
100g (3½oz) blue cheese,
  crumbled
100g (3½oz) mozzarella
  cheese, grated
6 fresh sage leaves, chopped

FLOWERING GREENS

These beautiful and stunning vegetable flowers are wonderful to eat. They should be made the most of when they are in season. There are tight-headed, milky-white cauliflowers, or various coloured ones with a sweet, cabbage-like flavour which are mostly organically grown in Cornwall (where the climate suits), or the milder-tasting, sensational romanesco with its lime-green, intricately pointed head that resembles an ancient Japanese headdress. Or perhaps you favour purple sprouting broccoli or the dark green clusters of calabrese? Get to know them all, and how to enjoy them at their best.

WHAT WHEN AND HOW

WHAT TYPES
Cauliflower: Familiar white curds or, now, bright purple, orange, and green. Miniature ones are also available.
Romanesco: Similar to cauliflower, but less hardy and made up of a collection of lime-green, intricate, symmetrical points.
Calabrese: Italian sprouting broccoli; a cluster of small florets forming a tight, dark green head.
Sprouting broccoli: Purple is the more common; white is also available. The main stem sprouts numerous small flower heads, some in clusters, and tender young leaves. Great plants to grow as the more you cut, the more they sprout.

WHEN IN SEASON
Cauliflower: All year; **Romanesco:** September–November; **Calabrese:** July–November (best August–October); **Purple sprouting broccoli:** January–April (best February)

HOW TO CHOOSE AND STORE
Cauliflower and romanesco: Choose tight, firm heads and bright green leaves. Avoid if discoloured, have cut curds, or are bolting.
Calabrese: Select dark green, firm heads. Avoid if yellowing even slightly. As you pay by weight, choose with short stalks. Avoid if pliable.
Sprouting broccoli: The stems should be thin, firm and snap easily. Avoid thick, woody ones. If purple sprouting has tiny, yellow flowers, it is old. Store in the chiller box in the fridge for up to 4 days.

Purple cauliflower The tight, purple head is best cut into florets and steamed rather than boiled, to keep its colour.

Orange cauliflower Bright orange curds, just like white, green, or purple ones. Buy several colours and use a bit of each for a colourful accompaniment.

Purple sprouting broccoli
The main stem sprouts
numerous small flower
heads. Cook as calabrese
or asparagus. The heads
go green when cooked.

Choose a head with
a short stalk.

Calabrese The tight, green heads are
separated into small florets before
cooking. It can also be eaten raw.

Romanesco It looks stunning and
tastes like a delicately flavoured
cauliflower. It can be treated in
the same way.

Lime-green head has
symmetrical points.

Choose
unblemished
curds.

White cauliflower Tight,
white curds and dark green
leaves. Eat raw, steam, or boil whole or
separated into florets. Cook it lightly and
you will avoid any sulphurous smell.

PERFECT PAIRINGS

All different types of **CHEESE** are good in a sauce or just crumbled or grated and tossed with the cooked florets. **OLIVE OIL** and **TOASTED FLAKED ALMONDS** as a dressing. **TOMATOES** as a sauce, or whole cherry ones, stir-fried with the florets. **EGGS** blended with cream for an omelette or quiche, or chopped hard-boiled as a garnish with toasted buttered breadcrumbs. **CURRY PASTE** or **GARAM MASALA** in sauces or stir-fries.

SIMPLE WAYS TO ENJOY

TO PREPARE

CAULIFLOWER AND ROMANESCO
Remove any outer leaves and separate into small, even-sized florets (the green parts can be stripped off the stalks and cooked with the florets). Can be cooked whole. For dips and stir-fries, cut into tiny pieces. Use the stalks for flavouring soup or stock.

CALABRESE
Cut off the stalk. Peel this and cut into fingers to cook with the florets. Separate the head into small, even-sized florets. To serve with dips or for stir-fries, cut into tiny pieces.

SPROUTING BROCCOLI
Cut off the base of the stalks. Separate any multiple florets into single heads so that all are similar sized for even cooking.

SPAGHETTI WITH SPROUTING BROCCOLI AND CHILLI FLAKES →
Cook the spaghetti according to the packet instructions. Drain. Return to the pan. Cut some white or purple sprouting broccoli into tiny florets and chop the stalks. Stir-fry with a chopped bunch of spring onions in a generous amount of olive oil until just tender. Tip everything into the spaghetti. Add dried chilli flakes, seasoning, and a good squeeze of lime juice. Toss lightly over a gentle heat. Serve with grated hard sheep's or Parmesan cheese.

NO-EFFORT GRATIN WITH TOMATOES
Boil or steam broccoli, cauliflower, or romanesco florets until just tender but still a bright colour. Drain, if necessary. Place in a flameproof dish. Add some seeded and chopped tomatoes. Mix a carton of thick cream with a handful of strong Cheddar cheese, a little made English mustard and seasoning to taste. Spoon over. Sprinkle with extra grated cheese and grill under a moderate heat until piping hot and golden on top.

CAULIFLOWER OR CALABRESE WITH WHITE BEANS AND LEEKS
Steam or boil the florets until just tender. Fry a sliced leek, a crushed garlic clove and a chopped onion in olive oil until soft, not brown. Add a drained can of haricot beans, a can of chopped tomatoes, a few chopped sun-dried tomatoes and a few sliced stuffed olives. Simmer. Season. Stir in the florets and some chopped basil. Serve sprinkled with grated hard goat's cheese.

FLOWER SOUP
Fry a chopped onion in butter. Add some florets, a diced potato, seasoning and a bouquet garni. Cover with chicken or vegetable stock. Simmer until tender. Discard the bouquet garni. Purée. Thin with milk. Season again.

PICKLED CAULIFLOWER AND BABY ONION SALAD

SERVES 4–6 **PREPARATION TIME** 10 minutes, plus salting and marinating. Make a day or two in advance. **VARIATION** Try using lime-green romanesco instead of cauliflower, or top with some chopped hard-boiled eggs for added creaminess. **SERVE WITH** cold meats, smoked mackerel, or cheeses.

1 Put the cucumber and shallots or onions in a colander. Sprinkle with salt and leave for 30 minutes. Rinse thoroughly and pat dry. Put in a plastic container with a lid. Meanwhile, blanch the cauliflower for 2 minutes. Drain, rinse with cold water, and drain again. Add to the container with the chillies.

2 Put the vinegar, wine, oil, honey, spices, and bay leaf in a pan. Bring to the boil and simmer for 4 minutes. Pour over the vegetables and stir well. Cover, leave to cool, then chill overnight or for up to 48 hours. Give the container a shake from time to time.

3 When ready to serve, spoon into a dish using a slotted spoon.

INGREDIENTS
1 small cucumber, diced
12 shallots or baby onions,
  peeled and halved
Salt
1 small white cauliflower, cut
  into tiny florets
1 red and 1 green jalapeno chilli,
  seeded and sliced
8 tbsp white wine vinegar
150ml (5fl oz) dry white wine
5 tbsp olive oil
2 tbsp clear honey
1 tsp black peppercorns
1 tsp coriander seeds
1 tsp ground turmeric
1 bay leaf

CREAMY CALABRESE AND BLUE CHEESE PUFFS

SERVES 4 **PREPARATION TIME** 20 minutes **COOKING TIME** 35 minutes
SERVE WITH new potatoes and a tomato salad for lunch, or make smaller ones for a starter. They can be served cold, but are best eaten hot from the oven.

1 Cook the calabrese in boiling, lightly salted water for 2 minutes until almost tender. Drain, rinse with cold water, and drain again. Preheat the oven to 220°C (425°F/Gas 7).

2 Cut the pastry in quarters. Pile the calabrese at one end of each oblong, leaving a border. Add the cheese and crème fraîche. Season with pepper and a few grains of salt (the cheese is quite strong).

3 Brush the pastry edges with water. Fold over the uncovered halves of pastry, press edges together to seal, and transfer to a dampened baking sheet. Make a few slashes in the tops and glaze with crème fraîche. Bake for 30 minutes until puffy, crisp, and golden.

INGREDIENTS
175g (6oz) calabrese, cut into tiny florets
375g (13oz) sheet ready-rolled puff pastry (about 23 x 40cm/9 x 16in)
100g (3½oz) creamy blue cheese, crumbled
6 tbsp crème fraîche, plus extra for brushing
Salt and freshly ground black pepper

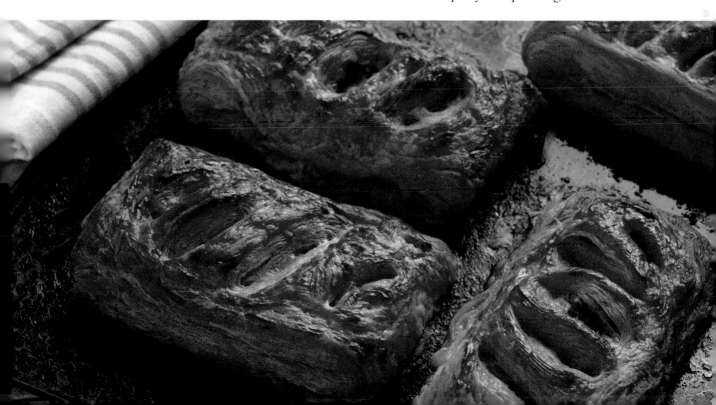

CELERY AND FENNEL

Celery has crisp juicy stalks, with a bitter hint and delicate leaves. It can be bright green or blanched white – if it is earthed up during growth to protect it against frost for a late harvest. Self-blanching varieties are also now available. White was highly prized as less bitter, but today green is often considered better for taste and texture. Fennel has short, fat stalks in a tight bulb with dark green, feathery fronds. It tastes of aniseed. It is mostly grown in the south, where conditions emulate its Mediterranean origins.

White celery More delicately flavoured than green, the outer stalks are best added to soups, stews, and casseroles; the hearts are more tender for eating raw, but can be braised.

Fresh green leaves: use for garnish.

Firm, white stalk

WHAT WHEN AND HOW

WHAT TYPES
Celery: Two types of the same plant. Green celery is grown naturally, with bright green stalks and leaves and a paler green heart. Blanched white celery has pale cream, thick outer stalks, a tender heart and yellow leaves.
Fennel: Commonly referred to as Florence fennel. Short, fat, white or pale green bulbs, made up of a series of stalks.

WHEN IN SEASON
Celery: September–February
Fennel: July–October

HOW TO CHOOSE AND STORE
Celery and fennel: Choose firm, tight, crisp heads with fresh-looking leaves/ fronds. Avoid ones with cracked or browning outer stalks. Store in a biodegradable plastic bag in the chiller box in the fridge for up to 2 weeks.

Green celery Crisp and fresh with a more pronounced flavour than white. As a rule, the deeper the colour, the stronger the flavour. Use as white celery.

Fennel Bulbs have a distinctive aniseed flavour. and can be enjoyed raw in salads, or braised, or roasted. Chop the fronds for garnish. Don't confuse with the herb, wild fennel, which does not form a bulb.

PERFECT PAIRINGS

CELERY CHEESES, either **CREAMY ONES** spread in the grooves of stems cut into short lengths, or serve long sticks of celery with a **CHEESE BOARD** at the end of a meal; **APPLES** and **WALNUTS**, chopped in a salad with chicken, cheese, or fish. **FENNEL SEAFOOD**, all kinds, but particularly **MUSSELS**, with a dash of Pernod in the sauce. **CELERY** and **FENNEL HARD CHEESES**, like Cheddar, as a sauce poured over, then glazed; **ORANGE SEGMENTS** in a salad with fish, chicken, or veal; **PUY LENTILS** and **ROOT VEGETABLES** in a braise.

SIMPLE WAYS TO ENJOY

TO PREPARE

CELERY
Cut off any browning root end. Pull the stalks off the root, then trim off the strings with a potato peeler. Chop or slice as required into soups, stews, stir-fries, or casseroles. The leaves can be chopped and used as a garnish or in salads. The heart can be separated into tender stalks for eating raw – there is no need to remove the strings – or it can be halved or quartered for braising.

FENNEL
No need to string. Trim off any browning root end, then slice, chop, or quarter the heads. Use the fronds chopped as a herb or for garnish.

ROASTED CELERY OR FENNEL WITH ORANGE AND WALNUTS
Quarter trimmed celery hearts or fennel bulbs. Put in a roasting tin. Add the finely grated zest and juice of an orange. Drizzle with a little olive oil and melted butter. Sprinkle with a spoonful of sugar and some chopped fresh thyme and chopped walnuts. Season well. Cover tightly with foil. Roast at 200°C (400°F/Gas 6) for 40 minutes. Remove the foil and brown for about 15 minutes until tender and glazed.

CELERY AND STILTON SOUP
Put a few chopped outer celery sticks, a couple of chopped potatoes and a chopped onion in a pan. Cover with hot chicken or vegetable stock. Simmer gently for 30 minutes until tender. Purée in a blender with diced Stilton (see p318) to taste. Strain through a sieve to remove any strings and return to the pan. Thin with milk, if necessary, and stir in a little single cream. Season to taste and serve garnished with snipped chives.

FENNEL AND PERNOD MAYONNAISE
Finely chop a head of fennel, reserving the green fronds. Mix with some mayonnaise and a splash of Pernod, and seasoning to taste. Spoon into a small serving bowl, chop the fronds and sprinkle over to garnish. Serve with grilled prawns, scallops, langoustines, turbot, or mackerel fillets.

BEANS

Some of the oldest known vegetables; clean-tasting with different subtleties of sweetness and fragrance. Beans are notoriously susceptible to pests, diseases, and rotting in wet weather, so yields can be variable – especially in rainy summers. Most are eaten pod and all, but broad beans, except when tiny, are shelled. If not picked to be used as a fresh vegetable, many types of bean are left to fatten until the swollen seeds are shelled and dried for legumes – a good source of vegetable protein.

WHAT WHEN AND HOW

WHAT TYPES
Broad: Pale green pods with a furry lining and swollen, nail-shaped beans.
Flat (helda): Long, stringless pods with underdeveloped beans inside.
French: Also known as green beans, these have small, stringless short pods, varying in thickness and shades of green.
Runner: Originated in South America; long, more swollen pods than flat beans; white or purple beans inside.
Purple (kidney): A heavy-podded, deep purple form of French bean with kidney-shaped beans inside.
Waxpod (white): Another French bean variety, also known as yellow wax beans.

WHEN IN SEASON
Broad: May–August; **Flat (helda):** June–October; **French:** June–October; **Purple (kidney):** May–October; **Runner:** July–October; **Waxpod (white):** June–November

HOW TO CHOOSE AND STORE
With broad beans, choose soft pods, evenly green with no black markings. The beans inside feel no bigger than your thumbnail. Fat, swollen beans will be tough-skinned and floury inside. For all other beans, the pods should snap cleanly when bent: if they are pliable, they are not fresh. Avoid any with brown patches or that are exceptionally large. Store all in the chiller box in the fridge for up to 3 days.

Runner beans Long, thin pods with a distinctive, sweet bean flavour.

The stringy edges need cutting off before slicing.

They have no stringy edges.

French beans All the pods have a distinctive flavour different from that of runner beans. Enjoy blanched in salads, steamed, boiled, or stir-fried.

Flat (helda) beans Taste like a cross between runner and French beans. Slice or cut into chunks.

Broad beans They should have soft pods and even-sized pale or green beans within.

Waxpod (white) beans Sweet, delicate flavour. They cook more quickly than green or purple varieties.

Purple (kidney) beans Plump pods with a good flavour. Best steamed or boiled.

FRENCH BEAN, GARLIC, AND TOMATO OMELETTE

SERVES 4 **PREPARATION TIME** 10 minutes **COOKING TIME** 20 minutes
VARIATION Top with fried or poached eggs instead of the omelette.
SERVE WITH grilled meat, fish, or chicken, using the filling on its own
as a saucy vegetable accompaniment.

1 Blanch the beans in boiling water for 3 minutes. Drain.

2 Heat the oil in a saucepan. Add the tomatoes and cook gently,
stirring, for 2 minutes until they start to soften. Add the wine,
tomato purée, garlic, sugar, and seasoning to taste. Bring to the
boil. Add the beans, reduce the heat, and simmer very gently
for 5 minutes, stirring occasionally, until the beans are just tender
and bathed in a thick sauce. Add the parsley and basil, taste, and
reseason. Cover with a lid and keep warm.

3 Beat 2 eggs at a time with a little salt and pepper. Add a dash of
cold water. Heat a little butter in an omelette pan until it foams.
Pour in the eggs. Cook over a moderate heat, lifting and stirring
until the base is set and golden, and the eggs are almost firm but
still slightly creamy.

4 Spoon a quarter of the tomato and bean mixture over one half
of the omelette. Tilt the pan over a warm plate. Flip the other
side of the omelette over the beans then slide out on to the plate.
Keep the omelette warm while you quickly make the others in
the same way.

INGREDIENTS
225g (8oz) thin French beans,
  topped and tailed
2 tbsp olive oil
2 tomatoes, roughly chopped
4 tbsp dry white wine or cider
1 tsp tomato purée
1 large garlic clove, finely
  chopped
A pinch of caster sugar
Salt and freshly ground
  black pepper
1 tbsp chopped fresh parsley
1 tbsp chopped fresh basil
8 eggs
A little butter

SUMMER PEA SOUP WITH MINT GREMOLATA

SERVES 6 **PREPARATION TIME** 10 minutes **COOKING TIME** 25 minutes
VARIATION This is lovely made with fresh peas, pods and all, but if time is short or they're not in season, you can use 450g (1lb) frozen ones. The gremolata adds a sophisticated touch and a lovely flavour, but you can omit it and serve the soup just with the swirl of single cream on top.

1 Soften the onion in the butter gently for 2 minutes, stirring. Add the remaining soup ingredients, apart from the cream. Bring to the boil, reduce the heat, part-cover, and simmer gently for 20 minutes until the peas and potato are really soft. Discard the mint.

2 Purée the soup in a blender or food processor. Pass through a sieve to remove the pod and pea skins. Taste and reseason, if necessary. Either reheat or chill.

3 Meanwhile, thoroughly mix together the gremolata ingredients. Ladle the soup into bowls. Add a swirl of cream and sprinkle with a little of the gremolata.

INGREDIENTS
FOR THE SOUP
1 onion, finely chopped
30g (1oz) butter
1 potato, roughly chopped
550g (1¼lb) peas in their pods, roughly cut up
1.2 litres (2 pints) chicken or vegetable stock
1 tsp caster sugar
A sprig of fresh mint
Salt and freshly ground black pepper
A little single cream, to serve

FOR THE GREMOLATA
2 tbsp finely chopped fresh flat-leaf parsley
2 tbsp finely chopped fresh mint
2 tsp finely grated lemon zest
1 garlic clove, very finely chopped

AN ORGANIC VEGETABLE BOX-SCHEME

NEIL MARSHALL, GROWING WITH GRACE

In the 1990s, Neil Marshall acquired 0.8 hectares (2 acres) of greenhouses at Clapham Nursery near Lancaster, on the edge of the Yorkshire Dales. At the same time as launching a vegetable-box scheme, he and some friends in the village set up a cooperative (an employee-owned business) that combined the need to be a successful business with an emphasis on social responsibility. They called it Growing with Grace.

Neil grows a wide range of produce, from salad and brassica crops, to roots, beans, and alliums. Their salad leaves have proved a bestseller. Growing up to 15 varieties of leaf salad at a time, Neil bags them up with plenty of watercress and sells them through the on-site shop and vegetable-box scheme. He often includes a few homegrown edible flowers, such as nasturtiums, to add a bit of colour.

The majority of produce is grown in greenhouses, sheltered from erratic British seasons, harsh frosts, and strong winds. This means Neil can stretch the season at both ends – enabling him to offer produce when conventionally farmed vegetables are no longer in season.

A strict five-year crop rotation plan means plants are not grown in the same bit of ground in a five-year period, which prevents the build-up of disease and weeds, and creates rich, fertile soil. After a busy spring sowing new plants, it's a matter of keeping up with the crops – harvesting and maintaining them – and holding weeds at bay. Compost acts as a mulch, playing an important part in weed control by stifling their growth. This compost comes from a sustainable composting scheme: the council delivers between 10 and 18 tons of local garden waste once a week, which Neil uses to return nutrients to the soil. Boxes of organic vegetables that have grown in this soil are then sold locally. "We sell vegetables to our community and get the green waste back from them to compost and use to grow their vegetables." Another innovative community venture is the on-site biodiesel plant. Volunteers make biodiesel from community waste vegetable oil, and then use it to run their delivery vans.

Growing with Grace has joined forces with local smallholders, so with more land to grow produce, and access to other selling points, they now grow everything from aubergines to chillies and garlic. Education also plays an important part in their business. Neil has created a "Forest Garden" in one of the greenhouses – a garden of exotic fruits such as peaches, almonds, and figs, and vegetables – which school groups are encouraged to visit for activity-based educational projects and discussions.

See p107 for Neil's *Traffic-light Risotto*.

OPPOSITE, ABOVE LEFT A stunning romanesco cauliflower.

ABOVE RIGHT Old tyres used to grow herbs and salad leaves.

BELOW LEFT The farm shop.

BELOW RIGHT Neil in one of his greenhouses.

SQUASHES

There are many varieties of squashes, from the small, tender courgettes and pretty little patty pans to the large, swollen butternuts, pumpkins and marrows. They are all grown organically throughout the UK and are a welcome addition to veg boxes in summer and winter. If you thought them watery and tasteless, think again. Courgettes simply sautéed with a sliver or two of garlic, or roasted butternut squash caramelizing at the edges, are sensational. They are such versatile ingredients: they can be used in soups, main courses and, even, desserts.

Green courgettes Traditional finger-shaped varieties. Can be eaten raw, steamed, boiled, griddled, fried, or stuffed and baked.

Courgette flowers The tender, golden flowers are either on a stalk (male) or attached to small courgettes (female). Stuff, or just dip in batter and fry.

Choose small ones for the best flavour.

WHAT WHEN AND HOW

WHAT TYPES
Summer squashes: Tender-skinned, immature squashes with creamy texture and undeveloped seeds. The most common are green and yellow long courgettes (zucchini) but also round ones like green eight ball, yellow one ball, yellow crookneck and patty pan (custard marrow). The flowers are edible.
Winter squashes: Hard-skinned, mature varieties with large seeds. (Included here is a good selection of pumpkins, marrows and colourful squashes.) Onion squashes, particularly Uchiki Kuri, are popularly grown here now.

WHEN IN SEASON
Courgettes: May–October (flowers May–September); **Patty pan, yellow crookneck squash:** July–September; **Butternut, acorn, harlequin, and gem squash:** September–December; **Marrow and spaghetti marrow:** August–October; **Pumpkin:** September–November

HOW TO CHOOSE AND STORE
Summer squashes: Choose small, firm, unblemished ones that feel heavy, with glossy skin. Avoid if shrivelling. Skin should pierce easily. Store in the chiller box in the fridge for up to 5 days.
Winter squashes: They should feel heavy and have hard, unblemished skin. If you can pierce the skin easily, it won't be sweet and ripe. Young, tender-skinned marrow has delicate flesh. If very large and hard-skinned, it can be fibrous. Store in a cool, dark place for up to 3 months. Do not chill.

Yellow courgettes Bright yellow skin. Sometimes slightly sweeter than green, but use in exactly the same way.

Eight ball courgettes Green and round, about the size of a tennis ball. Treat as you would long courgettes.

Yellow one ball courgettes Another colourful variety of round courgette. Good flavour.

Marrow An overgrown courgette with succulent flesh. Good sliced and stuffed, stuffed whole, roasted in chunks with butter, or steamed and served in a sauce.

Harlequin squash Cream and green, Sweet Dumpling variety, with high sugar content. Excellent roasted.

Spaghetti marrow Orange rugby ball best boiled whole, then split, the fibres scooped out in strands and topped with sauce.

Patty pan squash Pretty little squashes in different colours, with a slightly nutty taste. Good baked whole, or use as courgettes.

Gem squash Dark green, the size of a large cricket ball. Tastes very similar to acorn squash. Good stuffed or roasted.

Butternut squash Cream exterior and sweet, golden flesh. Halve and stuff, or peel, cut into chunks and steam, boil, roast, or purée.

Acorn squash Ridged skin, usually green but can be golden or white. Very sweet, orange flesh. Cook like butternut.

Bright yellow, bumpy skin.

Pumpkin Not just for carving for Halloween; the bright orange flesh can be cooked and puréed for soups or pumpkin pie. Also good roasted or steamed.

Yellow Crookneck squash Like a curved, swollen courgette, with sweet-tasting flesh that is more like winter squash.

Distinctive acorn shape.

Jack-be-little pumpkin These small pumpkins are best quartered, seeded, and roasted.

PERFECT PAIRINGS

MELTED BUTTER to dress cooked squashes. **POPPY SEEDS** sizzled in olive oil scattered over. **TOMATOES** and **ONIONS** as a sauce or stuffing. **GARLIC** to flavour when frying, roasting, or in stuffings. **SAUSAGEMEAT** as a stuffing. **NUTMEG**, **CUMIN**, and other sweet spices to flavour.

SIMPLE WAYS TO ENJOY

TO PREPARE

SUMMER SQUASHES
Top and tail, then halve, quarter, slice, or cut into fingers, as required. If stuffing, scoop out the seedy centre and use the pulp, chopped, as part of the stuffing.

WINTER SQUASHES
Halve or slice and remove the seeds. Peel thickly (except young marrows). Cut into chunks, if required.

SAUTÉED COURGETTES OR SUMMER SQUASHES WITH GARLIC →

Sauté sliced courgettes or summer squashes in olive oil with some crushed garlic. Toss and cook until golden on all sides. Grind black pepper over. Serve in the garlic oil, sprinkle with chopped parsley and coarse sea salt.

STUFFED COURGETTE FLOWERS

Mix chopped cooked spinach with chopped tomato and some soft goat's cheese. Season with grated nutmeg, salt and pepper. Spoon into courgette flowers. Dip the flowers in batter (p69); deep-fry, then drain on kitchen paper.

SPAGHETTI MARROW WITH FRESH TOMATO SAUCE

Pierce a spaghetti marrow twice. Boil in lightly salted water until tender. Make a quantity of fresh tomato sauce (p144). Drain the marrow. Cut in half, scoop out the seeds, and scrape the flesh into warm bowls. Spoon the sauce over. Sprinkle with grated hard goat's cheese or Parmesan.

RATATOUILLE

Soften a chopped red onion and garlic clove with some sliced summer squashes, peppers, and aubergine in a little olive oil, stirring. Add some skinned and chopped tomatoes, a little tomato purée and a splash of dry white wine. Season. Add a pinch of sugar. Cover, simmer gently, stirring occasionally, until tender. Add some chopped basil.

SIMPLE STUFFED WINTER SQUASH

Put thick, seeded marrow rings or halved smaller squashes in a baking tin with a little water in the base. Spoon in thick Bolognese sauce (p258). Smother with grated Cheddar cheese. Cover loosely with foil. Bake at 190°C (375°F/Gas 5) until tender. Remove the foil and allow to brown.

ROASTED GARLIC AND PUMPKIN HUMMUS

ALLEGRA MCEVEDY

Allegra is a chef, food writer, and co-founder of Leon, the healthy and ethical restaurant chain.

INGREDIENTS
FOR THE HUMMUS
400g (14oz) can chickpeas, drained
2½ tbsp lemon juice
1 garlic clove, finely chopped
1 tbsp tahini paste
5 tbsp extra virgin olive oil
1 tsp cayenne pepper
Salt and freshly ground
   black pepper

TO FINISH
850g (1lb 14oz) pumpkin, peeled,
   and cut into 5cm (2in) chunks
2 tbsp olive oil
¼ tsp cumin seeds
¼ tsp ground allspice
6 garlic cloves, peeled
½ red chilli, thinly sliced
A few pumpkin seeds
A little paprika

SERVES 4 **PREPARATION TIME** 15 minutes **COOKING TIME** 40 minutes.
This was a lovely idea of mine that didn't make our autumn menu. Try it on coarse bread sprinkled with a white, crumbly cheese, like Caerphilly or feta.

1 In a bowl combine all the hummus ingredients except seasoning, then purée in a food processor. Tip into the bowl, stir and season.

2 Preheat the oven to 180°C (350°F/Gas 4) with a roasting tin in. Put the pumpkin in a bowl with the oil, cumin, allspice, garlic cloves, chilli, and seasoning. Mix well to coat. Tip into the hot roasting tin.

3 Roast for about 40 minutes, giving it all a good stir once or twice during cooking. Take care with the garlic to make sure that it doesn't burn but just gets nicely caramelized, removing early if need be.

4 Purée the pumpkin and garlic in the processor, then fold into the hummus. Season to taste. Garnish with pumpkin seeds and paprika.

TRAFFIC-LIGHT RISOTTO

JO RHODES AT GROWING WITH GRACE

Neil Marshall is the founder of Growing with Grace, near Lancaster, a vegetable and fruit cooperative. See pp100–1.

SERVES 4–6 **PREPARATION TIME** 12 minutes **COOKING TIME** 30 minutes.
This is a fantastic, colourful dish that is very easy to prepare. Jo cooks it quite regularly for us at Growing with Grace to feed the hungry workers. It's quite filling, so will serve up to six people, depending on their appetites.

1 Cut the winter squash into 1cm (½in) cubes and discard the seeds and skin. Melt the butter in a large pan and fry the onions until transparent. Add the red pepper and squash and continue to cook for a further 2 minutes.

2 Add the rice and stir until the grains are coated in butter, then add the wine (if using), or a cup of stock, and stir. Add the fresh herbs and seasoning, and simmer until the wine (or stock) has evaporated.

3 Stir in 2 ladlefuls of stock and simmer until the liquid has evaporated again. Continue adding 2 ladlefuls of stock at a time and allowing it to evaporate until the rice is tender but al dente.

4 Add a further ladle of stock, the chopped spinach, and cherry tomatoes, and simmer for a further 2 minutes. Stir, taste, and reseason, if necessary. Serve the grated cheese separately, if using.

INGREDIENTS
675g (1½lb) any winter squash
75g (2½oz) butter
2 onions, chopped
2 red peppers, chopped
350g (12oz) arborio rice
Large glass white wine (optional)
Leaves from a large sprig of
  fresh thyme, chopped
8 fresh sage leaves,
  roughly chopped
Salt and freshly ground
  black pepper
1.2 litres (2 pints) hot vegetable
  stock
150g (5½oz) fresh spinach,
  chopped
8 cherry tomatoes, chopped
  into quarters
2 tbsp grated hard goat's cheese
  or Parmesan (optional)

ONIONS AND LEEKS

Onions are a fundamental ingredient for flavour and texture in cooking worldwide. They are one of the oldest vegetables and grow best in the cooler, dryer conditions in the east of Britain, giving them better keeping qualities. Leeks have been the national emblem of Wales since St David persuaded his men to wear one in their caps to distinguish them from the Saxon enemy in the Battle of Heathfield in 633AD. Organic varieties tend to be those most resistant to "rust" – a fungal disease. When cooked, both onions and leeks lose their pungency, taking on a sweet creaminess that is almost irresistible.

Spring onions Bunched, thin onions with green stalks. Use in salads, stir-fries, or chopped in savoury dishes.

Try using the white part in the dish and the green top chopped as a garnish.

WHAT WHEN AND HOW

WHAT TYPES
Bulb onions: Brown, white and red; baby (sometimes bunched) and standard-sized. Large, mild Spanish onions are also available.
Salad onions: Young onions on long, green stalks. Thin ones are called spring onions or scallions. Larger bulbs are often referred to as green onions.
Shallots: Members of the same family, like small mild onions; there are round ones and the long banana shallots. Many chefs prefer these to onions.
Leeks: Members of the onion family; numerous varieties available. Their white-and-green stems are actually leaf sheaths. Use baby leeks whole.

WHEN IN SEASON
Bulb onions: June–March (best June–September); **Salad onions:** March–September (best April–August); **Shallots:** September–March; **Leeks:** September–April (best September–February)

HOW TO CHOOSE AND STORE
Onions and shallots: Choose firm ones with dry outer skins. Avoid if wet, stained or smelling unpleasant. Store unwrapped in a vegetable rack in a cool, dark place. **Salad onions:** Buy crisp onions with firm stalks. Avoid if drying and brown on the outer skin or if the green tops are browning/yellowing. Store wrapped in a biodegradable plastic bag in the chiller box in the fridge for up to 5 days. **Leeks:** Need cool humidity, so store as salad onions, or wrapped in a cool, dark place.

Salad onions Larger than spring onions with a sweet, mild flavour. Good raw or cooked. Can also be trimmed and pickled.

Baby leeks Very sweet and tender. Excellent griddled, roasted, or steamed.

Known as poor man's asparagus.

Banana shallots Some say this is the classic shallot – griselle in French. Excellent, sweet, delicate flavour. Use as round shallots.

Round shallots sweet, mild, purple-tinged flesh. Best for finely chopping in any dish where you want a delicate flavour.

Red onions Red skin and layers right through the vegetable. Sweet, mild flavour; excellent for salads and roasting.

Brown onions Classic onions with gold to brown skins and a fairly strong flavour. Excellent all-rounders.

White onions Almost pure white flesh and sweet, mild flavour. Good for dishes where you don't want to fry them off first.

Spanish onions Large, sweet, mild, juicy onions, usually with straw-coloured skin but can be white or red. Excellent for frying and for eating raw.

Often gritty inside, so wash well before use.

Leeks Fat, sweet-tasting vegetable with a mild onion flavour. Use raw sliced, or chopped in salads, or sauté, roast, steam, or boil.

PERFECT PAIRINGS

CHEESES with pickled onions, in sauces, soups, dips, and relishes. **TOMATOES** fresh and sun-dried in sandwiches, salads, sauces, and soups. **SAGE** or **ROSEMARY** sprinkled over roasts and in stuffings, **BASIL** or **PARSLEY** before serving. **CHILLIES**, **LEMONGRASS**, **STAR ANISE**, or **CLOVES** and **GARLIC** in salsas, stir-fries, and curries. **GRILLED SAUSAGES**, **PORK CHOPS**, **STEAK**, or **OFFAL** with caramelized fried onions. **SORREL** in soup, salads, and a creamy sauce for fish or chicken. **LAMB** and **CHICKEN** with creamed onions or leeks.

SIMPLE WAYS TO ENJOY

TO PREPARE

ONIONS AND SHALLOTS

To chop: Peel off the skin, leaving the root intact. Cut in half. Put flat on a board. Make a series of cuts from the rounded end through to the root at intervals, then cut from the root to the rounded end downwards at intervals. Cut across the onion at intervals. Discard the root.
To cut into rings: Don't peel; slice thinly. Separate into rings, discarding the outer skin and first layer.

ONIONS AND SHALLOTS FOR PICKLING

Cover with boiling water and some salt, leave to stand until the water cools, then peel.

SPRING ONIONS

Trim the root end and tip. Discard any damaged outer layer. Cut into diagonal short lengths, or chop.

LEEKS

Trim the root end and top. For baby ones, leave whole. For large ones, make a slit down the centre of the leek through to the white part. Gently open under running water and rinse out any grit. Slice or chop.

ROASTED BABY LEEKS WITH SUN-DRIED TOMATO DRESSING →

Finely chop a couple of sun-dried tomatoes in oil. Mix with a little of the tomato oil, a little more olive oil, a splash of red wine vinegar, a few finely chopped black and green olives, and some chopped basil. Season. Blanch trimmed baby leeks in boiling water for 2 minutes. Drain well. Toss in a little olive oil in a roasting tin. Roast in the oven at 200°C (400°F/Gas 6) for 10 minutes until golden and tender. Spoon the dressing over to serve.

ONION SOUP WITH CHEESE AND MUSTARD CROÛTES

Gently fry quartered, sliced Spanish onions in a good knob of butter with a sprinkling of demerara sugar until soft and richly browned, stirring. Add beef stock, season, and simmer for 30 minutes. Taste, and reseason, if necessary. Toast slices of French bread. Spread with grainy mustard. Top with grated Cheddar. Grill until melting. Float on top of the soup to serve.

RED ONION BHAJIS

Mix 85g (3oz) plain or gram flour with ½ tsp salt, ¼ tsp ground turmeric, ¼ tsp garam masala and ½ tsp crushed dried chillies (optional). Blend in 120ml (4fl oz) tepid water. Add 2 chopped red onions. Fry spoonfuls in hot oil until golden. Drain on kitchen paper.

READY-IN-A-MONTH PICKLES

Prepare pickling onions or shallots. Pack in clean pickling jars. Add a bay leaf and dried chilli (optional) to each jar. Cover with cold pickling vinegar. Screw on the lids, and store in a cool, dark place for at least 1 month.

MUSHROOMS

On a dewy, autumnal morning, you may have experienced the thrill of coming across field mushrooms nestling in a meadow and, if you've cooked them, the mouthwatering magic of eating them. Make sure you know what you're doing if you go foraging, or seek them out in farmers' markets, supermarkets (or online). Local conditions favour different species. Scotland, for instance, has an abundance of chanterelles; Wales and Ireland have more ceps, and Kent is particularly good for horse mushrooms. There is also a variety of organic and carefully cultivated ones available, from common white and brown, to more exotic types.

WHAT WHEN AND HOW

WHAT TYPES
Cultivated: A small percentage is certified organic but all are grown in similar strict conditions. There are white mushrooms (button, cup, open cup, and large flat); brown (crimini, chestnut, breakfast, and portabello or "field"); fan-shaped, coloured oysters; fat-stemmed wood blewits; and Japanese, brown, firm shiitake and orange nameko.
Wild: Fungi gathered in their natural state. Don't collect unless you are in the know. The most popular culinary ones, featured here, are the very expensive, honeycomb-domed morel; field; dome-shaped horse; oyster; yellow or orange, frilly chanterelle (girolle); cep (penny bun, *Boletus edulis*) and wood blewit, but there are many others such as chicken-in-the-wood, parasol, and horn of plenty.

WHEN IN SEASON
Cultivated: All year; **Chanterelle:** June–January; **Morel:** April–May; **Rest:** September–November

HOW TO CHOOSE AND STORE
To forage wild, go with a guide. When buying, avoid shrivelled or wet mushrooms; choose firm and fresh-looking ones. They should smell earthy and "mushroomy". Some wild ones have distinctive scents (see individual entries). Store in a paper (not plastic) bag in the fridge, but not in the chiller box. Use within a few days.

White button Tight, little mushrooms with a mild flavour. Eat raw or cook whole.

White closed cup The next stage, standard mushrooms, used sliced or chopped, raw, or cooked.

White large flat Fully opened with best flavour. Good stuffed, fried, or baked whole, or cut into thick slices.

Tiny and firm. Good flavour.

Chestnut Brown cup mushrooms; meaty texture and good flavour. Use as cup mushrooms.

slight smell of apricots.

Crimini Brown, slightly meatier equivalent of button mushroom. Use in the same way.

Breakfast Open cup chestnut mushrooms, good fried or stuffed.

Nameko An Asian mushroom. Earthy flavour, silky texture.

shiitake Meaty mushroom originally from Asia with brown cap and white gills. Excellent flavour.

Oyster Delicate-flavoured, silky mushroom in grey, brown, yellow, or pink. Cut up or cook whole.

Morel One of the most highly prized. Found in woodlands. It has a honeycomb hood and rich flavour. Often sold dried.

Portabello Large, flat mushrooms, also called field; they are a good substitute for fields, with a strong flavour.

Field The familiar wild mushroom with pink through to almost black gills, depending on growth. Very good flavour.

Wood blewit White mushroom with blue-tinged, fat stalk and cap. Faint aniseed smell. Good flavour. Must eat cooked.

Chanterelle Yellow or orange trumpet shape with frilly top; gills running down the stem. Found in many woodlands. Delicious flavour.

Cep (penny bun or porcini) Looks like a brown bun on a thick stalk. Found in woodland clearings. Meaty and delicious. Excellent dried.

Horse White with a domed cap, and pink gills, or black when flat. Often found in "fairy rings" in meadows. Excellent flavour.

PERFECT PAIRINGS

GARLIC in **BUTTER**, to sauté, or to flavour soup, sauces, stews, or stuffings. **FRESH HERBS**, particularly oregano or marjoram, chives, parsley, and coriander. **BACON** grilled or fried with them for breakfast. **EGGS** baked in quiches, omelettes, or scrambled. **STEAK** grilled with them.

SIMPLE WAYS TO ENJOY

TO PREPARE

Wipe, don't wash or soak as too much water gets in the gills. Peel only if wild and open (or, if cultivated, open or flat ones seem tough). Trim the stalks. Leave whole, slice, or chop as required.

BAKED FLAT FIELD MUSHROOMS IN CREAM AND ROSÉ WINE

Put flat wild or portabello mushrooms in a buttered baking tin. Scatter over chopped garlic. Season. Combine equal amounts of double cream and dry rosé wine and pour over just to cover the mushrooms. Cover with foil. Bake at 190°C (375°F/Gas 5) for 20 minutes. Sprinkle with chopped parsley.

CHILLED MUSHROOMS WITH TOMATOES AND GARLIC

Fry a chopped onion in olive oil. Add button mushrooms, crushed garlic, some skinned and chopped tomatoes, and a little dry cider. Season. Simmer, stirring occasionally, until bathed in a rich sauce. Add chopped oregano. Taste and reseason. Cool, then chill. Drizzle with olive oil to serve.

MUSHROOM PÂTÉ

Fry a finely chopped, small onion in a good knob of butter. Add finely chopped cup or mixed mushrooms; cook, stirring, until soft and there is no liquid left. Sharpen with lemon juice. Cool. Beat in some cream cheese and chopped parsley to form a fairly stiff mixture. Season. Pack in a pot. Chill.

MUSHROOM SALAD WITH CORIANDER

Mix sliced button or crimini mushrooms with some chopped spring onions and chopped cucumber. Drizzle with olive oil, a splash of white balsamic condiment, and a few roughly crushed coriander seeds. Toss and season. Garnish with torn coriander leaves.

WILD MUSHROOM SOUP

Soften some chopped shallots in butter. Add roughly cut up wild mushrooms. Cook gently to soften. Add some chicken or vegetable stock, a bouquet garni, and some seasoning. Simmer for 30 minutes. Discard the bouquet garni. Slightly thicken with cornflour, water, and just a dash of tomato purée. Add a splash of brandy. Reseason. Garnish with parsley.

ALL-YEAR MUSHROOM BARLEY RISOTTO

INGREDIENTS

1 tbsp dried morel or
  cep mushrooms
1 onion, chopped
1 garlic clove, crushed
15g (½oz) butter
225g (8oz) chestnut
  mushrooms, sliced
150ml (5fl oz) dry white wine
200g (7oz) pearl barley
2 tsp chopped fresh thyme, plus
  a few leaves, to garnish
750ml (1¼ pints) chicken or
  vegetable stock
Salt and freshly ground
  black pepper
2–3 tbsp single cream
A little grated hard sheep's
  cheese or Parmesan,
  to serve

SERVES 4 **PREPARATION TIME** 10 minutes, plus soaking **COOKING TIME** 45 minutes **VARIATION** In season, omit the dried mushrooms and substitute half the chestnut mushrooms with chanterelles or ceps.

1 Soak the dried mushrooms in boiling water for 30 minutes. Drain and chop.

2 Soften the onion and garlic in the butter, stirring for 2 minutes. Add the sliced fresh mushrooms and wine. Simmer for 2 minutes. Stir in the pearl barley and chopped thyme. Add the stock. Season. Bring to the boil, then simmer until the barley is tender but with bite and liquid is almost absorbed, about 40 minutes, stirring twice.

3 Add the chopped soaked mushrooms and the single cream. Garnish with thyme leaves. Serve with grated cheese.

NEW POTATOES

The first earlies appear in late spring and early summer. The most famous and highly prized is the Jersey Royal, with its unmistakable earthy flavour. As it comes from Jersey, it is not, technically, British, but we must embrace this little beauty as it has always graced our tables. We have also included here the firm speciality salad varieties, some grown organically, perfect to enjoy with summer meals. Apart from in the Channel Islands, many varieties are grown in Cornwall and near the East coast, where the sea breezes protect them from frost.

WHAT WHEN AND HOW

WHAT TYPES
First earlies: Planted in January to March for harvesting during the summer, with thin skins that scrape or rub off.
Speciality salads: Waxy, firm varieties; some are early croppers, others take longer to mature and can be stored.

WHEN IN SEASON
First earlies: May–July; **Speciality salads:** May–October (some are available most of the year)

HOW TO CHOOSE AND STORE
Choose firm, smooth potatoes. The skin of first earlies should scrape off easily with your nail. Avoid any that have green patches. Buy in small quantities and use within a few days. Store in a cool, dark place where air can get to them freely. Do not store in the fridge – the cold can make the starch turn to sugar and they'll blacken on cooking.

Good all-rounder.

Accent First early. Yellow tubers with fairly waxy, yellow flesh.

Jersey Royal First early. Flaky skin, white flesh and a sweet, distinctive, earthy flavour.

Best boiled or steamed.

Maris Bard First early. Pale
skin and creamy-white flesh
with a waxy texture.

Best boiled
or steamed.

Good served
hot or cold.

Duke of York First early. An excellent waxy
potato with lovely yellow flesh. If left in the
ground it becomes a good all-rounder maincrop.

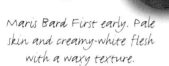

Best fried or
mashed.

Charlotte Speciality
salad. A lovely waxy
potato with yellow skin
and flesh.

Salad Blue First early. Not a salad
potato at all. Deep bluish purple
throughout. Floury texture. Good flavour.

Boil, steam, or
sauté whole. Serve
hot or cold.

Cook like Pink
Fir Apple.

Good boiled or
steamed and
in salads.

Anya Speciality
salad. Cross between
Pink Fir Apple and
Desirée.

Pink Fir Apple Speciality
salad. Pinky-red skin
with distinctive,
long, knobbly shape.
Has fairly sweet,
creamy-yellow flesh.

NEW POTATOES 117

PERFECT PAIRINGS

MELTED BUTTER, plain or flavoured with **PESTO** (see p161) to toss them in when cooked.
MAYONNAISE, **YOGURT**, or **CRÈME FRAÎCHE** to dress warm or cold; plain or flavoured with
HERBS, **GARLIC**, or **GRATED LEMON ZEST**. **MINT** to cook with them; **CHOPPED PARSLEY**,
THYME, or **SNIPPED CHIVES** to scatter over when cooked. **PICKLED**, **SALTED**, and **SMOKED FISH**
in warm and cold salads.

SIMPLE WAYS TO ENJOY

TO PREPARE

Scrub to remove any dirt and loose skin. You can scrape new varieties completely, if you prefer. Leave small ones whole, cut larger ones into bite-sized pieces. Place in water immediately or they will discolour.

← POTATO AND MACKEREL SALAD NIÇOISE

Boil baby salad potatoes and a couple of scrubbed eggs in lightly salted water for 5 minutes. Add some topped and tailed French beans, cut into short lengths; boil for 5 minutes more until tender. Drain. Plunge the eggs into cold water. Rinse the potatoes and beans with cold water; drain again. Put in a bowl with some flaked smoked mackerel, thinly sliced red onion, separated into rings, some halved cherry tomatoes, diced cucumber, black olives, a few torn Little Gem lettuce leaves, and some shredded basil leaves. Add French dressing flavoured with Dijon mustard. Toss. Shell the eggs, cut into wedges, and arrange on top.

BABY NEW POTATOES WITH SPRING ONIONS AND MINT

Boil or steam scrubbed baby potatoes until tender. Fry chopped spring onions in butter until golden and tender. Add the potatoes and some chopped fresh mint, and toss gently.

WARM POTATO SALAD WITH HERBS

Boil or steam prepared speciality salad potatoes until tender. Mix equal quantities of Greek-style plain yogurt and mayonnaise with some chopped parsley and thyme and a splash of white balsamic condiment. Add to the warm potatoes and toss gently. Season with pepper. Garnish with a little extra chopped parsley.

ROASTED POTATOES WITH SESAME SEEDS

Toss scrubbed chunks of new potatoes in a little olive oil in a roasting tin. Sprinkle liberally with sesame seeds. Roast in a fairly hot oven until tender and golden, turning once. Serve sprinkled with coarse sea salt.

AN OXFORDSHIRE VEGETABLE FARM

IAIN TOLHURST, TOLHURST ORGANIC PRODUCE

 For 30 years Iain Tolhurst has been farming organically, making him one of the longest-standing organic fruit and vegetable farmers in Britain. He and his family run a 7-hectare (17-acre) farm on the Hardwick Estate in Oxfordshire, on the edge of the Chiltern Hills. They began by supplying local greengrocers, then started a vegetable box scheme.

A small farm, their idea was always to stay local, sustainable, and not to be reliant on livestock – particularly for feeding the soil. "We used to bring in manure from local stables, but I am very fussy about my inputs and when I saw what goes into horses' diets it became a problem for me." After investigating various alternatives, Iain decided to introduce a green manure system into the seven-year crop rotation, growing 35 per cent green manure crops, like legumes and clover, and 65 per cent vegetables, at any one time. On seven plots, seven crops are grown on a yearly rotation, which means that the same crop is not grown in the same place for seven years. Different crops take different nutrients from the soil, so this system allows respite and a chance to replenish nutrients. The green manure helps this process, returning nitrogen and fertility to the soil.

Iain has seen a marked decrease in pests and disease since introducing the green manure technique, and is leading the field of closed-system stock-free organic farming: scientists and farmers from all over the world visit him to see how it works.

With over 80 varieties of vegetable growing at any one time on the Hardwick Estate, from potatoes, roots, and brassicas, to alliums and sweetcorn, Iain is kept busy all year round. For the intensive planting and harvesting period of June and July, Iain brings in some extra manpower to lend a hand. With winter field crops, and more exotic produce growing in the 2-acre walled garden, harvesting takes place all year round. The salad and leaf crops in the walled garden's protective environment are particularly plentiful over the winter months.

The walled garden's greenhouses and tunnels are home to over 35 crops all year round: tomatoes, peppers, cucumbers, and oriental salad leaves have all been a success, and very popular with Iain's customers. 85 per cent of Iain's produce is sold through a local box scheme, with the rest being sold in local shops. He keeps their business local, minimizing food miles, and none of the produce is sold further than 25 miles away from the farm.

See p127 for Iain's *Leek and Potato Soup*.

OPPOSITE, ABOVE LEFT Iain checking a young crop of Corni di Rosso peppers in the polytunnel.

ABOVE RIGHT Squash ripening in the field: just one of nine different varieties grown.

BELOW LEFT A fine crop of winter brussels sprouts coming up to maturity.

BELOW RIGHT Just a few of the 16 tons of potatoes grown on the farm. The varieties are chosen for flavour and disease resistance.

MAINCROP POTATOES

We've used this term to embrace second earlies as well as maincrop potatoes, eaten fresh or stored over the winter. Some commercial farmers select fast growers for a high yield with little consideration for flavour and texture. Organic farmers choose more hardy, blight-resistant varieties that some people think have a more interesting flavour. We're featuring some well-known varieties you'll find everywhere, and a selection of more unusual ones available in farmers' markets and veg boxes. Some are all-rounders, others superb for specific purposes. When buying meat you choose the right cut for the right dish – do the same for potatoes.

Estima Second early. Pale, firm, moist flesh. Boil or bake.

Vivaldi Second early. The wonder potato. Over a third less carbohydrate and half the calories of others. Sweet, buttery flavour. Best jacket-baked.

WHAT WHEN AND HOW

WHAT TYPES
Both types range from floury with a mealy texture to waxy with a firm texture.
Second earlies: These are planted slightly later than the first crop – February to May – then dug after the first earlies and eaten fresh or stored for use over the winter.
Maincrop: Grown later, between March and May, harvested from September onwards and then stored for use over the winter.

WHEN IN SEASON
Second earlies: July–October, available all year; **Maincrop:** September–October, available all year

HOW TO CHOOSE AND STORE
Choose firm, smooth potatoes. Avoid any that are cracked, wrinkled, damp, sprouting, or have green patches. Store in a cool, dark place, in a thick paper or natural-fibre bag where air can get to them freely. Don't store potatoes in the fridge: the starch will turn to sugar and they'll taste unpalatably sweet and may go black.

Good for salads, but also for chips, baking in wedges, and boiling.

Maris Peer Second early. Creamy flesh and pale skin. Neither waxy nor floury, but firm even when cooked.

Boil, chip, roast, or mash.

Wilja Second early. Dryish texture but not too floury. Golden skin, pale yellow, fairly firm flesh.

Best for baking, but good for boiling and wedges, too.

Marfona Second early. Pale yellow skin and flesh. Good, waxy texture and buttery flavour.

Excellent boiled or in salads.

Carlingford Second early. Not a new potato, but it behaves and tastes like one. Good, waxy texture and flavour.

Good all-rounder but great for chips, roasts, and mash.

British Queen Second early. Old variety, now quite rare, but still Ireland's favourite. Wonderful flavour and floury texture. Pale skin and flesh.

Great all-rounder.

Dunbar Rover Second early. Rare, as low yielding, but very high quality with superb flavour. White skin and flesh.

Purple Eyed Seedling Second early. Conservation potato. Distinctive purple patches on the skin, and creamy flesh. Best boiled or steamed.

Lady Balfour Maincrop. Fabulous earthy flavour, creamy flesh, thin skin. Great all-rounder.

Best for roasting and boiling.

Red Magic Maincrop. Distinctive, bright red, oval tubers with white flesh.

Good all-rounder but best for roasts, bakes, and chips.

Good all-rounder.

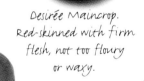

Desirée Maincrop. Red-skinned with firm flesh, not too floury or waxy.

Remarka Maincrop. Golden skin, fairly floury. Best for baking.

Excellent for roasts, bakes, and chips.

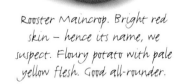

King Edward Maincrop. Famous floury potato with pale brown skin flecked with pink, and cream-coloured flesh.

Rooster Maincrop. Bright red skin – hence its name, we suspect. Floury potato with pale yellow flesh. Good all-rounder.

Maris Piper Maincrop. Creamy flesh, fairly floury texture and light brownish-gold skin.

Good for most purposes, but best for chips.

Good all-rounder.

Peach Bloom Maincrop. Distinctive, pinky-red-and-yellow-patched skin with white flesh. Medium texture.

Boil, bake, or mash.

Yukon Gold Maincrop. Originated in America. Distinctive gold skin and yellow flesh with a buttery flavour.

Vitelotte Maincrop. Ancient black-skinned variety with deep purple, slightly waxy flesh and a nutty flavour.

Excellent fried or roasted.

PERFECT PAIRINGS

GARLIC, cooked with or in a topping or dressing. **CHEESES**, all types for topping jackets, in baked dishes, on or in mashed potato. **EGGS**, fried with chips or sautéed, in omelettes; **OTHER VEGETABLES** boiled, then beaten with them for flavoured mash, such as carrots, Jerusalem artichokes, celeriac, swede, or leeks. **CHILLI** and sweet spices such as **CUMIN** and **NUTMEG** to flavour mash, to toss in roasts, wedges, and fries.

SIMPLE WAYS TO ENJOY

TO PREPARE

Scrub or peel thinly, as required. Remember, the skin gives added fibre and lots of goodness sits just beneath it. Leave small potatoes whole, cut large ones into even-sized pieces. Dice, slice, cut into wedges or chips, as required. If not cooking immediately, cover with water to prevent browning, If boiling for mash, cut into smallish pieces, as they will cook more quickly.

PERFECT FLUFFY MASH

Thinly peel fairly floury potatoes. Cut up evenly. Boil in lightly salted water until tender. Drain. Return to the pan and dry out briefly over a low heat. If you have one, put through a potato ricer and return to the pan, or else mash thoroughly with a potato masher. Add a good knob of butter, a splash of double cream or milk, and plenty of freshly ground black pepper. Beat with a wooden spoon until fluffy.

PERFECT CHIPS

Scrub or peel large, fairly floury potatoes, cut into thick slices, then into chips. Soak in cold water for 30 minutes. Drain and dry thoroughly. Heat oil for deep-frying to 190°C (375°F) or until a chip dropped into the oil rises sizzling immediately. Cook in batches until they are just beginning to colour. Remove from the oil. Reheat the oil. Fry all the chips together until crisp and golden. Drain on kitchen paper.

PERFECT ROAST POTATOES

Cut peeled, fairly floury potatoes into large pieces. Boil in lightly salted water for 3 minutes. Drain. Put the lid on pan, shake the potatoes to rough up. Heat some goose fat or olive oil in a roasting tin in the top of the oven preheated to 190°C (375°F/Gas 5). When almost smoking, add potatoes and turn in the sizzling fat. For added crunch, dust with plain flour before adding to the hot fat. Roast for about 1 hour, turning twice, until crisp and golden.

CAJUN POTATO WEDGES

Halve scrubbed, firm-fleshed potatoes and cut again into 4 wedges. Put in a baking tin. Toss in some olive oil. Mix a little ground cumin, paprika, garlic, salt, and dried oregano with chilli powder to taste. Sprinkle over and toss. Spread the potato wedges in the tin. Bake in the oven at 220°C (425°F/Gas 7) for about 30 minutes until crisp and golden, turning once.

SAUTÉED POTATOES WITH GARLIC

Dice scrubbed, firm potatoes. Boil in water for 3 minutes until almost tender. Drain and dry thoroughly. Heat a little butter and sunflower oil in a frying pan. Add 1 or 2 peeled garlic cloves and the potatoes. Fry, tossing, until golden. Drain on kitchen paper. Discard the garlic.

CREAMY POTATO AND LANCASHIRE CHEESE GRATIN

Boil thinly sliced, scrubbed all-rounders for 2 minutes. Drain. Layer in a greased ovenproof dish with some crushed garlic, grated Lancashire cheese and seasoning. Finish with cheese. Beat 1 or 2 eggs with some milk and/or single cream; pour over. Bake at 180°C (350°F/Gas 4) until golden and set.

POTATO CAKES WITH CELERY SEEDS

Boil 2 large potatoes and mash with a pinch of salt, a good knob of butter and enough flour to form a dough. Pat out to 1cm (½in) thick. Cut into rounds. Gently press on celery seeds. Cook on a griddle, 3 minutes each side.

POTATO AND CELERIAC ROSTI

Grate equal quantities of floury potatoes and celeriac. Mix with grated onion and chopped fresh sage leaves. Season. Bind with beaten egg. Put spoonfuls in hot oil in a frying pan. Press flat. Fry until golden and cooked, turning once.

CRISPY POTATO SKINS WITH CHILLI AND CORIANDER DIP

Mix some chopped coriander with finely chopped tomato, dried chilli flakes, and a splash of lime juice and olive oil. Season. Jacket-bake potatoes. Halve, scoop out, leaving a 5mm (¼in) shell. Cut into wedges. Deep-fry until crisp and golden. Drain on kitchen paper. Sprinkle with salt.

POTATO GNOCCHI

Season mashed potatoes. Mix with beaten egg. Add flour to form a soft dough. Roll into small ovals. Drop into a pan of boiling water. Cook until they float. Remove with a slotted spoon. Put in flameproof dishes. Top with melted butter and grated hard or crumbled blue cheese. Grill until bubbling.

LEEK AND POTATO SOUP

IAIN TOLHURST AT TOLHURST ORGANIC PRODUCE

Iain runs Tolhurst Organic Produce, a vegetable farm in Oxfordshire. See pp120–1.

SERVES 4 **PREPARATION TIME** 15–20 minutes **COOKING TIME** 1 hour
SERVE WITH plenty of warm wholemeal bread. **An economical and simple dish. Good, substantial, peasant-style winter food to keep out the chill and sustain you through a long afternoon's work or comfort you after a hard day. It's an unusual way of making soup, but it works a treat.**

1 Peel the potatoes, but leave whole. Wash the leeks thoroughly and cut into shreds. Put the prepared potatoes, chopped leeks, onion, and stock (or water with Marmite) in a large pan. Season lightly. Bring to the boil, reduce the heat, cover, and simmer for 30 minutes.

2 Using a slotted spoon, lift the potatoes out of the pan and mash with the margarine or butter. Return the mashed potatoes to the pan, stir thoroughly, and simmer for a further 25–30 minutes, stirring occasionally. If the soup gets too thick, simply add a little extra water to thin down to the required consistency. Taste and reseason with salt, if necessary. Ladle into warm bowls. Add a good grinding of black pepper to each.

INGREDIENTS
1kg (2¼lb) potatoes
500g (1lb 2oz) leeks
1 large onion, chopped
1.5 litres (2¾ pints) vegetable
   stock, or water and 2 tsp
   Marmite
50g (1¾oz) margarine or butter
Salt and freshly ground
   black pepper

JERUSALEM ARTICHOKES

These ugly-looking tubers have a secret — they taste superb. Originally from eastern America, they are a member of the sunflower family, and the plants grow incredibly tall. They also have the advantage of growing in just about any soil conditions, so can be grown at home easily — try to remove all tubers from the soil when harvesting, though, or they will grow like weeds. When cooked, they have a sweet, almost smoky flavour, similar to that of globe artichoke hearts but more intense. The flesh is almost translucent when cooked.

WHAT WHEN AND HOW

WHAT TYPES
Odd-shaped tubers in all forms and sizes; with pale skin and knobs.

WHEN IN SEASON
October–March (best November–February)

HOW TO CHOOSE AND STORE
Choose firm tubers with the fewest knobs (for ease of preparation). A knob should snap off easily if fresh. Avoid those caked in mud, or shrivelled, or sprouting, or that have soft patches on the skin. Store in the chiller box in the fridge, or in a paper bag in a cool, dark place for up to 2 weeks.

Thin skin can be scrubbed or thinly peeled.

Jerusalem artichoke strange-shaped tubers with thin skin and white flesh. Cook like potatoes; particularly good puréed, in soups, fried, or roasted.

The flowering plant of the Jerusalem artichoke.

PERFECT PAIRINGS

GAME and **RED MEATS** taste good with a purée. **NUTMEG** complements the smoky flavour. **SAGE**, **THYME**, **ROSEMARY**, and **BAY** are excellent added when roasting or to flavour mash (best mixed with potatoes). **LOVAGE** in soups. **CREAM** or **BUTTER** to enrich mash, purées, or soups. **SMOKED BACON**, **SAUSAGE**, or **FISH** tossed with boiled or roasted artichokes, or served with a purée.

SIMPLE WAYS TO ENJOY

TO PREPARE

Scrub well to remove dirt. No need to peel unless you want a pure white purée. (French Rounder variety is easiest to clean and peel.) Cut into even-sized chunks and place immediately in water with a squeeze of lemon juice, to prevent browning.

CURRIED ARTICHOKE SOUP WITH CRÈME FRAÎCHE

Soften a chopped onion gently in butter. Add a little Madras curry paste and fry briefly. Add scrubbed and roughly chopped artichokes, a chopped potato, some vegetable stock, a good grating of nutmeg, and a bay leaf. Simmer until tender. Discard the bay leaf. Purée, then thin with milk and stir in some crème fraîche and seasoning to taste. Reheat. Ladle into bowls, garnish with a dollop of crème fraîche and some chopped parsley.

ROAST ARTICHOKES WITH SMOKED PORK LOIN AND SAGE

Sauté artichoke chunks in olive oil until lightly golden. Add some chopped garlic, a splash of white balsamic condiment, diced smoked pork loin, a little chopped sage, some salt and freshly ground black pepper. Cover and cook very gently until everything is tender, shaking the pan occasionally. Remove the lid and cook over a high heat for a minute or two, shaking the pan, to remove any moisture. Serve with wilted spinach.

ARTICHOKE DAUPHINOISE WITH BACON AND THYME

Fry chopped onions, bacon and garlic until lightly golden, stirring. Add diced artichokes, a little chicken stock and some chopped thyme. Season and simmer until tender and most of the stock has gone. Add some double cream. Put in an ovenproof dish. Bake at 190°C (375°F/Gas 5) until golden.

JERUSALEM ARTICHOKE PURÉE

Boil scrubbed artichokes (peeled if you want a white purée) in lightly salted water until tender. Drain. Return to the pan and dry out over a low heat. Purée or mash with a good knob of butter, lots of black pepper and a dash of double cream. Add a grating of nutmeg to taste.

SWEET PEPPERS

Capsicums are bell-shaped or long and pointed, and come in a variety of colours. They're picked at different stages of ripeness – green through yellow to orange and red, but you may come across new white or purple varieties too. In Britain, they need to be grown in polytunnels or glasshouses to do well. But although they are high maintenance with a short season, their versatility and flavour mean they are in great demand, so organic producers find they are worth growing.

WHAT WHEN AND HOW

WHAT TYPES
Bell peppers: These are the familiar capsicums with faintly undulating stalk ends, rounded sides and tapering slightly at the base. They vary in size and the skins can be tough, so these can be removed before cooking (see opposite). **Long, pointed Ramiro or Romano peppers:** These are long, flatter, and thinner, tapering to a point. Usually sold red, they resemble some of the large chilli peppers but are sweet, not hot.

WHEN IN SEASON
July–October

HOW TO CHOOSE AND STORE
Choose bright, shiny peppers that feel firm. Avoid any with pale, soft spots or that are shrivelling.

Red peppers The sweetest of the four. The skin is often removed before use so their texture can be fully enjoyed.

The stalk and seeds are removed before cooking.

Yellow peppers sweeter than green, they are good mixed with all other colours and roasted.

Green peppers The immature fruit, with a sharp, slightly bitter taste. slice or stuff whole.

Ramiro or Romano peppers Longer and flatter and very sweet. Good stuffed whole, or split first, then grilled or roasted.

PERFECT PAIRINGS

CHICKEN, **VEAL**, or **FISH** in a casserole or stir-fry. Finely chopped in a salsa with **CHILLIES**, **CUCUMBER**, and **CORIANDER**. **GARLIC** and **ROSEMARY**, **OREGANO**, or **BASIL** griddled, roasted, or stir-fried. In soups, sauces, and casseroles with **TOMATOES**, **OLIVES**, and **ONIONS**.

SIMPLE WAYS TO ENJOY

TO PREPARE

Cut off the stalk end and remove the seeds. Stuff or cut into wedges, slice or dice as required. **To remove the skins:** Put the whole peppers under the grill or hold on a fork over a gas flame, turning until blackened in places and the skin is blistering. Put in a bag immediately and leave until cool enough to handle. Pull off the skin, remove the stalk and seeds.

ROASTED PEPPERS WITH GARLIC AND ROSEMARY

Cut prepared, mixed, coloured peppers into wedges. Place in a roasting tin and drizzle with olive oil. Sprinkle with some finely chopped garlic, a little chopped fresh rosemary and a good grinding of black pepper. Roast in the oven at 200°C (400°F/Gas 6) for about 45 minutes, until tender and browning in places, turning once. Scatter with coarse sea salt before serving.

PÂTÉ-STUFFED PEPPERS

Mash together equal quantities of smooth liver pâté and cream cheese. Pack into whole, seeded peppers and wrap in foil. Chill to firm. Cut into round slices and arrange on plates.

PEPPER AND TOMATO SAUCE

Fry a chopped red onion, a red and a green pepper, both chopped, and a crushed garlic clove in a little olive oil until softened but not browned. Add some skinned and chopped tomatoes, a little tomato purée, a splash of white wine and a pinch of caster sugar. Bring to the boil, reduce the heat and simmer gently, stirring, until pulpy and the peppers are tender. Add a little water if becoming too dry. Throw in a handful of sliced stoned olives, if liked, and add a few chopped leaves of fresh basil or marjoram. Season to taste. Serve with pasta, grilled chicken, veal, fish, or other seafood.

STUFFED ROMANO PEPPERS WITH CAERPHILLY

Cut the tops off Romano peppers and remove the seeds. Mash some Caerphilly cheese together with a little chopped fresh mint, a small handful of currants, a splash of olive oil, and seasoning to taste. Pack into the peppers and brush with a little more oil. Place on foil on the grill rack, and grill until the peppers are soft and going brown in places, turning once.

ROASTED RED PEPPER AND CHICKPEA SOUP

SERVES 4 **PREPARATION TIME** 25 minutes **COOKING TIME** 35 minutes
VARIATION If you prefer, you can add raw, diced peppers at step 2, to save
roasting them. It's much quicker, but what you gain in time you lose in flavour.

1 Roast the peppers under the grill for about 15 minutes, turning
occasionally until blackened. Remove from the grill, place them
straight into a biodegradable plastic bag and leave until cold. Rub
off the skins and discard the stalks and seeds. Rinse under the tap
to remove any black flecks, then chop.

2 Soften the onion, carrots, and garlic in the oil in a large pan,
stirring, for 2 minutes. Add the peppers and all the remaining
ingredients, except the olives. Bring to the boil, then reduce the
heat, part-cover, and simmer gently for 30 minutes.

3 Purée in a blender or food processor, return to the pan and
reheat. Taste and reseason, if necessary. Ladle into warm bowls,
add a trickle of olive oil and a sprinkling of chopped olives and
thyme to each.

INGREDIENTS
3 red peppers
1 Spanish onion, chopped
2 carrots, chopped
1 large garlic clove, chopped
3 tbsp olive oil, plus extra
  to garnish
1 tsp ground cumin
1 tsp ground cinnamon
2 tsp paprika
½ tsp grated fresh root ginger
400g (14oz) can chickpeas,
  drained
750ml (1¼ pints) chicken or
  vegetable stock
1 tbsp tahini paste
1 tbsp chopped fresh thyme,
  plus extra to garnish
1 tsp clear honey
Salt and freshly ground
  black pepper
2 tbsp black olives, stoned and
  finely chopped

CHILLIES

Not native to these shores, chillies still grow very well here in polytunnels, which protect them from the elements. You can enjoy many of the varieties you would expect to find in far-flung places such as Mexico or Thailand. If you're a chilli fanatic, you will appreciate the nuances between the really fiery, red, pointed piri piris and the undulating, rounder habaneros. You'll be able to detect the more intricate flavour of the yellow Hungarian hot wax or a milder jalapeño. We can't list every variety available here, but we have included some of the most popular.

WHAT WHEN AND HOW

WHAT TYPES
Mild and moderately hot: These will tickle your palate, or, at best, give a bit of a kick. They're the ones to go for if you can't take too much heat. Many of the larger, fleshy varieties come into this category. But it's not as easy as saying small is hot, large is mild; you do need to be able to recognize which ones you are choosing, such as pimientos de Padrón, poblano, jalapeño, Hungarian hot wax.
Hot and extremely hot: These are for the chilli lovers. They add intense flavour and fire and will make your body tingle! Our selection includes serrano, red cherry bomb, ring of fire, piri piri, and Scotch bonnet or the very similar habanero.

WHEN IN SEASON
July–November

HOW TO CHOOSE AND STORE
Choose fresh, bright, shiny-looking chillies, avoiding any with soft patches or that look wrinkled. Store wrapped in the chiller box in the fridge for up to 2 weeks. To get the best flavour from chillies, particularly in main meals, it is recommended that you buy the dried and fresh varieties and use a little of each, as the flavours change and deepen when dried.

Pimientos de Padrón These little, green peppers are a delicacy in Spain. Tradition says that one in 30 of them is fiery, the rest are sweet. VERY MILD.

Their fat shape makes them perfect for stuffing.

Poblano Large, fleshy, green chilli up to about 15cm (6in) long. FAIRLY MILD.

Jalapeño Shiny, green or red, cone-shaped chilli. Can be stuffed, but is often sliced; can also be chopped. MODERATELY HOT.

Often served sliced, and also pickled.

Ring of fire Thin, tapering, green or red cayenne chilli up to 9cm (3½ in) long. HOT.

Thin chillies are often hotter than large, fat, fleshy ones.

Red cherry bomb Short, fat, pendant-shaped, red chilli. Excellent for stuffing. HOT.

said to resemble a tam o'shanter.

Scotch bonnet Crinkly, roundish chillies in a variety of colours. EXTREMELY HOT.

Piri Piri Tiny, fiery, bird's eye chilli. VERY HOT.

Aji limon Yellow and crinkly with a distinctive herby, citrus flavour. Good with white meats and fish. HOT.

Serrano Sold in various colours from green, yellow, brown, orange, or red, and ranges from about 2.5–10cm (1–4in) in length. It is about five times hotter than the jalapeño. HOT.

Hungarian hot wax A fat, fleshy chilli, around 12cm (5in) long. It can be chopped, sliced, or stuffed. FAIRLY HOT.

Distinctive bullet shape.

PERFECT PAIRINGS

CHEESE, particularly hard ones like Cheddar, or any of the sheep's ones sprinkled over a chilli-flavoured meat dish or use to zip-up cheese on toast. **SEAFOOD** loves the kick of chillies (and lime juice) in raw dishes like ceviche or when sautéing scallops, prawns, or squid; or in a dipping sauce for cooked seafood (see below). **TOMATOES**, use red or orange ones with them in sauces, or any colour with them in a salsa with chopped cucumber, olives, and maybe some chopped apricots or plums to serve with grilled meat, duck, or chicken.

SIMPLE WAYS TO ENJOY

TO PREPARE

People often say that removing the seeds reduces the fire of the chilli. Experts say this isn't necessarily the case. So split and remove the seeds if you prefer, then slice or chop. The recommendation is that the hotter the chilli, the finer you should chop it. For very hot ones, like Scotch bonnet or piri piri, you are advised to wear rubber gloves when preparing them. Whatever you do, don't rub your eyes or other areas of delicate skin after chopping.

PIMIENTOS DE PADRÓN

Rinse and pat dry. Heat enough olive oil to coat the base of a wok or large frying pan. Sauté the whole peppers, tossing until tender and golden brown in patches, about 5 minutes. Tip into a shallow dish and sprinkle with coarse sea salt. Pick up in your fingers by the stalk and nibble off the pepper.

SWEET CHILLI AND TOMATO DIPPING SAUCE

Skin, seed, and finely chop a couple of ripe tomatoes. Mix with a seeded and finely chopped red chilli (choose the type according to how hot you want the sauce), a couple of tablespoons of tomato ketchup, and a couple of teaspoons each of white balsamic condiment and clear honey. Season.

ROASTED CHEESE-STUFFED CHILLIES

Select some large, fat chillies that are suitable for stuffing, such as poblano, Hungarian hot wax, or jalapeño. Cut off the tops and remove the seeds. Mix equal quantities of soft and Cheddar cheeses. Season lightly and add a little chopped thyme or sage. Use to fill, but not over-stuff, the chillies. Lay them on foil under the grill and drizzle with olive oil. Grill until browning in places and softening. Carefully turn and grill the other sides.

QUICK BEEF CHILLI

Brown lean minced beef steak with some chopped onion and garlic. Add a chopped mild or hot chilli, a pinch of crushed dried chillies, a little ground cumin and dried oregano, canned chopped tomatoes, drained and rinsed canned red kidney beans, some tomato purée, a pinch of caster sugar, and seasoning. Simmer until rich and thick. Serve with rice, grated Cheddar cheese, and shredded lettuce.

FIERY PEANUT AND PEPPER NOODLES

INGREDIENTS

1 red pepper
1 green pepper
1 tbsp sunflower oil
4 spring onions, chopped
1 garlic clove, finely chopped
1 courgette, finely chopped
1 or 2 green jalapeño or poblano
  chillies, seeded and chopped
1 tsp grated fresh root ginger
1 tbsp chopped fresh flat-leaf
  parsley
1 tbsp chopped fresh coriander,
  plus a few torn leaves, to serve
Grated zest and juice of 1 lime
4 tbsp crunchy wholegrain
  peanut butter
3 tbsp soy sauce
1 tbsp dry sherry
9 tbsp water
500g (1lb 2oz) fresh egg noodles
60g (2oz) chopped roasted
  peanuts, to serve

SERVES 4 **PREPARATION TIME** 20 minutes **COOKING TIME** 4–5 minutes
VARIATION You can use hotter chillies, if you prefer. Experiment with aj limon, for instance, for added citrus flavour with the heat. If you don't have fresh noodles, reconstitute about half the weight of dried ones.

1 Grill the peppers, turning once or twice until blackened in places, about 15 minutes. Put in a biodegradable plastic bag and leave until cold. Rub off the skins and dice the flesh, discarding stalk and seeds.

2 Heat the oil in a wok or large frying pan. Add the spring onions, garlic, and courgette and stir-fry for 1 minute. Add the peppers, chillies, ginger, herbs, lime zest and juice, peanut butter, soy sauce, sherry, and water. Stir until the peanut butter melts. Add the noodles and toss for 2 minutes until piping hot. Pile into warm bowls and sprinkle with peanuts and a few torn coriander leaves.

MARSH SAMPHIRE

Vibrant marsh samphire is an amazing sea plant that grows wild mainly along the coast of East Anglia and on Humberside on muddy sea flats. It has delicious fleshy fronds that taste of iodine and the sea. It is a highly prized delicacy that you can buy in some specialist greengrocers, fishmongers, and farmers' markets during the summer months, but if you can, gather it yourself (see the note below). Don't confuse it with rock samphire, which is a different edible plant found at the edge of shingle beaches around Britain and is a member of the carrot family. It's nothing like as good.

WHAT WHEN AND HOW

WHAT TYPES
Also known as glasswort, sea fennel, and poor man's asparagus. It has knobbly, bright green, fleshy fronds and looks like a sprig of coral or a shiny cactus.

WHEN IN SEASON
June–September

HOW TO CHOOSE AND STORE
Choose young, bright green plants, avoiding any that look dry, dark, or wilting. It can be kept wrapped in a paper bag in the chiller box of the fridge for up to 2 days, but it is best eaten very fresh.

Note: If you find samphire yourself, never pull it up by the roots, as that is illegal. You can cut some, but don't take too much, and make sure you leave plenty of the plant for regrowth.

Choose young, bright green plants.

Marsh samphire Young shoots can be eaten raw but are very salty. Traditionally samphire is pickled in vinegar, but the succulent stalks are fabulous lightly cooked and eaten fresh like asparagus, or with fish dishes.

PERFECT PAIRINGS

MELTED BUTTER tossed with lightly steamed or boiled samphire. **VINEGAR** or **FRENCH DRESSING** drizzled over warm or cold fronds. **WHITE** and **OILY FISH** and **SHELLFISH** served with it as a vegetable or sauce.

SIMPLE WAYS TO ENJOY

TO PREPARE

Wash well in cold water. Nibble a bit, and if it is still very salty you can soak it in several changes of cold water for a few hours. Cut the fronds off the woody stems if they are still there.

STEAMED SAMPHIRE WITH GARLIC AND LEMON BUTTER

Melt a good knob of unsalted butter (enough for the quantity of samphire you are using) in a small pan. Stir in a small or large crushed garlic clove, the finely grated zest of 1 lemon, and a good grinding of black pepper (no salt!). Lay the prepared samphire in a steamer or metal colander over a pan of simmering water and steam for 2–3 minutes until tender but still with some bite. Lay the stalks on plates. Drizzle the melted butter over the stalks.

SAMPHIRE SAUCE FOR FISH

Boil 175g (6oz) prepared samphire in 150ml (5fl oz) water for about 3 minutes until tender. Drain. Purée with a good knob of unsalted butter and a splash of white balsamic condiment, adding a little water, if necessary, to give a thick pouring consistency.

PICKLED SAMPHIRE

Blanch 115g (4oz) prepared samphire in boiling water for just 1 minute. Place in a shallow sealable container. Put 6 tbsp cider vinegar, 6 tbsp medium-sweet cider, and 1 tsp pickling spices in a small pan and bring to the boil. Pour over the samphire, stir well, cover, and leave until cold, then leave to marinate in the fridge for 24–48 hours, turning occasionally. Drain. Lovely with grilled red mullet, Cornish sardines, or smoked mackerel, but eat within 2 days as it is not for keeping.

SWEETCORN

A succulent cob, ribbed with creamy yellow, plump, sweet kernels is a seasonal delight. There is nothing nicer than sinking your teeth into it, dripping with butter. It has been grown widely in the south for many decades, but with climate change it is creeping north. The season's short, so enjoy it while you can. Although frozen and canned corn is good, it can't compare to fresh. Delicately flavoured, immature baby sweetcorn cobs are now grown here too.

No more than 10cm (4in) long.

Baby corn sweet, nutty, immature cobs cooked whole or cut in chunks.

Choose creamy yellow kernels, as they will be the sweetest.

WHAT WHEN AND HOW

WHAT TYPES
Corn-on-the-cob: A variety of maize with a high sugar content. The cobs, wrapped in tightly fitting, pale green leaves, called the husk, are harvested when the kernels are just ripening.
Baby corn: A specialist vegetable, grown so that it is harvested as soon as the silks appear, before the kernels develop.

WHEN IN SEASON
Corn-on-the-cob and baby corn: August–September

HOW TO CHOOSE AND STORE
Best eaten very fresh, as the minute the cob is cut, the sugar starts to turn into starch, so it becomes less sweet. Deep gold kernels are overripe and the sugar will already be turning to starch.

Corn-on-the-cob can be cooked whole then picked up in the fingers and the kernels bitten off the cob, or the kernels can be removed before cooking.

PERFECT PAIRINGS

CORN-ON-THE-COB The traditional accompaniment is **MELTED BUTTER** drizzled over; **BACON** wrapped round before barbecuing or grilling; kernels with **CHEDDAR CHEESE** in a sauce as a vegetable, in soup, or as a topping for pizza. **BABY CORN SESAME OIL** and **SOY SAUCE** tossed with the cooked baby cobs, other **BABY VEGETABLES** such as **CARROTS**, **COURGETTES**, **MANGETOUT**, and **ONIONS**, steamed, stir-fried, or as crudités with dips. **FOR BOTH CHICKEN** grilled with pieces of corn cobs, sautéed, or casseroled with kernels, or stir-fried with baby cobs.

SIMPLE WAYS TO ENJOY

TO PREPARE

CORN-ON-THE-COB
Cut off the stalk, then remove all the leaves and the silks. To remove the kernels, hold the cob upright on a board and cut them off with a knife, working downwards around the cob.

BABY CORN
Cut into short lengths, halve lengthways, or leave whole.

QUICK CORN CHOWDER

Soften a chopped onion with some diced potatoes in a good knob of butter. Add corn kernels from 3–4 cobs. Simmer in chicken stock until tender. Either mash the potatoes into the liquid or purée the soup. Season, and add a splash of cream. Top with crumbled crisp bacon, if liked.

BARBECUED OR ROASTED CORN COBS IN THEIR HUSKS

Put the whole cobs in their husks in a roasting tin and roast in the oven preheated to 180°C (350°F/Gas 4), or on the rack over a hot barbecue for about 30 minutes, turning once. Pull back the husks, add a knob of butter and freshly ground black pepper.

CREAMED CORN

Cut the kernels off some corn cobs. Melt a good knob of unsalted butter in a saucepan. Add the corn, cover, and cook gently for 5 minutes, shaking the pan occasionally until the corn is tender but not brown. Add a little double cream and a pinch of freshly grated nutmeg. Simmer gently, stirring until the corn is bathed in a rich, creamy sauce. Season to taste.

CHICKEN WITH CHARGRILLED BABY CORN

Cut chicken breasts in half lengthways and flatten. Sprinkle with soy sauce. Fry both sides in sunflower oil until golden and cooked through. Meanwhile, toss some baby corn in a little more oil, salt, and freshly ground black pepper. Cook in a hot griddle pan, turning once or twice until browned and cooked through. Pile the cobs on the chicken breasts and serve.

TOMATOES

Tomatoes were first cultivated by the Aztecs and Incas in South America in 700AD. Until fairly recently, the only tomatoes you could buy in the UK were perfectly round and not particularly flavoursome. Now, we grow myriad varieties in different shapes and sizes, many sold still on the vine to maximize their flavour. There are tiny, ultra-sweet cherry or baby plums right through to standard ones and huge slicing tomatoes, in colours from bright green or creamy white, through yellow, orange, and red, to deep mahogany. Included here are just a few of those available in farmers' markets and veg boxes. Go organic for great flavour, but also because a recent study showed that organically grown tomatoes contain more antioxidants than conventionally grown ones.

Firm flesh.

Golden Queen This is a bright yellow, juicy cherry, but you can also get much larger ones.

Brandywine An old beefsteak variety, considered to be the finest tasting of all.

Pinky-red flesh.

WHAT WHEN AND HOW

WHAT TYPES
Cherry: These are tiny versions of standard tomatoes, some no bigger than a thumbnail.
Cocktail: Slightly larger than cherries, they can be stuffed as a cocktail snack (hence their name), or can be cooked whole.
Plum: These are oval and plum-shaped. The Italians have long used them in cooking; they have more pulp and less juice, so make great tomato sauce. Use baby ones with pasta.
Standard: The classic tomato, uniformly round and juicy, a good all-rounder for salads, grilling or frying.
Beefsteak: These are big, fat tomatoes that can weigh as much as 450g (1lb). They are good stuffed, baked, or sliced for salads and sandwiches.
Vine tomatoes: Any of the above types can be found sold as small trusses, just as they were grown, rather than individually picked off the plants.

WHEN IN SEASON
All varieties: July–October (June–November under cover)

HOW TO CHOOSE AND STORE
Choose ones that smell of the vine. They should be firm, not too soft, with no bruises. The calyces should be fresh and bright green, not shrivelled. Apart from naturally striped tomatoes, avoid any that are tinged with too much green as these are under-ripe, or store them in a paper bag with a ripe banana and they'll ripen quickly (but won't taste as good as if ripened on the plant). Storing in the fridge impairs their flavour, so store in a bowl like other fruit.

Red cherry The classic baby heritage or heirloom tomato, with a good sweet taste, perfect for popping in the mouth whole.

Uniform bright red skin.

Cindel A classic tomato
with firm flesh and
bright red skin.

If the fruit
turns too
yellow, it is
over-ripe.

White beauty This is a rarer tomato,
with creamy white flesh all the way
through. It has a delicate flavour
and is very sweet.

Gardener's delight A very popular
cherry tomato with a bright red
colour and sweet flavour.

Beam's yellow pear An
attractive, little, yellow
tomato with a distinctive
shape. It looks great halved
in salads.

Unusual
pear-shaped fruit.

Mr Stripey (Tigerella)
A distinctive tomato with
delicious, sweet, juicy flesh. Good
for salads and sandwiches.

Green Zebra
A good-sized green
tomato, with greenish-gold
stripes and spots and an
excellent, tangy flavour. Good used
raw in salads and salsas.

Sanmarzano The classic
Italian plum tomato
– the one you find in
cans too! It has few seeds,
so is perfect for cooking.

Black Russian
A standard-sized fruit
with a mahogany-coloured
skin. It has a superb sweet
flavour but with lovely
acidic overtones.

Big Rainbow A large beefsteak tomato
with golden flesh, streaked with red.
It is very juicy, sweet, and succulent.

TOMATOES 143

PERFECT PAIRINGS

SOFT CHEESES like **MOZZARELLA** and **GOAT'S CHEESE**; **HARD CHEESES** like **CHEDDAR**; or crumbled **BLUE CHEESES** like **STILTON** or **BLUE CHESHIRE**, melted on cooked ones, as part of a topping or together in a salad. **BASIL**, torn and scattered over raw tomatoes, or added at the end of cooking. **ORANGE** is a favourite flavouring, particularly in tomato soup. **VODKA** turns tomato juice into a Bloody Mary with plenty of ice, a splash of Worcestershire sauce and Tabasco, a pinch of celery salt, and a squeeze of lemon or lime juice; try **VODKA** in soup or sauce for a real kick.

SIMPLE WAYS TO ENJOY

TO PREPARE

To skin: Put the fruit in a bowl and just cover with boiling water. Leave to stand for 30 seconds, drain, rinse with cold water, then peel off the skins. Halve, quarter, slice, or chop, as required.

FRESH TOMATO SAUCE

Fry a chopped onion in a little olive oil for 2 minutes, stirring until softened, not browned. Add lots of chopped tomatoes, skinned, if liked, a squeeze of tomato purée, and a good pinch of sugar. Season. Bring to the boil, reduce the heat, simmer until pulpy. Purée, if liked. Add chopped basil or oregano.

FRESH TOMATO JUICE

Purée some quartered ripe tomatoes in a blender with a little tomato purée, a pinch of caster sugar, and celery salt. Strain through a sieve to remove the seeds and skin. Season to taste and pour over lots of ice. Add a splash of Worcestershire sauce, if liked.

PAN-ROASTED VINE TOMATOES WITH BALSAMIC VINEGAR

Heat some olive oil in a large frying pan. Add sprigs of red or yellow cherry or cocktail tomatoes on the vine and fry gently, shaking the pan for 1 minute. Sprinkle over a little light soft brown sugar and a good splash of balsamic vinegar. Fry gently, spooning the juices over the fruit once or twice, until the tomatoes are soft but still hold their shape. Season, transfer to warm plates, and spoon the juices over.

SEMI-DRIED TOMATOES IN OLIVE OIL

Halve very sweet, ripe, standard tomatoes. Arrange cut-sides up in a large roasting tin. Drizzle with some olive oil. Sprinkle each tomato with a pinch of caster sugar and add a good grinding of black pepper. Bake in the oven at 150°C (300°F/Gas 2) for 2 hours until meltingly tender. Serve warm or cold scattered with torn fresh basil; and crusty bread, or store in the fridge.

YELLOW TOMATO AND PEPPER BRUSCHETTA

Roast a yellow pepper under the grill, turning occasionally until the skin blisters and blackens. Wrap in a biodegradable plastic bag and leave to cool, then peel off the skin. Skin 6 yellow cherry tomatoes. Seed and finely chop the pepper and tomatoes, then mix with a splash of olive oil and some chopped fresh thyme. Season. Toast slices of French bread and rub with a halved garlic clove. Spoon the tomato mixture on top and leave to soak into the bread for 5 minutes before serving.

TOMATO AND GRILLED GOAT'S CHEESE SALAD

Slice some beefsteak tomatoes and arrange overlapping on small plates. Drizzle with olive oil and just a splash of sherry vinegar. Scatter with torn fresh basil leaves. Season lightly. Put a disc of goat's cheese per person on oiled foil and flash under a preheated grill until melting and lightly golden. Quickly transfer to the salads and serve.

LINGUINE WITH BABY PLUM TOMATOES AND CHILLIES

Cook about 85g (3oz) linguine per person. Drain and return to the pan. Meanwhile, melt some butter and olive oil in a pan. Add a little finely chopped onion and fry gently to soften, stirring. Add some chopped red chillies to taste and baby plum tomatoes. Toss briefly to soften slightly. Blend some tomato purée with a little apple juice, a splash of amaretto liqueur, brandy, and some double cream to form a creamy sauce. Add to the pan. Bring to the boil. Season. Pour over the pasta. Toss gently. Serve sprinkled with chopped parsley.

TOMATO AND ONION TART

SERVES 4–6 **PREPARATION TIME** 25 minutes **COOKING TIME** 25 minutes
VARIATION To make it more substantial, you could top each portion with
a lightly poached egg. **SERVE WITH** a crisp green salad. You can serve the
tart warm or cold.

1 Preheat the oven to 200°C (400°F / Gas 6). Mix the flour, salt, and
cinnamon together. Rub in the butter until the mixture resembles
breadcrumbs. Mix with enough cold water to form a firm dough.
Knead gently on a lightly floured surface. Roll out and use to line
a 23cm (9in) shallow flan dish or tin. Fill with crumpled foil or
line with greaseproof paper and fill with baking beans. Bake in
the oven for 10 minutes. Remove the foil or paper and beans
and cook for a further 5 minutes to dry out.

2 Meanwhile, fry the onions gently in the oil, stirring, for
5 minutes, until soft but not brown. Add the tomatoes, tomato
purée, sugar, and some seasoning and simmer gently, stirring
occasionally, for 10 minutes until pulpy. Stir in the parsley, taste
and reseason, if necessary.

3 Spoon into the flan case and spread out. Arrange the anchovies
in a lattice pattern on top with the olives dotted around. Bake for
10 minutes. Serve warm or cold.

Note: Anchovies are endangered in some areas. Make sure you buy
sustainably fished ones. Look for Fish4Ever in good supermarkets
or online. For more information, go to www.fish-4-ever.com.

INGREDIENTS
175g (6oz) wholemeal flour
A good pinch of salt
1 tsp ground cinnamon
100g (3½oz) butter, diced
2 Spanish onions, roughly
  chopped
3 tbsp olive oil
1 garlic clove, crushed
450g (1lb) tomatoes, skinned
  and chopped
1 tbsp tomato purée
½ tsp caster sugar
Salt and freshly ground
  black pepper
2 tbsp chopped fresh parsley
60g (2oz) can anchovies
  in olive oil, drained
A few black olives

SALAD LEAVES

We used to have only soft, round lettuce or the crisper Webbs Wonderful and, maybe, chicory in winter. Now there's an unbelievable variety of tasty leaves; some are grown all year, while others have overlapping seasons so there is always a supply, thanks to the help of glasshouses and polytunnels. Some are crisp and juicy, others tender and delicate; some are mild, others peppery. They add contrasts of texture and flavour to salads, sandwiches, and wraps, act as a bed for just about anything savoury and can be used as a colourful garnish. Some are delicious in soups, braised, or stir-fried.

Little Gem small, tight lettuce with juicy, round leaves. Keeps well. Good sautéed in halves or quarters, as well as raw.

WHAT WHEN AND HOW

WHAT TYPES
Whole head: All the different varieties, grown and cut whole. The leaves can still be separated and used as required. They include: crispheads, like iceberg, batavia, frisée, Cos (romaine), Chinese leaf (cabbage), radicchio and chicory; and soft or butterheads like round, curly, oakleaf, Little Gem, and lollo rosso.
Other leaves: The loose-leafed ones that can be bought in packs, bunches, or still growing. They include baby spinach leaves and Swiss chard (see p76), rocket, watercress, salad cress, red mustard cress, lamb's lettuce, dandelion, and the Asian mustards like mizuna and mibuna (and baby tat soi and mustard greens, see p76).

some are dark red, others just tinted at the tips.

WHEN IN SEASON
Dandelion: March–May; **Little Gem, lollo rosso, oakleaf:** April–September; **Lamb's lettuce:** May–November; **Cos (romaine), iceberg, frisée, Batavia:** June–September; **Chinese leaf (cabbage):** September–December; **Radicchio:** September–March; **Chicory:** October–April; **Round and curly lettuce, watercress, salad cress:** All year; **Asian mustards:** All year (best September–May); **Rocket:** All year (best May–October)

Lollo rosso soft lettuce without a heart and with crinkled, red-tipped leaves.

HOW TO CHOOSE AND STORE
Choose fresh-looking leaves with a firm heart, if relevant. Avoid if wilting or bruised. Heads will keep in the chiller box in the fridge for a week or more (discard any wilted leaves before use). Unwashed leaves will keep in a biodegradable plastic bag in the fridge for several days, but ready-washed must be eaten within a day or so, as they rot quickly.

Frisée Member of the chicory family with crisp, spiky leaves. Classic for French bistro salad with poached egg and bacon (see p153).

slightly bitter heart.

The classic for Caesar salad.

Cos (romaine) Crisp, tall leaves surrounding a paler heart. Keeps well.

Crunchy texture and juicy, sweet flavour.

Chinese leaf (cabbage) Pale green leaves with thick, fleshy, white stalks. Excellent for stir-fries as well as raw.

Has a mild, delicate flavour.

Tight head, keeps well.

Iceberg Hearty, pale, juicy, crisp lettuce. Webbs Wonderful (mentioned in introduction) is a variety of iceberg.

Oakleaf similar to lollo rosso but with undulating, rather than crinkly, leaves. The green leaves are tinged with red.

Radicchio Tight-headed member of the chicory family. Cabbage-like texture makes it robust for warm salads.

Red with white ribs.

Base can be bitter (see To Prepare, p152).

Chicory Tight, spear-shaped cluster of blanched-white, crisp leaves. Red Treviso variety also available. Good raw, or braised wrapped in ham and in a cheese sauce.

Choose ones with as firm a heart as possible.

Round lettuce The traditional soft-leaf butterhead lettuce with silky, slightly firmer heart. Good for soup and salad.

They remain crisp long after they are cut.

Batavia Frilly-leafed lettuce with a good nutty flavour, and excellent keeping qualities.

Mizuna When young, the dark green, serrated leaves with thin, white stalks have a mild, slightly spicy, mustardy taste, similar to rocket.

150 SALAD LEAVES

Try throwing on a pizza margarita just before serving.

Rocket Serrated-edged leaves with a pronounced peppery flavour.

Lamb's lettuce Clusters of small, soft leaves with a sweet, nutty flavour.

Salad cress The sprouting leaves of cress seeds. Usually grown in compost. Mild, sweet, and slightly nutty. Good in salads, sandwiches, and garnishes.

Stalks have a stronger, peppery flavour than the leaves.

Watercress Sprigs of shiny, round leaves on thick stalks. Good in salads, sandwiches, and chopped in sauces or soup.

Red mustard cress Looks like large-leafed, red-flecked cress but is the sprouted seeds of mustard, with a pronounced mustard flavour. Can also be all green.

Dandelion Familiar, pointed leaves with indentations. Best if young and small. Taste one: if it is bitter, soak in warm water for 15 minutes, then rinse and drain before use; or blanch and serve like spinach.

PERFECT PAIRINGS

EXTRA VIRGIN OLIVE, **SUNFLOWER**, or **GRAPESEED OILS**, alone or mixed with speciality ones such as **CHILLI**, **GARLIC**, **SESAME**, **WALNUT**, or **TOASTED PUMPKIN**, drizzled over with or without vinegar or citrus juice. Speciality **VINEGARS** such as **RASPBERRY**, **APPLE CIDER**, **AGED BALSAMIC**, **SHERRY**, **CIDER**, **WINE VINEGARS**, or **WHITE BALSAMIC CONDIMENT** with oils for dressing. Fresh whole or torn **HERB LEAVES**, thrown in to add flavour.

SIMPLE WAYS TO ENJOY

TO PREPARE

A clear advantage of organic vegetables is that there are no chemicals to remove, so don't wash unless necessary. For all salads, dress at the last minute to preserve crispness.

HEADS

Cut off the stump and separate into leaves, discarding any damaged outer ones. Tear rather than cut, so as not to bruise the leaves, unless you need to shred with a sharp knife. Wash and pat dry with kitchen paper, only if necessary.
For chicory: Cut a cone shape out of the base with a pointed knife to remove the bitter core before separating.

LEAVES

Pick over and discard any damaged leaves. Trim off the feathery stalks of watercress, and use to flavour stock or soup. Snip off growing cress with scissors.

CRUNCHY GREEN SALAD WITH HONEY MUSTARD DRESSING

Whisk 3 parts olive oil, 1 part lemon juice, with a small spoonful each of clear honey and grainy mustard. Season. Mix some crisphead lettuce, torn into bite-sized pieces, a small handful of coriander leaves, chopped green pepper and diced cucumber in a bowl. Add a little dressing and toss gently.

CAESAR SALAD

Boil a large egg for 1½ minutes. Drain, and rinse in cold water. Crack over a blender; scoop into a goblet. Add 2 anchovy fillets (see note, p147), a dash of Worcestershire sauce, and 3 tbsp sunflower oil. Blend until creamy. Sharpen with lemon juice. Season. Fry bread cubes in olive oil until golden. Drain on kitchen paper. Tear a Cos lettuce into a salad bowl. Add the croûtons and some hard sheep's cheese or Parmesan shavings. Dress, toss.

BABY LEAF SALAD WITH PEAR AND TOASTED PUMPKIN SEEDS

Put a large handful of mixed baby leaves, per person, into a salad bowl. Add some chopped spring onions, peeled and diced ripe pears and toasted pumpkin seeds. Whisk 2 parts olive oil with 1 part toasted pumpkin seed oil, and 1 part white wine vinegar. Season to taste. Pour over. Toss gently.

CHICORY NACHOS

Put chicory spears in a shallow, flameproof dish. Fill with tomato salsa. Sprinkle with grated Cheddar. Grill until bubbling. Serve immediately.

WATERCRESS OR LETTUCE SOUP

Soften a chopped onion and a chopped potato in butter. Add 2 chopped bunches watercress, or 1 butterhead lettuce with 4 parsley stalks, and a light stock. Season. Simmer until tender. Purée. Thin with milk. Reheat or chill.

BISTRO SALAD WITH FRISÉE LETTUCE

INGREDIENTS
4 eggs
1 tbsp lemon juice
Olive oil
2 thick slices bread, crusts
  removed, diced
1 garlic clove, halved
5mm (¼in) slice fresh root
  ginger (optional)
115g (4oz) smoked lardons
½–1 frisée lettuce, torn
Leaves of 3 sprigs fresh thyme
1 small handful of fresh flat-leaf
  parsley
1 small handful of fresh
  coriander
1 small red onion, thinly sliced,
  separated into rings

FOR THE DRESSING
2 tbsp red wine vinegar
¼ tsp dried chilli flakes
2 tsp Worcestershire sauce
¼ tsp caster sugar
Salt and freshly ground
  black pepper

SERVES 4 **PREPARATION TIME** 5 minutes **COOKING TIME** 10 minutes
VARIATION Replace the soft-cooked eggs with hard-boiled ones, or try other
crisp lettuce varieties in place of the frisée.

1 Poach the eggs in gently simmering water with the lemon juice for
about 3 minutes. Scoop out and put straight into cold water.

2 Heat a little olive oil in a non-stick frying pan. Add the bread,
garlic, and ginger, if using, toss and stir until golden. Drain on
kitchen paper. Discard the garlic and ginger. In the same pan,
dry-fry the lardons until crisp and golden. Drain on kitchen paper.

3 Put the lettuce in a salad bowl, and tear in the herbs. Add the
onion, lardons and croûtons. Add 5 tbsp olive oil to a pan with the
dressing ingredients. Heat gently, stirring. Add to the salad, toss. Put
into four bowls. Top each with a poached egg.

LEAF, CHANTERELLE, AND COBNUT SALAD

SKYE GYNGELL

Originally from Australia, Skye is the award-winning head chef at Petersham Nurseries Café, Surrey, where she works with seasonal and local produce. She is also food writer for the *Independent on Sunday*.

SERVES 4 **PREPARATION TIME** 15–20 minutes. **This is a light and simple salad using all the ingredients that are good in the first few weeks of September. It's important that you buy the very best ingredients that you can afford.**

1 Place the celery, fennel, and salad leaves in a mixing bowl. Add the chanterelles, lemon zest and juice, and season well with salt and pepper. Pour over the olive oil and toss together lightly with your hands. Add the cheese and cobnuts and toss again.

2 Divide half the salad among four plates. Spoon a good tablespoon or so of crème fraîche over each and top with the rest of the salad. Finish with the chopped parsley and serve at once.

INGREDIENTS
2 celery sticks, cut into
  fine slices
1 fennel bulb, fibrous outer
  leaves removed, cut into
  fine rounds
A handful of lamb's lettuce
A handful of baby red chard,
  or torn radicchio
20 chanterelle mushrooms ,
  gently wiped clean with a dry
  cloth (don't wash them)
Grated zest and juice of
  1 unwaxed lemon
Sea salt and freshly ground
  black pepper
3 tbsp extra virgin olive oil
100g (3½oz) hard goat's cheese
  or Parmesan, finely sliced
12 cobnuts, shelled and
  roughly chopped
90ml (3fl oz) crème fraîche
1 tbsp chopped fresh parsley

CUCUMBERS AND RADISHES

The cooling cucumber is a member of the squash family, so it could have been put with courgettes and marrows but it isn't prepared or cooked in the same way. Crisp, peppery radishes could have gone with root vegetables, as that's what they are, but, although you *can* boil them like turnips, you don't prepare them like that and that's not how we think of them. So, as they are both such traditional British salad crops, we thought we'd give them their own page, with some delicious suggestions for serving them.

WHAT WHEN AND HOW

WHAT TYPES
Cucumbers: Two types – smooth, indoor, or European cucumbers and ridge, or outdoor varieties. The long, smooth cucumbers grown in hothouses have fairly tender, green skin, pale green flesh and hardly any seeds. Ridge are short and knobbly with tougher skins and large, white seeds. When ripe, the flesh turns creamy yellow. Try "burpless" varieties.
Radishes: Here are the familiar red, round and the long, red and white, French Breakfast types. Numerous varieties are available.

WHEN IN SEASON
Cucumbers: June–October (best August–September); **Radishes:** April –December (best April–October)

HOW TO CHOOSE AND STORE
Cucumbers: Choose firm ones; avoid if pliable or the ends feel soft. Ridge cucumbers have knobbly, marked skins, but avoid if scabby. Keep for a week in a paper bag in the fridge.
Radishes: Bunches should have fresh, not limp, leaves. Radishes should feel firm; soft ones will be dry and "woody". Remove the leaves, and store for 2–3 days in the fridge chiller box.

French Breakfast radishes Long-bodied, with a milder, sweeter, but still peppery flavour and crisp texture.

Particularly good for dipping.

Red round radishes Traditional, small, red sphere, with hot, peppery taste.

smooth, green skin and hardly any seeds.

smooth cucumbers Long and slender. They have a cool, mild, delicate flavour. Good in salads and sandwiches, and can also be lightly cooked.

Ridge cucumbers Crisp, firm texture and more intense, almost lemony, flavour. Tough skins.

Tough skins and large white seeds.

PERFECT PAIRINGS

CUCUMBERS **VINEGAR** and freshly ground **BLACK PEPPER** for a simple salad; **FISH** and **SEAFOOD**, particularly in salads as a sauce or garnish; **SOY SAUCE** and **GINGER** in stir-fries, **YOGURT** or **SOURED CREAM** for a dip, sauce or soup, **MINT** or **DILL** to flavour salads, soups, sauces, dips, and pickles; **CHEESE** all types in sandwiches and salads. **RADISHES** **LETTUCE**, **TOMATO**, **CUCUMBER**, and **SPRING ONION** with sliced red ones for a British salad; **UNSALTED BUTTER** and **FRESH CRUSTY BREAD** with French Breakfast radishes.

SIMPLE WAYS TO ENJOY

TO PREPARE

CUCUMBERS
Smooth ones need just washing or slicing. Some people like to pare off strips of the green skin before slicing for an attractive finish. They can be peeled, then grated, diced, or chopped, as required. Ridge should be peeled before use then cut as required. If stuffing, or just for preference, scoop out the seeds using a teaspoon.

RADISHES
Cut off the leaves and trim the roots. Slice, or leave whole.

CHILLED CUCUMBER SOUP
Grate a peeled cucumber. Squeeze out the moisture. Mix with a couple of spoonfuls of white wine vinegar, some chopped fresh dill, a pinch of sugar, and ½ large carton of Greek-style plain yogurt. Season. Chill well. Thin with ice-cold milk. Garnish with dill.

CUCUMBER GRATIN
Peel ridge cucumbers and cut into chunks. Boil in a little dry cider with a knob of butter in a covered flameproof casserole until just tender. Remove with a slotted spoon. Make the cider into a sauce with some milk, thickened with cornflour. Stir in grated Cheddar cheese, a dash of English mustard, and season with salt and pepper. Add the cucumber, sprinkle with a little more cheese and a handful of crushed cornflakes. Grill until golden.

PICKLED CUCUMBER
Cut cucumber into thumb-sized pieces. Put in a colander with some sliced onion. Sprinkle with salt, toss, and leave for 2 hours. Rinse and pat dry. Pack in a clean screw-top jar. Add some chopped fresh dill, a few peppercorns, and a mace blade. Sweeten malt vinegar to taste with honey; pour over. Screw on the lid. Chill for 3 days before use.

RADISH, CUCUMBER, AND MINTED YOGURT SALAD
Mix some Greek-style yogurt with a little lemon juice, honey, and plenty of chopped mint. Add roughly diced radishes and diced cucumber. Season to taste. Serve with lamb or cheese.

HERBS

Used judiciously, herbs impart fabulous fragrance and flavour. Experiment at will, but you'll discover certain ones go particularly well with certain foods. Some are best added during cooking; others stirred in just before serving, to preserve the taste. Dried varieties are much more pungent and should be used sparingly. Some are more difficult to grow than others. Basil, for instance, likes sunshine so is usually grown in polytunnels to keep it warm. Mint, on the other hand, will grow absolutely anywhere. We have also included garlic and horseradish here as, although not technically herbs, they are the other most popular UK-grown seasonings.

Basil Bright green or purple annual; shiny leaves with a warm, heady, slightly peppery flavour. There is also a tiny-leafed Greek variety. The leaves are often torn or shredded and are always added at the end of cooking.

WHAT WHEN AND HOW

WHAT TYPES
Can be cooked: Bay, bouquet garni (sprig of parsley, thyme, and a bay leaf tied together) removed before serving; coriander, garlic, mint, oregano, parsley, rosemary, sage, tarragon, and thyme.
Best used raw: Basil, borage, chervil, chives, dill, horseradish, marjoram.
For garnishing: Use the same herb as in the dish or, for delicately flavoured savoury dishes, a sprig of or a little chopped parsley, or some snipped or whole chives; with spices, use coriander; for desserts, mint, rosemary or pretty herb flowers.

WHEN IN SEASON
Bay, rosemary, sage and thyme: All year;
Basil: June–September; **Borage, dill, wild fennel, lovage, and garlic:** May–September;
Chives: March–November; **Chervil, coriander, and tarragon:** May–October;
Horseradish: October–December; **Marjoram, oregano, mint, and parsley:** March–October

HOW TO CHOOSE AND STORE
Buy pots or grow on windowsills or in the garden. Buy cut herbs in small quantities as they don't keep long. Place bunches in water and store sealed packs in the chiller box in the fridge. Use within 1 week. Can be frozen to use in cooking, but not as a garnish. Keep garlic and horseradish in a cool, dry place.

Chives Perennial herb with an aroma and flavour that is a cross between onions and leeks. Add just before serving. Usually snipped with scissors rather than chopped.

The whole stalks and purple flower heads are used for garnishing, too.

The thin, frilly-edged leaves are similar to those of flat-leaf parsley.

Coriander sweet and pungent – usually loved or hated. A semi-hardy annual known as bug-bane because the smell is repulsive to bugs. Its seeds are dried and used as a spice, too.

Long, soft, thin leaves.

Tarragon Perennial with spicy-sweet fragrance and a pungent aniseed flavour. French tarragon has a better flavour than the coarser Russian tarragon. Use sparingly.

Rosemary Hardy perennial with a warm, flowery fragrance that gives stunning flavour to savoury and sweet dishes. Good for drying. Use sprigs whole and remove after cooking, or add chopped leaves.

Dill An annual with a delicate, mild aniseed flavour. Wild fennel is almost identical but smells much more strongly of liquorice. Its seeds are also used for flavouring.

Sage A strong perennial herb with stringent, spicy, sweet yet bitter taste that should be used sparingly. Good for drying.

Mint Numerous varieties. A rampant perennial. Spearmint or garden mint are most popular here for flavouring. Good for drying. Don't confuse with peppermint, with rounder, serrated-edged leaves, and a menthol flavour.

Parsley Two types of hardy biennial: common curly-leaf and Italian flat-leaf. Flat-leaf has a more delicate flavour. Every cook uses parsley; it's perfect for garnishing just about any savoury dish, chopped, in sprigs, or deep-fried.

Green garlic Mild new-season garlic looks a bit like spring onion and is used in the same way.

The cloves are covered in a papery skin, removed before use.

Dry garlic The mature crop has a head divided into pungent cloves which are used individually. Whole heads roasted, then mashed, will become creamy and mild.

Bay Perennial tree; sweet, recognizable fragrance, reminiscent of cloves and basil mixed together. The leaves are not eaten and are usually removed before serving the dish. Good for drying.

Marjoram Sweet marjoram is the most popular variety in Britain. The scented flavour fades quickly, so it is best added just before serving.

Oregano Also known as wild marjoram, a perennial with a similar but stronger flavour. Good for drying.

Thyme A perennial, garden thyme is the most common type, with a sweet, spicy, soothing scent. Lemon thyme has a faintly citrus scent. The tiny leaves are stripped off the stem and added whole or chopped.

Borage Perennial (also grows wild) with hairy stem and leaves and bright blue, starry flowers. If you rub a leaf there's the distinct smell of cucumber. The classic herb for Pimm's.

Horseradish Peel away the outer skin to reveal pure white flesh which, when grated, has a strong piquant taste and smell, reminiscent of mustard.

↖ Looks like a piece of gnarled brown bark.

Chervil Never cooked, chervil is an annual with an unusual, sweet, spicy aroma and feathery leaves.

Lovage Tall perennial with ribbed, hollow stems and yellowy-green leaves that look, smell, and taste a bit like celery.

↖ Use the leaves sparingly as they can overpower.

PERFECT PAIRINGS

BAY All **MEAT**, **FISH**, and **POULTRY**, and in **SWEET CREAMS** and **CUSTARDS**. **ROSEMARY** and **MINT LAMB** Rosemary sprinkled over, mint as a sauce; rosemary roasted with **VEGETABLES**; mint boiled with **POTATOES** and **PEAS**; add to **FRUIT CAKE**. **SAGE ONIONS**, **CHEESE**, and rich meats like **PORK** or **GOOSE**. **THYME**, **TARRAGON**, and **PARSLEY** Thyme and parsley in **STUFFING**, tarragon or parsley in sauce for **CHICKEN** and **FISH**. **BASIL**, **MARJORAM**, and **OREGANO TOMATOES**, **GRIDDLED AUBERGINES**, **MINCED MEAT** creations, and **CHEESE DISHES**. **DILL**, **BORAGE**, **LOVAGE**, and **CHERVIL** in a sauce for **FISH**, **POTATOES**, or **ROOT VEGETABLES**; in a dressing for **CUCUMBER**. **GARLIC** with chopped fresh herbs in **BUTTER**, **OLIVE OIL**, or **SOFT CHEESE**. **CORIANDER** add to any spicy dishes like **CURRIES**, **CHILLIES**, and **TAGINES**. **HORSERADISH** as a relish with strong meats like **BEEF** and **GAME**, or **SMOKED MACKEREL** and **BEETROOT**.

SIMPLE WAYS TO ENJOY

TO PREPARE

Strip the leaves off woody stalks (fleshy stalks, like parsley and coriander, can be used, too). Put in a cup and snip with scissors, or chop on a board. Hold chives in a bunch and snip with scissors. Basil is best torn, not chopped. Bay should be used whole.

GARLIC AND HERB BUTTER

Mash a crushed garlic clove into one-third of a block of softened butter with some black pepper and chopped mixed herbs. To serve in bread, cut a baguette in slices, but not quite through its base and spread the mixture between the slices and over the top; wrap in foil and bake until crisp on the outside. For a sauce with grilled fish or chicken: melt and pour over.

PAIN TOMATE WITH GREEN GARLIC

Mash the white part of a green garlic. Spread on toasted French bread. Drizzle with extra virgin olive oil and top with skinned, seeded, and finely chopped tomatoes. Sprinkle with coarse sea salt.

BASIL, CORIANDER, OR PARSLEY PESTO

In a blender or food processor, chop a bunch of coriander with a handful of pine nuts and a halved, large garlic clove. Slowly blend in olive oil to form a thick paste. Scrape the sides. Add a small chunk of freshly grated hard sheep's cheese or Parmesan, and seasoning to taste. Stir into cooked pasta or use as required.

HORSERADISH CREAM

Mix grated horseradish with a splash of vinegar and some cream. Add a pinch of sugar, if liked.

FRUIT, NUTS & HONEY

APPLES

Like other tree fruit, apples are grown mainly in orchards in Sussex, Kent, Suffolk, and up in Worcester and Hereford, with several in Wales, Ireland, the West Country, and some hardy ones as far north as Scotland. Resilient varieties, such as the popular Discovery, are produced organically. However, some well known varieties, such as Royal Gala and Spartan, are susceptible to a fungal infection called scab – so organic growers avoid them. We have chosen numerous crisp, juicy, mouthwatering British apples – dessert types and cookers – to encourage you to seek them out instead of buying imported interlopers. We grow specialist cider apples, too, of course.

WHAT WHEN AND HOW

WHAT TYPES
Dessert: Numerous varieties to eat straight from the tree. Pippin is an old English word for "seedling"; all pippins, like many old varieties, were grown by chance from planting apple pips.
Cooking: Sour or sharp varieties that pulp when cooked. Larger than dessert varieties. Bramley's Seedling, first grown (also by chance) in Nottingham in the 19th century, accounts for 95 per cent of the crop but there are a few others too.

WHEN IN SEASON
Dessert: August–February (best August –December), depending on variety
Cooking: October–April (best October –December), depending on variety

HOW TO CHOOSE AND STORE
Choose both dessert and cooking varieties that are firm with tight, unbroken skin. Avoid if bruised. They don't have to be bright and shiny, as if waxed, just fresh and apple-smelling. All apples are best stored in a cool larder or fridge in a biodegradable plastic bag rather than a fruit bowl. They'll retain their flavour and juiciness much longer.

DESSERT

Discovery One of the earliest-cropping varieties, developed from Worcester Pearmain. Delicate flavour with a hint of strawberry. Best eaten very fresh.

Classic russeted skin.

Egremont Russet Golden, rough-skinned apple with a dryer, but excellent, sweet-sharp flesh.

Natural patches of brown russet are not a sign of poor quality.

Cox's Orange Pippin One of our most famous varieties. Green-gold with flashes of red. Sweet, juicy flesh. Can be cooked.

Cevaal Good cropper; yellowish skin flashed with red. Good flavour, similar to Cox's.

Fiesta Also known as Red Pippin. Developed in Kent. Another Cox's offspring. Good cropper, excellent for juicing.

Worcester Pearmain Red and yellow but can be almost all red. Good, very sweet strawberry flavour if ripened fully on the tree.

Orleans Reinette Originally from France but grown here for a long time. Crisp, sweet, and slightly nutty with gold, flecked-red skin with some russeting.

Laxton's Superb Similar to a Cox, with sweet, aromatic flesh.

Lord Lambourne Very sweet, mid-season apple with predominantly red skin with patches of greenish yellow.

Ribston Pippin Flushed red and gold with some russeting. Fragrant, Cox-like taste.

APPLES **165**

Don't be put off by its appearance: it has a wonderful flavour.

Chivers Delight Excellent, crisp, juicy apple that keeps well.

Ashmead's Kernel An old, greenish-gold, traditional variety with excellent flavour that keeps well.

Braddick's Nonpareil An exciting, rich but sharp flavour, very different from the Cox types.

King of the Pippin An excellent all-rounder; just as good cooked as raw, and ideal for cider.

Royal Gala Cross between Golden Delicious and Cox's Orange Pippin. Crisp, sweet, and juicy.

Spartan Late-cropping; dark red skin, sometimes with a dash of green. Crisp and juicy.

COOKING

Newton Wonder Red-and-green cooker, can grow quite large. Excellent, acidic flavour and golden flesh when cooked.

Edward VII Late-cropping cooker, green-skinned with delicate taste. Good with added flavourings such as blackberries or sweet spices.

Bramley's Seedling Classic cooking apple. Large, green-skinned with acid, fragrant flesh.

Howgate Wonder Very big cooking apple with red-and-green skin. A tart but sweetish flesh that some like eating raw.

PERFECT PAIRINGS

CHOCOLATE goes surprisingly well, nibbled with it for a simple dessert. **SWEET SPICES**, like **CINNAMON**, **CLOVES**, **NUTMEG**, **GROUND MIXED SPICE**, **GINGER**, and **STAR ANISE**, to enhance the flavour in pies and purées. **CHEESES**, particularly hard ones like **FARMHOUSE CHEDDAR**, as part of a ploughman's lunch, quick snack, or try an apple pie with cheese pastry. **LOVAGE** and **MINT** to add fragrance to purées and poached fruit. **CARAMEL** to coat like toffee or as a syrup.

SIMPLE WAYS TO ENJOY

TO PREPARE

Peel (unless you want the skin for colour in a dish), quarter, core, and slice or dice. Toss in lemon juice or, if cooking later, put in a bowl of acidulated water to prevent browning. For baking whole, remove the core with an apple corer or cut out with a long, sharp knife. Score a line through the skin round the girth of the fruit to prevent splitting during cooking.

TOFFEE APPLES

Push a stick into 3–4 eating apples. Melt 225g (8oz) demerara sugar, 1 tbsp golden syrup, 30g (1oz) butter, 1 tsp vinegar, and 5 tbsp water. Boil until golden and a spoonful dropped in cold water forms a hard, but not brittle, ball. Dip apples in toffee. Swirl round. Put on baking parchment to set.

APPLE AND CELERIAC SALAD

Mix some shredded celeriac with chopped red apple, roughly chopped hazelnuts, and snipped chives. Dress in mayonnaise with a pinch of curry powder added.

BRAISED APPLE AND RED OR WHITE CABBAGE

Mix shredded red or white cabbage with chopped apple, chopped onion, a few sultanas and a little brown sugar in a casserole. Add just a splash of red or white wine vinegar and water. Season. Stir and dot with butter. Cover tightly. Bake at 160°C (325°F/Gas 3) for up to 2 hours until tender. Stir before serving.

APPLE, PARSNIP, AND LEEK GALETTES

Grate a dessert apple, parsnip, and leek. Season, add some chopped sage and beaten egg to bind. Fry spoonfuls pressed out into flat cakes in a little butter and oil until golden and cooked through, turning once.

APPLE SAUCE FOR PORK, DUCK, OR GOOSE

Put just enough water in a pan to cover the base. Add peeled, cored, and sliced cooking apples, cover and cook very gently until pulpy, stirring occasionally. Sweeten to taste and beat in a knob of butter.

APPLE, RAISIN, AND PUMPKIN SEED BREAKFAST BARS

MAKES 12 bars **PREPARATION TIME** 10 minutes **COOKING TIME** 40 minutes
VARIATION You can add some chopped nuts in place of the seeds, if you prefer,
or experiment with other dried fruits, like blueberries or chopped dried apricots.

1 Preheat the oven to 180°C (350°F/Gas 4). Grease an 18 x 28cm
(7 x 11in) shallow baking tin.

2 Don't peel the apples; grate them straight into a large bowl,
working round the cores. Add the oats, spelt, flour, raisins, pumpkin
seeds, salt, bicarbonate of soda, cinnamon, and sugar. Mix well.

3 Add the sunflower oil and beaten egg and mix with a wooden
spoon until thoroughly blended. Spoon the mixture into the
prepared tin. Spread out right to the edges using your fingertips,
pressing down well.

4 Bake in the oven for about 40 minutes until golden brown and
fairly firm. Remove from the oven and leave to cool in the tin for
about 10 minutes. Cut into bars with a sharp knife, then transfer
to a wire rack to cool completely. Store in a sealed container
in the fridge.

INGREDIENTS
4 dessert apples
115g (4oz) rolled oats
60g (2oz) spelt
30g (1oz) plain flour
60g (2oz) raisins
30g (1oz) pumpkin seeds
½ tsp salt
¼ tsp bicarbonate of soda
½ tsp ground cinnamon
85g (3oz) light soft brown sugar
2 tbsp sunflower oil
1 large egg, beaten

APPLE CUT-AND-COME-AGAIN CAKE WITH CINNAMON SUGAR

SERVES 8–12 **PREPARATION TIME** 30 minutes **COOKING TIME** 20–25 minutes
VARIATION Try it with not-too-ripe pears and sprinkle with mixed spice instead
of cinnamon. **SERVE WITH** some double cream, ice cream, or custard.

1 Preheat the oven to 200°C (400°F/Gas 6). Grease a large baking
tin, about 24 x 20 x 5cm (9½ x 8 x 2in) and dust with flour.

2 Peel, core, quarter, and slice the apples and put in a bowl of water
with the lemon juice added to prevent browning.

3 Whisk the eggs and 225g (8oz) of the sugar until thick and pale
and the whisk leaves a trail when lifted out of the mixture.

4 Put the butter, milk, and cream in a pan and heat until the butter
melts, then bring to the boil. Stir into the egg mixture. Sift the
flour and baking powder over the surface and fold in with a metal
spoon. Pour into the prepared tin.

5 Drain the apples and arrange attractively over the batter. Mix
the remaining sugar with the cinnamon and sprinkle over. Bake for
20–25 minutes until golden and cooked through. Leave to cool in
the tin, then cut into squares.

INGREDIENTS
115g (4oz) butter, diced, plus
  extra for greasing
200g (7oz) plain flour, plus
  extra for dusting
3–4 cooking apples
  (depending on size)
1 tbsp lemon juice
3 eggs
250g (9oz) caster sugar
6 tbsp milk
4 tbsp single cream
1 tbsp baking powder
2 tsp ground cinnamon

BERRIES

Cream clusters of elderflowers with an indescribable subtle fragrance tell us that berries – the epitome of the British summer – are on their way. Almost simultaneously, plump gooseberries ripen on their prickly plants, and sweet, juicy, outdoor strawberries are ready for picking. As the season wears on, blueberries, raspberries, and loganberries appear, then blackberries, bilberries, and elderberries take us through to autumn. Fruits for supermarkets are often harvested when hardly ripe, to prevent damage in transit, but their flavour never develops. If you want perfect fruit, pick your own or buy organic berries from farmers' markets.

Green gooseberries An acquired taste with an acidic, perfumed flavour. Green ones are suitable only for cooking with plenty of sweetening.

WHAT WHEN AND HOW

WHAT TYPES
Blackberries: Large cultivated and smaller wild varieties.
Gooseberries: Firm green, sour, or soft purple sweet ones.
Raspberries: Many varieties; orangey red to deep crimson.
Strawberries: Numerous varieties, some of which are illustrated here, selected for flavour.
Loganberries (or tayberries): A hybrid of a blackberry and a raspberry.
Blueberries: This North-American native is now grown here.
Bilberries: Looks like a mini blueberry; grows on dense bushes on moors and heaths.
Elderberries: Elder trees are prolific in hedgerows, with clusters of green, then purple berries following creamy flowers.

WHEN IN SEASON
Blackberries: July–October; **Gooseberries:** June–August; **Raspberries:** July–November, extended by polytunnels; **Strawberries:** May–September; **Loganberries:** July–September; **Blueberries:** July–August; **Bilberries:** August–September; **Elderflowers:** May–June; **Elderberries:** August–October

HOW TO CHOOSE AND STORE
Avoid any berries with brown patches; they should all be plump, shiny, and a rich uniform colour. Running juices indicate bruised or overripe fruit. Ideally, cook or eat when freshly picked, or store in the fridge.

Purple gooseberries Dessert varieties which can be eaten raw or cooked.

sweeter than green gooseberries.

Raspberries They have a long season and are delicious on their own or to complement other sweet and savoury foods. Difficult to grow organically because they are susceptible to pests and diseases.

They should be deep purple and juicy.

Kent Driscoll Jubilee strawberries Award-winner with excellent shape, colour, and flavour.

Wild blackberries Smaller than cultivated ones, these have a more acidic, fuller flavour. Don't pick them by dusty roadsides because they will be polluted.

Sonata strawberries Elsanta cross, with large, uniform fruit and stunning aroma and flavour.

They look like dark red, elongated raspberries.

Evie strawberries Dark red, full-flavoured, sweet, and juicy.

Loganberries have an intense, sweet-sharp flavour and are delicious cooked in compotes and pies.

Each flower changes into a berry that turns from green to deep purple.

Blueberries Berries are of varying sizes and deep blue in colour, with a grey bloom. They have great antioxidant properties and a distinctive, sweet flavour.

Elderflowers Creamy-white clusters with a delicate fragrance.

The berries hang down when ripe.

Elderberries have a sweet, perfumed flavour and are popular with home wine makers, being known as "the Englishman's grape". Like blackberries, they should not be picked on roadsides.

PERFECT PAIRINGS

BLACKBERRY sauce with **PORK** and **PEARS**; stew with **APPLES** for compôtes and pies. **GOOSEBERRIES** and **ELDERFLOWER** heads (remove heads before serving) in a sauce with **GOOSE** (how they got their name), or with **MACKEREL**. **FRESH RASPBERRIES** (or blueberries) with **DUCK**, grilled and sliced in a warm salad, dressed with olive oil and raspberry vinegar. **STRAWBERRIES** Pour **CHAMPAGNE** over whole or sliced fruit, marinate in **ORANGE ZEST** and juice for an hour or two before serving. **LOGANBERRIES** **ALMOND-FLAVOURED SPONGE** or shortcake topped with them or stewed in sweet white wine.

SIMPLE WAYS TO COOK

TO PREPARE

GOOSEBERRIES
Top and tail.

RASPBERRIES, BLACKBERRIES, LOGANBERRIES, AND STRAWBERRIES
Pull off any calyces. Slice strawberries if large.

BLUEBERRIES AND BILBERRIES
Pick over, but no extra preparation needed.

ELDERBERRIES
Pull the berries off the stalks with the prongs of a fork.

ELDERFLOWERS
Discard any with brown flecks. Rinse and pat dry.

BERRY SAUCE FOR ICE CREAM OR OTHER DESSERTS
Simmer 225g (8oz) berries with 5 tbsp water (add 2–3 elderflower heads to gooseberries, if liked). Stir occasionally until pulpy. Sweeten to taste. Add a small knob of butter. (Discard the elderflowers, if using). Sharpen with lemon juice, if necessary. Strain through a sieve to remove seeds.

QUICK BERRY AND CREAM CAKE
Beat together 175g (6oz) each self-raising flour, caster sugar, and softened butter, 3 eggs, and 1 tsp each baking powder and natural vanilla or almond extract, until fluffy. Transfer to two greased 18cm (7in) round sandwich tins. Level the surfaces. Bake at 190°C (375°F/Gas 5) for 20 minutes until risen and the centres spring back when pressed. Cool on a wire rack. Sandwich with whipped cream and sliced or lightly crushed red berries. Top with a little more cream and some whole berries.

BERRY AND APPLE COMPÔTE
Put 2 large peeled and thickly sliced cooking apples in a pan with 115g (4oz) berries (blue/purple ones are best). Add some water, sugar to taste, a cinnamon stick and a thick lemon slice. Cook gently until apples are tender but hold their shape. Discard cinnamon stick and lemon. Serve hot or cold.

ELDERFLOWER CORDIAL
Dissolve 450g (1lb) sugar with 900ml (1½ pints) water, the zest of 1 lemon and the juice of 2. Boil for 2 minutes. Add 12 elderflower heads. Stir, cover, leave until cold. Strain into a bottle. Chill. Serve diluted.

CHOCOLATE STRAWBERRY SHORTCAKES

MAKES 6 **PREPARATION TIME** 15 minutes **COOKING TIME** 10 minutes
VARIATION You can make plain shortcakes by omitting the cocoa powder
and increasing the flour accordingly.

1 Preheat the oven to 230°C (450°F/Gas 8).

2 Sift the flour, cocoa, and baking powder into a bowl. Add the
butter and rub in with the fingertips. Stir in the sugar. Beat the egg
with the vanilla and stir in. Add enough milk to form a soft, but not
sticky, dough. Knead gently until smooth.

3 Pat out to about 1cm (½in) thick. Cut into 6 rounds using
a 7.5cm (3in) cutter, rekneading and cutting the trimmings as
necessary. Place on a lightly greased baking sheet. Bake in the
oven for about 10 minutes until risen and the bases sound hollow
when tapped. Transfer to a wire rack to cool for 5–10 minutes.

4 Halve 3 strawberries for decoration, leaving the calyces intact,
and reserve. Slice the remaining strawberries, discarding the
calyces, and sweeten with a little caster sugar, if necessary. Split
the shortcakes, sandwich with the sliced strawberries and some of
the cream. Top with the remaining cream and decorate with the
reserved, halved strawberries.

INGREDIENTS
200g (7oz) plain flour
30g (1oz) cocoa powder
2 tsp baking powder
60g (2oz) unsalted butter, diced
60g (2oz) caster sugar, plus extra
  for sweetening
1 large egg, beaten
1 tsp natural vanilla extract
About 6 tbsp milk
225g (8oz) strawberries
150ml (5fl oz) double cream,
  whipped

RASPBERRY AND HAZELNUT CRÈME BRULÉE

SERVES 4 **PREPARATION TIME** 10 minutes, plus chilling **COOKING TIME** 30 minutes **VARIATION** Try using chopped pears in the base and walnuts in the cream, or apricots in the base and ground almonds in the cream.

1 Divide the raspberries among 4 ramekins. Sprinkle with 1 tbsp of the sugar and the lemon zest.

2 Whisk the cream with the eggs, hazelnuts, vanilla extract, and a further 1 tbsp of the sugar. Pour over the raspberries. Stand the dishes in a large frying pan with enough boiling water to come halfway up the sides of the dishes. Cover the pan with a lid or foil and cook very gently for about 30 minutes or until set. Don't let it boil or the custards will curdle. Leave to cool, then chill.

3 Either sprinkle liberally with the remaining sugar and put under a preheated grill until caramelized, or put the remaining sugar in a small, heavy-based pan. Heat very gently until the sugar melts and turns pale golden. Do not stir. Swirl the pan gently to allow it to brown evenly and continue to cook until it turns a rich brown colour. Don't allow to burn. Quickly pour the melted sugar over the creams. Blast with a blow torch to scorch in places, tilting so burnt caramel runs to the edge. To eat, crack the caramel with a spoon and dig in.

INGREDIENTS
115g (4oz) raspberries
140g (5oz) caster sugar
1 tsp finely grated lemon zest
400ml (14fl oz) double cream
2 eggs
60g (2oz) ground hazelnuts
½ tsp natural vanilla extract

STONE FRUITS

Lovely, sweet, juicy fruits with a single central stone, all related to each other. The majority of the UK crop is grown in Kent and Herefordshire. There are little, deep purple damsons; numerous varieties of purple, red, or golden plums; shiny, plump cherries; silver-bloomed gages, pinky-gold apricots and wild sloes. When ripe, all except sloes, damsons (unless very ripe) and some cooking plums are delicious eaten raw on their own or in fruit salads, but they are also excellent cooked in delectable desserts and preserves that bring out their exceptional flavours.

Ripe when the leaves have dropped.

Sloes The purple berries are used to flavour gin, preserves, and wine.

WHAT WHEN AND HOW

WHAT TYPES
Plums: The most famous, and most widely grown in the UK, is Victoria, with distinctive red-and-yellow-tear-shaped fruit with green-gold flesh. We've also featured the smaller but similar Opal, a delicious early-fruiting variety, the deep blue Czar and the relatively new Great Yellow, originally from California, for contrast. But look out for other varieties too.
Damsons: Small and oval with dark-blue skin, greenish-yellow flesh and a pronounced bloom. (Look for bullaces – cultivated or in hedgerows and thickets – too. They're wild damsons, mottled red and white, green or greeny-yellow; use them in the same way.)
Greengages: Bright green and round, with greenish-yellow or gold flesh.
Cherries: Mostly deep reddish purple, sweet cherries are such a British fruit but, sadly, in decline. We import far too many. Support CherryAid and demand British – they're fabulous.
Apricots: Distinctive fruit with soft, velvet skin and yellow–orange flesh. Not as juicy as the other stone fruits.
Sloes: Small, purple fruit of the wild blackthorn tree.

WHEN IN SEASON
Plums: August–October; **Damsons:** August–September; **Greengages:** August; **Cherries:** May (late)–July; **Apricots:** July–August; **Sloes:** October–November

HOW TO CHOOSE AND STORE
The skin should be firm but the flesh should give when gently squeezed. Avoid if wrinkled, split, wet, or with any brown patches. If properly ripe, store in the fridge for a few days. If underripe, store in a fruit bowl.

Damsons Quite sharp even when ripe. Excellent flavour when cooked. Use for desserts, cheese, jam, and chutney.

Distinctive bloom.

Great Yellow plums Large, round plum; sweet and juicy. Good dessert, plum but can be cooked.

Cherries Sweet, round fruit with slightly crisp texture. Delicious raw or cooked. Sour cherries (like Morello) are great for jam, but not so widely available.

Green patches mean it's not quite ripe.

Apricots Fleshy fruit with a subtle flavour that blossoms when cooked. Good poached, puréed, or in jam.

Victoria plums The most British of plums with juicy, sweet flesh. Good all-rounder.

Czar plums Deep blue with an outstanding flavour. Excellent for cooking.

Greengages Beautiful sweet-scented fruit when ripe. Use instead of plums for desserts and preserves.

Opal plums Sweet, early-cropping variety with juicy, golden flesh. Delicious raw but good for cooking, too.

STONE FRUITS 181

PERFECT PAIRINGS

CHERRIES and APRICOTS with **COCONUT**. **DAMSONS** and **PLUMS** as chutney with **CHEESES**, **COLD MEATS**, and **POULTRY**. **FOR ALL** as sauces, relishes, or stuffings for rich meats and game like **PORK**, **VENISON**, **DUCK**, and **HAM**; **ALMONDS**, flaked and sprinkled over or ground in crumbles, cakes, and pastry; **KIRSCH**, **BRANDY**, or **AMARETTO** splashed in syrup.

SIMPLE WAYS TO ENJOY

TO PREPARE

Slit in half with a sharp knife. Twist to separate. Ease out the stone with the knife point or, if it is loose, with your fingers. This is not necessary when making jam, as the stones rise to the surface when boiled with the sugar and can be skimmed off with a slotted spoon. For cherries, you can buy a stoner that removes them, keeping the fruit whole.

To skin apricots: Make a nick in the skin with a knife. Put the fruit in a bowl, cover with boiling water, leave for 30 seconds, drain, and peel off the skin.

STONE FRUIT JAM (NOT CHERRIES, UNLESS MORELLO)

Halve 1.8kg (4lb) fruit. Crack a few stones and remove the kernels. Crush. Put the fruit and stones, crushed kernels, juice of 1 lemon (for apricots) and 450ml (15fl oz) water in a pan. Bring to the boil, reduce heat; simmer until pulpy. Remove from heat. Stir in 1.8kg (4lb) sugar. Stir to dissolve. Boil rapidly until setting point is reached. Skim off the stones. Pot and label.

PLUM, DAMSON, OR GREENGAGE CHUTNEY

Halve 900g (2lb) fruit. Put in a large pan with a chopped large onion, chopped garlic, 2 good handfuls of sultanas, a peeled and chopped apple, 450g (1lb) dark brown sugar, 1 tsp dried chilli flakes, 2 tsp salt, 1 tsp ground ginger, and 600ml (1 pint) pickling vinegar. Heat, stirring, until sugar dissolves. Boil, reduce the heat, and cook slowly for a long time, stirring occasionally, until really thick and pulpy. Skim off the stones. Pot and label.

SPICED FRUIT PRESERVED IN BRANDY

Rinse a clean skewer in boiling water. Prick fruit all over with it. Make a syrup with half sugar to water. Add the fruit, a cinnamon stick and a clove, cover, and simmer for 3 minutes. Discard the spices. Lift out the fruit with a slotted spoon. Put in a bowl. Add the same amount of sugar again to the syrup. Dissolve, boil for 5 minutes. Leave to cool. Pour over the fruit. Add a really good slug of brandy. Stir gently. Spoon into jars. Screw on the lids. Store in a cool, dark place for at least 3 weeks.

POACHED PLUMS, GREENGAGES, OR APRICOTS WITH KIRSCH

Put some prepared fruit in a pan. Add a glass of white wine and a good splash of kirsch. Bring to the boil, reduce the heat, cover, and simmer very gently until tender but not pulpy. Serve warm or chilled.

CHERRY STRUDEL

Brush 4 sheets of filo pastry with melted butter and put one on top of each other on a sheet of greaseproof paper. Mix 225g (8oz) stoned cherries with 3 tbsp demerara sugar and 4 tbsp ground almonds. Spoon along the pastry, just in from the edge. Roll up using the paper to help. Put on a buttered baking sheet in a horseshoe shape. Brush with melted butter. Bake at 190°C (375°F/Gas 5) for 20–25 minutes until golden.

FRUIT AMBER

Gently stew plenty of quartered, stoned fruit, the zest and juice of a lemon, a good knob of butter, and a little sugar until pulpy. Add more sugar to taste. Beat until smooth. Beat in 2 egg yolks. Put in an ovenproof dish. Make the meringue with 2 egg whites and 4 tbsp caster sugar. Pile on top of the fruit and bake at 150°C (300°F/Gas 2) until crisp and biscuit-coloured.

FRUIT CHARLOTTE

Line a dish with buttered bread triangles. Top with halved or quartered stoned fruit. Sprinkle well with sugar. (Add a squeeze of lemon juice if using apricots.) Butter a couple more bread slices. Dice. Scatter over. Sprinkle with more sugar. Bake at 180°C (350°F/Gas 4) until golden and tender.

ALL CREAM FRUIT FOOL

Stew some stoned fruit in a splash of water. Sweeten with sugar. Purée. Leave to cool. Fold in some whipped cream. Spoon into glasses.

FRUIT SAUCE FOR ICE CREAM

Stew some stoned fruit in a little sweet white wine or apple juice with the grated zest of a lemon until soft. Sweeten with honey or sugar to taste. Boil to evaporate excess liquid, stirring. Purée. Serve warm or cold.

FRUIT RELISH FOR DUCK, GAME, OR LAMB

Simmer 2 finely chopped spring onions, 8–10 chopped stoned fruits, plus 2 tbsp each balsamic vinegar and hoisin sauce very gently until soft. Sweeten with honey. Add soy sauce and chopped coriander to taste. Serve warm or cold.

APRICOT TOFFEE BRIOCHE PUDDING

SERVES 4 **PREPARATION TIME** 10 minutes **COOKING TIME** 8–10 minutes
VARIATION You can use any stone fruit for this recipe, but with tart ones add
a tablespoon of water instead of lemon juice. You can also use ordinary bread
if you prefer, but brioche gives a lovely richness and texture. **SERVE WITH** thick
plain yogurt, or indulge with West Country clotted cream or vanilla ice cream.

1 Put the butter in a non-stick wok or large frying pan. Place over
a moderate heat until melted. Add the sugar and lemon zest and
juice. Continue to heat, stirring, until the sugar has melted. Turn
down the heat. Add the brioche and very gently fold in, keeping the
brioche as whole as possible.

2 Add the fruit and lightly fold through the mixture. Cover and
cook gently until the apricots are tender, about 5 minutes. Leave
to cool slightly and serve warm, or cool completely and then chill
before serving.

INGREDIENTS
60g (2oz) butter
225g (8oz) light soft brown sugar
Finely grated zest and juice
  of ½ lemon
4 thick slices brioche, cut in
  large cubes
450g (1lb) apricots, stoned
  and quartered

PLUM AND MARZIPAN CLAFOUTIS

SERVES 6 **PREPARATION TIME** 30 minutes **COOKING TIME** 50 minutes
VARIATION This is equally delicious made with cherries or damsons, but instead of putting the marzipan in the fruit cavities, dot little pieces in between. (You can use bought organic white marzipan for quickness.) **SERVE WITH** whipped cream, flavoured with a little sugar and grated orange zest.

1 Mix the marzipan ingredients together with enough of the egg white to form a stiff paste. Push a tiny piece of the paste into the cavity in each plum half.

2 Grease a shallow, ovenproof dish, large enough to hold the plums in a single layer, with 15g (½oz) of the butter. Arrange the plums cut-side down in the dish, with the marzipan underneath. Melt the remaining butter and leave to cool.

3 Preheat the oven to 190°C (375°F/Gas 5). Put the remaining egg white from the marzipan with the eggs and egg yolk. Add the sugar and whisk until thick and pale. Whisk in the melted butter, the flour, milk and cream to form a batter. Pour over the plums. Bake in the oven for about 50 minutes until golden and just set. Serve warm, dusted with caster sugar.

INGREDIENTS
FOR THE MARZIPAN
115g (4oz) ground almonds
60g (2oz) caster sugar
60g (2oz) icing sugar
A few drops of natural
   almond extract
½ tsp lemon juice
1 egg white, lightly beaten

FOR THE CLAFOUTIS
675g (1½lb) plums, halved
   and stoned
75g (2½oz) butter
4 eggs and 1 egg yolk
115g (4oz) caster sugar, plus
   extra for dusting
85g (3oz) plain flour, sifted
450ml (15fl oz) milk
150ml (5fl oz) single cream

DAMSON "SOUP" WITH BLACKBERRIES AND VANILLA ICE CREAM

SALLY CLARKE

Sally Clarke is a restaurateur and chef. As founder of the eponymous, world-famous Clarke's restaurant, deli, and bakery in London, Sally was one of the first chefs to introduce seasonal cooking to British restaurants.

SERVES 8 **PREPARATION TIME** 20 minutes **COOKING TIME** 40 minutes
This is not really a soup in the classic sense, but it has the consistency of a slightly robust, autumnal one. Serve chilled in soup plates, ideally, rather than deep bowls. If strawberries, raspberries, or loganberries are available, they make a lovely addition to this dessert.

1 Wash the damsons well and place them in a stainless-steel pan with the red wine, sugar, and cinnamon stick. Cover and simmer gently until the fruits are very soft. This will take about 40 minutes. Remove the stones, which will have risen to the top, and the cinnamon stick, push the remaining contents of the pan through a plastic or stainless-steel sieve with the back of a ladle, pressing as much of the solids through as possible. Taste and check the consistency – it should have the thickness of a puréed soup. Chill.

2 Cook the blackberries in a stainless-steel pan with the water for 2–3 minutes, until the juice runs. Taste for sweetness and add a little sugar, if required. Cool.

3 To serve, divide the damson "soup" among 8 soup plates and place one large scoop of vanilla ice cream on top of each. Arrange the blackberries around the dollops of ice cream, decorate with a sprig of mint and dust with icing sugar.

INGREDIENTS
1kg (2¼lb) damsons
1 bottle of inexpensive red wine, such as Beaujolais or other light style
175g (6oz) granulated sugar
1 cinnamon stick
300g (10oz) blackberries
2 tbsp water

TO SERVE
Vanilla ice cream (home-made or good-quality bought)
8 sprigs of fresh mint
Icing sugar, for dusting

Recipe reproduced with permission from Sally Clarke's *Recipes from a Restaurant, Shop and Bakery*, published by Grub Street.

CURRANTS

Black-, red-, and whitecurrants are packed with goodness and have been recognized for centuries for their health-giving properties. They all grow on trusses with their fingernail-sized fruit hanging down. Black are the most common and are brimming with vitamin C and antioxidants. Their deep purple, almost black, shade depicts their intense flavour. Red- and whitecurrants are not so common but are worth buying when you see them. They all thrive in organic systems as they're not susceptible to pests, but they are labour intensive to pick.

WHAT WHEN AND HOW

WHAT TYPES
Blackcurrants: They grow in clusters of deep purple fruit. Modern hybrids are not as sour as old varieties. Usually sold without stalks.
Redcurrants: Not grown as extensively as blackcurrants, they are highly prized for their clusters of translucent, bright red, shiny berries. They are sold on the stalks.
Whitecurrants: Not so widely available; they are the albino of the currant world, almost colourless, and are worth looking out for in farmers' markets.

WHEN IN SEASON
July and August.

HOW TO CHOOSE AND STORE
Select trusses where all the fruit is ripe. Avoid those with green berries still attached, particularly if others are only just turning colour. Can be kept in the fridge for up to 5 days, but don't wash before you store. Best eaten or cooked when fresh. Preserve by making into jam or jelly, or freeze the whole fruits.

Glossy, red berries.

Redcurrants A more subtle flavour than blackcurrants, they are often used for redcurrant jelly but can be added raw to sweet and savoury dishes. The glossy berries are lovely gently stewed with honey or sugar, or frosted for a garnish, or served as a dessert (see opposite).

Choose plump, dark purple berries.

Blackcurrants Perfect for numerous desserts, jams, jellies, and cordial. They are slightly acidic, so need cooking and sweetening with sugar, honey, pure fruit juice, or liqueur before eating.

The berries are sweeter than those of other currants.

Whitecurrants Good dessert fruits, particularly with raspberries and blueberries.

PERFECT PAIRINGS

BLACKCURRANTS Chop **MINT** and put it in a pie with them, add a sprig or two when making jam. **REDCURRANTS** Serve **LAMB** with redcurrant jelly – throw a few into the pan juices, with a little redcurrant jelly added too, and spoon over chops; use the berries as a lovely garnish. **WHITECURRANTS** Toss the berries in grated **LEMON** zest mixed with sugar before serving as a dessert; use the lemon sugar to flavour some sweetened cream to serve alongside them.

SIMPLE WAYS TO ENJOY

TO PREPARE

Hold the stalk of the truss over a bowl and run the prongs of a fork down it to remove the berries so that they fall into the bowl below.

BLACKCURRANT BRULÉE

Stew 225g (8oz) blackcurrants in 3 tbsp apple juice until tender. Sweeten to taste with caster sugar. Blend 2 tsp cornflour with 2 tsp water, stir in and cook for 1 minute to thicken. Spoon into 4 small flameproof dishes. Leave to cool. Top with a layer of thick vanilla yogurt, then cover with an even layer of light soft brown sugar. Flash under a grill until the sugar melts and caramelizes, or use a blow torch.

FROSTED REDCURRANTS OR WHITECURRANTS

Brush small trusses of the fruit with lightly beaten egg white. Sprinkle liberally with caster sugar, then leave to dry on non-stick baking parchment. Serve for dessert, as a garnish, or with cheese.

REDCURRANT OR WHITECURRANT JELLY

Simmer 900g (2lb) redcurrants in a pan with 400ml (14fl oz) water and 1 tbsp lemon juice for about 30 minutes until soft, stirring occasionally. Put in a jelly bag and leave to drip for 12 hours or overnight (don't squeeze!). Measure the juice and put it in a pan with 450g (1lb) sugar per 600ml (1 pint) juice. Heat, stirring, until the sugar dissolves, then boil until setting point is reached. Remove any scum. Pot and label.

FRAGRANT BLACKCURRANT AND ROSEMARY CHEESECAKE

SERVES 8–10 **PREPARATION TIME** 20 minutes **COOKING TIME** 1–1¼ hours
VARIATION Ring the changes by using chopped mint instead of rosemary, and blackberries instead of blackcurrants. Add a splash of lemon juice when cooking the fruit to bring out the flavour.

1 Mix the crushed biscuits with the chopped rosemary and stir in the melted butter. Press the mixture into the base and about 2.5cm (1in) up the sides of a buttered 20cm (8in) springform tin. Preheat the oven to 150°C (300°F/Gas 2).

2 Beat the cheese with the sugar, eggs, and vanilla extract. Spoon into the prepared tin. Level the surface. Bake for 1–1¼ hours until set. Turn off the oven and leave until cold. Chill.

3 Stew the blackcurrants in 4 tbsp water until the juices run. Sweeten to taste. Blend the arrowroot with 1 tsp water and stir in. Cook, stirring, until thickened and clear. Leave to cool.

4 Remove the cheesecake from the tin and place on a serving plate. Spoon the blackcurrant topping over so that the fruits trickle down the sides a little. Lay a sprig of rosemary alongside, if liked.

INGREDIENTS
FOR THE CHEESECAKE
200g (7oz) digestive biscuits,
  crushed
1 tbsp chopped fresh rosemary
85g (3oz) butter, melted, plus
  extra for greasing
675g (1½lb) cream cheese
225g (8oz) caster sugar
2 eggs
1 tsp natural vanilla extract

FOR THE TOPPING
225g (8oz) blackcurrants
Granulated sugar, to taste
1 tsp arrowroot
A small fresh rosemary sprig,
  to decorate (optional)

GRAPES AND FIGS

Figs and grapes conjure up images of biblical times and dry, dusty Mediterranean hillsides. But they also thrive in sunnier spots of southern Britain. Here we're featuring the delicate, almost sensuous Brown Turkey fig and juicy, green, red, and black dessert grapes. They're not grown commercially on a large scale but you'll find some in farmers' markets and many people's gardens. We grow wine grapes – some organic – in England and Wales, too. They're different varieties, produced specifically for the purpose. Some vintages match many European equivalents and some sparkling ones are considered a rival to Champagne.

WHAT WHEN AND HOW

WHAT TYPES
Green (white) dessert grapes: Pale, frosted green to greenish yellow. Seeded and seedless.
Black dessert grapes: Deep purple-black skin and pale greeny-yellow flesh; paler red varieties, too. There are seedless varieties, but classic black ones have one or two large seeds.
Wine grapes: Many varieties, but Chardonnay is the most popular for white wine, and Pinot Noir for red. Wines are often blended from more than one type to get the desired balance.
Figs: Brown Turkey is most common with brownish-purple skin and red flesh, or there are green ones, like Brunswick, with pink flesh.

WHEN IN SEASON
Grapes: September–October
Figs: August–September

HOW TO CHOOSE AND STORE
Dessert grapes should be firmly attached to their stem; if tumbling off, they're too ripe. Check the stalk ends: avoid any with softness or browning. The main stalk should be fresh and brownish green, not withered. Figs should have unblemished skin and give gently to pressure, but they are delicate. Store in the chiller box in the fridge; eat within 2–3 days. Remove about an hour before eating.

Green (white) dessert grapes some can be quite tart, others sweet and juicy with a crisp texture. Good with chicken (including liver), fish, and soft cheese.

All grapes should have a definite bloom.

Chardonnay wine grapes Their wine is fruity and dry when young, and often oak-aged to give a more rounded, deep, buttery flavour.

Black dessert grapes They have a more robust flavour and can be very juicy and sweet. Larger varieties can be cooked. They have a good colour to go with many meats, cheeses, or game.

Brown Turkey figs sweet, fragrant, and delicate when ripe. Eat whole or cut into quarters. Can be poached in syrup or topped with sweetened butter or soft cheese and grilled.

PERFECT PAIRINGS

FOR ALL Serve with **CHEESE** at the end of a meal, in salads or canapés, as an accompaniment to strong meats like **LIVER**, **GAME**, and **PÂTÉS**, or mixed with **OTHER FRUITS** for fruit salad, in syrup, wine, or pure fruit juice.

SIMPLE WAYS TO ENJOY

TO PREPARE

GRAPES
Wash and dry. Leave on the bunch if serving with cheese. **To seed whole:** Use a clean hair grip, insert in the stalk end and scoop out the seeds. Alternatively (and easier), halve the grapes and gently flip out the pips with the point of a knife, taking care not to remove the flesh too.

FIGS
Eat whole when ripe or peel back the skin first, if liked. Cut into halves or quarters if serving as an accompaniment. Dice or slice for fruit salads.

CHICKEN WITH CREAM AND GREEN GRAPE SAUCE
Roast some chicken portions. Spoon off all but a good spoonful of fat from the tin. Add some dry white wine and boil until syrupy, stirring. Stir in some crème fraîche, halved seedless green grapes, and chopped tarragon. Season to taste. Serve the chicken with the sauce. Garnish with tarragon sprigs.

BRIE AND RED GRAPE SALAD
Put 4 good handfuls of lamb's lettuce in a bowl. Add some halved red or black grapes, seeded, if necessary, a little finely chopped red onion and some cubed Brie. Drizzle with a little olive oil and a splash of raspberry vinegar. Season and toss gently. Pile on to individual plates.

CHICKEN LIVER AND GRAPE CROSTINI
Sauté trimmed and roughly cut-up chicken livers in a little butter for 4 minutes until cooked but soft. Add a splash of grape juice, a little chopped sage, and a few halved, seedless grapes. Bubble for 1 minute. Season. Spoon on buttered, toasted French bread, rubbed with a garlic clove.

FRESH FIGS WITH SMOKED DUCK BREASTS
Lay slices of smoked duck breasts on plates. Quarter figs and open out starburst fashion and put them alongside. Garnish with sprigs of parsley and drizzle with a little French dressing.

GRILLED FIGS WITH SOFT CHEESE AND RAISINS
Halve ripe figs and put in a flameproof dish. Mix soft cheese with a little honey and some raisins. Sharpen with grated lime zest. Spoon over. Pour in enough sweet sherry to cover the base of the dish. Grill until the cheese is melting. Transfer to serving dishes and spoon the sherry around.

SUSSEX APPLES AND PEARS

MATTHEW AND CAROL WILSON, OAKWOOD FARM

Matthew Wilson grew up at Oakwood Farm, near Hastings, East Sussex, which was then a commercial, non-organic farm growing apples, and now has about 20 hectares (50 acres) of orchards, including apples, dessert and perry pears, and plums. In 1997 he and his wife, Carol, decided to take the plunge and go organic. The business was fully certified in 2000.

They have seen a noticeable change in their orchards since going organic. One of the biggest challenges for organic growers is controlling pests and diseases, however, the range of wildlife and insects on their farm and in their hedgerows has exploded, creating a diverse ecosystem which has helped keep pests under control naturally, and maintain soil fertility. Checking earthworm population is a good indicator of soil health, and the Wilsons' soil has them in abundance. Another way to deal with pests and diseases is to choose strains that are least susceptible. As Matthew explains: "Jonagold is a good cropper and a popular variety, but prone to disease, so we worked until we found a solution, which was to graft the trees with other strains."

As well as apples and perry pears, they grow dessert pears. They are particularly fond of the pears, but are beginning to widen their range to include other fruits. They grow about

Just-harvested dessert pears.

50 varieties of culinary and cider apples, and about 20 varieties of perry and dessert pears. Their most popular varieties include Jonagold, Bramley, Cox, Falstaff, Discovery, Fiesta, Russet, and Spartan. Matthew recently grafted some old Sussex varieties, and is planning to grow quinces, medlars, apricots, and nuts – including cobnuts, almonds, walnuts, and chestnuts. Almonds are not normally grown here, but he hopes they will thrive in the moderate Sussex climate and be cropping in five to six years.

The autumn harvest season is hectic but short, and they pull in dozens of pickers to lend a hand. The rest of the year is spent grading fruit, pruning, making juice (cider and perry), and selling their produce. Over 70 per cent of their fruit is sold whole, with the rest juiced and bottled. Their juices are made from pulped apples pressed through woven cloth, then pasteurized. They are one of only a few organic producers in Sussex, and sell all over the county through box schemes, farmers' markets, and other organic outlets.

See p199 for Carol's *Pear and Cream Pie*.

OPPOSITE, ABOVE LEFT Matthew, Carol, and their dog Rosie, in the orchard.

ABOVE RIGHT King of the Pippins.

BELOW LEFT Queen Cox.

BELOW RIGHT Apples are packed into and stored in wooden "bins", which hold up to 300 kilos of fruit.

PEARS, QUINCES, AND MEDLARS

Sweet, juicy pears; firm, fragrant quinces and soft, ripe, sharp medlars are the flavours of a British autumn. A lot of our produce comes from Hampshire, Kent, East Sussex, and East Anglia where the climate suits them. Quinces can withstand frosts and need temperatures of below 7°C (45°F) to flower and then fruit in late autumn. Quinces and medlars need "bletting" for several weeks (they are left in a dark place to ripen and go soft) before being eaten as a dessert fruit.

Rough russet patches are a natural feature of the skin.

WHAT WHEN AND HOW

WHAT TYPES

Pears: Related to apples, there are four main varieties developed and grown in the UK: Conference, originated in the 19th century; Doyenne de Comice, another 19th-century variety; Concorde, a cross between Conference and Comice, first grown in Kent in 1970s; and Williams Bon Chrétien, the oldest of these, an 18th-century introduction.

Quinces: A relative of apples and pears, the quince has similar-shaped fruits, sometimes with down on the skin. Japonica is an ornamental quince whose small fruit can be used like quinces.

Medlars: Another relative of the same family; the medlar is a small, strange-looking, round fruit with wide-spread sepals that give it a hollow appearance at one end.

Conference Green, often irregular-shaped fruit. Juicy, sweet, white flesh when ripe, with a good flavour.

WHEN IN SEASON

Pears: September–February (best September–November)

Quinces and medlars: October–November

HOW TO CHOOSE AND STORE

If just ripe, they should smell fragrant and give slightly to gentle pressure. The rough, brown russeting on some skins is normal and does not denote poor quality. If overripe they will be soft and the flesh soft and pappy. For cooking, choose firm, slightly underripe fruit. Avoid those with damaged skin.

skin turns more yellowy as it ripens.

Doyenne de Comice Rounded shape with green-and-brown skin. Creamy, almost buttery, juicy flesh.

Medlars The fruit is hard and
tart until bletted. Eat ripe and
raw for dessert, or cook like quinces.
The fruit rarely ripens on the tree.

More russet patches
than Conference.

Concorde Looks like a more regular,
pear-shaped Conference pear.
Exceptionally good flavour.

The flesh
turns pink
when cooked.

Classic
pear
shape.

Quinces Yellow-skinned pear- or
apple-shaped fruit with hard,
tart flesh. Use for cheese
(membrillo in Spain), jelly,
or to flavour apple and
pear dishes.

Williams Bon Chrétien
Golden-skinned with a deep
flavour and good, juicy flesh.

PERFECT PAIRINGS

PEARS **CHOCOLATE** as a sauce, mousse, or sponge; **WALNUTS** to add crunch in salads, cakes, and desserts; **BLUE CHEESE** in a dressing, stuffing, or salad. **QUINCES** and **MEDLARS** **APPLES** and **PEARS**, slice one and add to the fruit in tarts or pies; **HARD SHEEP'S** and **GOAT'S CHEESE** with quince or medlar cheese; **LAMB**, **PORK**, **GAME**, and **CURED MEATS**, poached then sautéed in butter or as jelly or cheese. **FOR ALL** **CINNAMON**, **STAR ANISE**, **GINGER**, **CARDAMOM**, and **CLOVES** for spicing poached or to flavour crumbles, pies, or sponges.

SIMPLE WAYS TO ENJOY

TO PREPARE

PEARS AND QUINCES
Wipe off any down from quinces. Peel. Leave whole or quarter, core, and slice or dice, as necessary.

MEDLARS
As dessert, after "bletting" to ripen; wash, halve, and scoop the flesh out with a spoon.

SPICED POACHED PEARS IN RED WINE
Lay peeled pears in a casserole dish. Sweeten some red wine with light soft brown sugar and sharpen with a dash of lemon juice. Pour over the fruit, add 1 star anise and 1 cinnamon stick. Cover and cook at 160°C (325°F/Gas 3) until tender, turning once. Discard the spices. Serve hot or chilled.

GRILLED PEARS WITH IRISH CREAM LIQUEUR TOPPING
Whip equal quantities of double cream and thick plain yogurt. Flavour with Irish cream liqueur and ground cinnamon. Chill. Coat cored, thickly sliced, firm pears in melted butter. Sprinkle with demerara sugar. Put on a foiled grill rack; grill until golden. Serve topped with cream and chopped walnuts.

PEAR AND GINGER UPSIDE-DOWN CAKE
Thickly butter a 20cm (8in) sandwich tin. Sprinkle liberally with light soft brown sugar. Lay peeled, cored pear halves attractively on top. Beat 115g (4oz) each softened butter, light soft brown sugar, wholemeal self-raising flour, with 2 tsp ground ginger, 1 tsp baking powder and 2 eggs. Spread over. Bake at 190°C (375°F/Gas 5) for 20 minutes until just firm. Turn out.

QUINCE OR MEDLAR CHEESE
Wash and chop quinces, cores and all; leave medlars whole. Steam until tender. Purée with lemon juice. Add 450g (1lb) sugar per 500ml (16fl oz) pulp. Heat gently in a pan, stirring, until the sugar dissolves. Simmer, stir until a line is left when drawn through cheese. Rinse plastic lidded boxes in boiling water. Dry. Brush with oil. Pack in cheese. Cover and store in fridge.

PEAR AND CREAM PIE

CAROL AT OAKWOOD FARM

Matthew Wilson grows organic apples and pears at Oakwood Farm, East Sussex, and sells fruit, juice, cider, and perry. See pp194–5.

INGREDIENTS
FOR THE PASTRY
225g (8oz) plain flour
A good pinch of salt
1 tsp ground cinnamon
½ tsp ground mixed spice
75g (2½oz) walnuts, finely chopped
140g (5oz) unsalted butter, softened and diced
115g (4oz) caster sugar, plus extra for finishing
1 egg

FOR THE FILLING
3 Comice or William pears
4 tbsp double cream
Natural vanilla extract

SERVES 6–8 **PREPARATION TIME** 15–30 minutes, plus chilling **COOKING TIME** 40 minutes. **My wife Carol has been making this for years. I love it. If chopping walnuts in a processor, don't grind them too finely: you want some texture.**

1 Whiz all the pastry ingredients, except the egg, in a food processor. Then add the egg to make a dough. Wrap in foil or greaseproof paper and chill for at least 30 minutes. Preheat the oven to 190°C (375°F/Gas 5).

2 Peel, quarter, and core the pears. Take the pastry, cut off a third and set aside. Roll out the rest and line a 20cm (8in) loose-bottomed flan tin. Arrange the pears cut-side down. Roll out the remaining pastry and use as a lid. Trim. With a sharp knife, cut lines in the centre of the lid to make a star. Fold back the points to form a flower with a central hole. Brush with water, sprinkle with caster sugar. Bake for 40 minutes until golden. Cool. Whip the cream, flavour with 1 tsp sugar and a few drops of vanilla extract. Spoon into the centre.

RHUBARB

Rhubarb originated in Asia but has been popular in Britain since the 17th century. Technically it is a vegetable, but it is usually served as a fruit. This perennial is propagated by splitting and replanting the crown in winter. It's a good organic crop as slugs in its first year are the only pests that bother it. There are two types: the lovely pink, tender, forced stalks – grown in the dark so they shoot quickly and become tall, slender and succulent – and outdoor rhubarb, with thicker green and red coarser stalks, with a more acidic flavour.

WHAT WHEN AND HOW

WHAT TYPES
Forced rhubarb: The plants are covered with a bin as soon as the shoots appear. The warm, dark conditions encourage rapid growth, producing pink, tender shoots with yellow leaves.
Outdoor rhubarb: Much coarser, green-red stalks, with dark green leaves, grown naturally.

WHEN IN SEASON
Forced: February–April
Outdoor: April–July

HOW TO CHOOSE AND STORE
Choose firm, straight stems that snap easily. Avoid any that are very pliable. The leaves of forced rhubarb should be pale yellow and fresh. They are often trimmed before you buy, but if the leaves are still on outdoor rhubarb, they should be fresh and green, not wilting. Avoid any stems with brown patches. Store in the fridge for up to 2 weeks.

The stalks may need peeling.

Outdoor rhubarb The stalks can be used in the same way as forced rhubarb, but are best puréed for sauces and desserts. Some people add a dash of pink food colouring to the cooked pulp for a more pleasing colour.

Forced rhubarb Tender, thin, pink stalks that are perfect for all desserts from compotes, pies, tarts, and crumbles to ice cream, sorbets, fools, and mousses.

All rhubarb leaves are toxic.

PERFECT PAIRINGS

GINGER, fresh, ground, or crystallized, or ginger wine when poaching, or in other desserts.

ORANGE zest and juice added to it in when poaching, or in pies, flans, and mousses.

STRAWBERRIES or **RASPBERRIES** puréed with the cooked fruit for mousses, fools, or ice cream.

Add just a pinch of chopped fresh or crushed dried **LAVENDER FLOWERS** to poached fruit at the end of cooking for a fragrant spiced flavour. With **OILY FISH**, use the purée as a sauce to offset the richness of grilled or pan-fried mackerel or herring (see p212).

SIMPLE WAYS TO ENJOY

TO PREPARE

Cut off and discard the leaves (they are poisonous) and the base of the stems. Cut the stems into short lengths. If outdoor rhubarb is very thick you may need to pull off the skin too. (It will be obvious if the skin is tough when you try to cut it into lengths.) Use as required.

POACHED RHUBARB

Layer 450g (1lb) prepared forced rhubarb in a casserole dish with 60g (2oz) caster sugar and add 3 tbsp apple juice. Cover tightly and cook in a preheated oven at 180°C (350°F/Gas 4) for about 30 minutes until tender but still holding its shape. Serve with pouring cream.

RHUBARB AND ORANGE YOGURT FOOL

Put 450g (1lb) prepared forced or outdoor rhubarb in a pan. Add 85g (3oz) caster sugar and the grated zest and juice of an orange. Cover and cook gently for about 10 minutes until the fruit is really pulpy. Purée in a blender or food processor. Leave until cold. Gently fold into 300ml (10fl oz) thick Greek-style yogurt, then spoon into glasses. Chill. Drizzle a tiny swirl of clear honey on top just before serving.

RHUBARB AND ALMOND CRUMBLE

Put 450g (1lb) prepared rhubarb in an ovenproof dish. Sprinkle with 60g (2oz) caster sugar and add 2 tbsp water. In another bowl, rub 60g (2oz) butter into 115g (4oz) plain flour until it resembles breadcrumbs. Stir in 60g (2oz) light soft brown sugar and a handful of flaked or chopped almonds. Sprinkle over the fruit and press down well. Bake in a preheated oven at 190°C (375°F/Gas 5) for about 35 minutes until crisp and golden and the fruit is tender. Serve with custard or cream.

RHUBARB AND CUSTARD ICE CREAM

SERVES 4–6 **PREPARATION TIME** 30 minutes, plus chilling and freezing time
VARIATION You can add some grated fresh root ginger or the zest of an orange
if you want to enhance the flavour, but it's perfect with just the tartness of the
rhubarb and the vanilla-tasting custard.

1 Gently stew the rhubarb with 60g (2oz) of the sugar and 2 tbsp
water in a covered pan until really tender, about 10 minutes, stirring
occasionally. Purée in a blender or food processor. Leave to cool.

2 Beat the egg yolks, remaining sugar, and salt in a large bowl with
an electric beater or balloon whisk until thick and pale. Heat the
milk and cream until hand hot and stir into the mixture with the
vanilla. Put the bowl over a pan of gently simmering water and stir
with a wooden spoon until the custard just coats the back of the
spoon and a finger drawn through it leaves a clear line. Remove
from the pan and leave to cool.

3 When the custard is completely cold, mix with the rhubarb purée
and freeze in an ice-cream maker, according to the manufacturer's
directions. Or, pour into a shallow freezer-proof container with
a lid, and freeze for about 2 hours until frozen around the edges.
Beat well with a fork to break up the ice crystals, freeze for a
further 2 hours, beat again, then freeze until firm. The ice cream
is best eaten fresh but can be stored in the freezer for up to 1 week
and taken out 15 minutes before serving to soften slightly.

INGREDIENTS
450g (1lb) forced rhubarb, cut
  into short lengths
225g (8oz) caster sugar
5 egg yolks
175g (6oz) caster sugar
Pinch of salt
450ml (15fl oz) milk
150ml (5fl oz) single cream
1 tsp natural vanilla extract

smaller flakes
than cod.

Pollack An underrated fish with
a surprisingly good flavour. Can
be substituted for cod or haddock.
Usually sold in fillets.

Haddock Slightly sweeter
flavour than cod. Usually sold
in loins or fillets. Can be cooked
in exactly the same way.

Large,
moist flakes.

Cod Has firm, white, highly prized
flesh. Usually sold in fillets, loin, or
steaks. Poach, steam, fry, or bake.
Steaks can be stuffed.

Coley (saithe) Has a good fish
flavour. Often cheaper than other
varieties. Good all-rounder. Usually
sold in large fillets.

The slightly grey
flesh turns white
when cooked.

Whiting A more delicate fish with an
excellent flavour. Usually sold in fillets.
Good poached, or crumbed and fried.

NUTS

A nut is a seed or fruit with an oily kernel inside a hard shell, used for food. Technically they are not all true nuts (peanuts, for instance, are legumes), but the ones grown in Britain are. Enjoy the mahogany-brown chestnut, our traditional, heart-warming nut, roasted on an open fire or a street brazier; crinkly walnuts with their hard, brown shells and intense flavour, and the little, round cobnuts and hazelnuts with their sweet, milky taste that deepens when toasted. Perfect for so many sweet and savoury dishes, so make the most of them.

WHAT WHEN AND HOW

WHAT TYPES
Chestnuts: The fruit of the sweet chestnut tree, not to be confused with the horse chestnut tree. On the tree, the nuts are encased in pale green, spiky cases.
Hazelnuts and cobnuts: Hazelnuts are the original wild nut, still widely found. Cobnuts are a cultivated variety, Kentish cobs being the most well known. Until a decade ago they were in decline, but are now being revived.
Walnuts: Mainly grown in the south, walnuts first develop in a bright green, shiny outer husk that gradually goes dark brown as the fruit ripens.

WHEN IN SEASON
Chestnuts: September–December; **Hazelnuts and cobnuts:** green, August; brown, September–October; **Walnuts:** green, June–July; brown, September–January (best October–November)

HOW TO CHOOSE AND STORE
In their shells they should feel heavy; if light, they may be rotten inside. Avoid chestnuts with signs of mould on the shell or any cracks. Store in a cool, dark place and use within a few weeks. Buy prepared nuts in small quantities. Store in a cool, dark place in an airtight container, not the fridge.

Sweet chestnuts Sweet and floury, perfect for puréeing for savoury dishes and desserts. They can also be roasted whole in their skins, or shelled and boiled or baked.

The hard, brown shell and bitter inner skin must be removed before eating.

The crinkly, brown shells split into two clean halves.

Walnuts The bright green, unripe fruit with soft, milky nuts inside can be pickled whole. The dry, brown, ripe fruits are used in many sweet and savoury dishes, but usually as whole halves or chopped, rather than ground.

Hazelnuts and cobnuts These small nuts have a distinctive flavour. Used chopped or ground in stuffings, cakes, biscuits, creams, and other desserts.

The flavour of the nut is enhanced with toasting.

PERFECT PAIRINGS

ALL NUTS with **CHOCOLATE** in desserts, cakes, biscuits, and sweetmeats. HAZELNUTS and COBNUTS with **RASPBERRIES** as a topping, or sauce for hazelnut-flavoured desserts; **CREAM CHEESE** for savoury and sweet dishes. WALNUTS with **BLUE CHEESE** in tarts, dressings, and in a sauce for pasta; with **COFFEE** in desserts and cakes.

SIMPLE WAYS TO ENJOY

TO PREPARE

CHESTNUTS
To peel: Make a small slit in the skin at the pointed end. Cover with boiling water. Leave until cool enough to handle (at least 5 minutes), lift out one at a time, then peel off the shell and the inner thin, brown skin.
To cook before use: Boil in water for about 30 minutes until tender but still holding their shape. Or roast in their skins in a heavy pan, shaking and turning until blackened all over, or roast in the oven at 200°C (400°F/Gas 6) for about 30 minutes.

HAZELNUTS, COBNUTS, AND WALNUTS
Crack open the shells and remove the nuts. Use whole, or chop or grind as required. To toast whole or chopped hazelnuts or cobnuts, toss them in a hot non-stick pan, shaking all the time until they turn golden. Tip out immediately so they don't burn.

CARAMELIZED CHESTNUT AND ORANGE BROCHETTES
Thread cooked chestnuts on to soaked wooden skewers. Mix melted butter with some grated orange zest and juice and sweeten well with light soft brown sugar. Brush all over the nuts. Put on foil on the grill rack. Grill until golden, turning and brushing frequently. Serve with clotted cream.

NUTTY CHEESE AND HERB BITES
Toast some chopped hazelnuts or cobnuts. Coarsely grind in a blender or clean coffee mill. Mix two-thirds of the nuts with some cream cheese, chopped parsley, snipped chives, and a pinch of cayenne. Season to taste. Roll into small balls with damp hands. Roll in the remaining chopped nuts and chill until ready to serve with drinks.

CHOCOLATE WALNUT BROWNIES
Sift 12 tbsp self-raising flour with ¼ tsp salt and 2 tbsp cocoa powder in a large bowl. Melt ¼ block butter with 12 tbsp caster sugar, 2 tbsp milk and a 100g (3½oz) bar of 70-per-cent-cocoa-solids chocolate, stirring. Add to the flour mixture with 2 beaten eggs and a handful of chopped walnuts. Beat until smooth. Turn into a dampened 18 x 28cm (7 x 11in) shallow baking tin lined with baking parchment. Bake at 180°C (350°F/Gas 4) for 20 minutes until just firm and cracking on top. Cool slightly, then cut into squares and cool on a wire rack.

PICKLED WALNUTS
Wearing rubber gloves, prick green walnuts twice with a fork. Soak in well-salted water for 2 weeks, changing the salt water twice. Drain and spread on a tray to dry and turn black. Put in a pan and cover with 2 parts vinegar to 1 part brown sugar. Add some pickling spices. Bring to the boil and simmer for 10 minutes. Spoon into jars and cover with the pickling syrup. Cool, then cover, label, and store in a cool, dark place.

HONEY

There are over 35,000 British beekeepers harvesting honey. It's difficult to class as organic since it depends on the bees' origin and the apiary must be on certified organic land with only organic crops or uncultivated land for a 6.4-km (4-mile) radius (the distance bees travel). Any pollutants must be outside this range. Honey is getting scarce. Worldwide, bees are under threat from pesticide use on farms and are being decimated by a killer varroa mite. Warwick University researchers think they've found a natural fungus that destroys the mite. Bees are vital for pollinating every fruit and vegetable, so without them our food sources would be very scarce. If you buy organic, you protect our bees.

Honeycomb A chunk of comb with the honey still inside. The most natural way to eat honey. Nothing added, nothing taken away. You can spread it on hot toast, wax and all, and let it melt in.

WHAT WHEN AND HOW

WHAT TYPES
Two types: clear and set. Honey is 80 per cent sugar – mostly a mixture of fructose and glucose. Those high in fructose stay runny; those with more glucose set. But they vary from very runny to creamy to solid. They can be monofloral – the most highly sought after, sourced from one type of pollen – or polyfloral – from various types. There's also blended honey – different types blended after production. Here are a couple of British monoflorals, but there are others that are highly sought after, such as cherry blossom, with a slight almond flavour, and hawthorn, with a slightly bitter aftertaste, supposed to be good for insomnia. We've shown a couple of polyflorals here, too, to show how diverse they can be.

WHEN IN SEASON
Collected June–August, depending on the blossom.

HOW TO CHOOSE AND STORE
Choose set or clear according to your own preference (no nutritional difference). Store in a cool, dark place (but not the fridge). If it crystallizes, stand the jar in hot water or microwave very briefly on Medium to warm, but don't let it boil.

Borage honey Clear monofloral honey; pale with a delicate hint of cucumber.

Ling heather blossom honey This is the connoisseurs' choice for set monofloral honey, made from the smaller, late-flowering moorland heather. It tastes of toffee and never crystallizes but stays as a gel, the consistency of non-drip emulsion paint. Rare and expensive.

shropshire set polyfloral honey Deep brownish-gold and thick with a high glucose content. It's not blended, but taken from hives in the county and from Herefordshire.

sussex clear multifloral honey Local honey collected from the countryside, so it can include a range of wild flowers – anything from clover to blackberry. There's a set version, too.

PERFECT PAIRINGS

NUTS and **DRIED FRUITS** to stuff apples and pears or on breakfast cereal. Drizzled over thick **PLAIN YOGURT**. **LEMON** and **LIME** in dressings or warmed to trickle over pancakes. Instead of sugar (it's twice as sweet, so you need far less) in **CAKES** and **BISCUITS**. Sweet, fragrant herbs such as **ROSEMARY** and **MINT**, or sweet spices such as **GINGER**, **CINNAMON**, and **STAR ANISE** in syrups and sauces. With **GRAINY MUSTARD** and **OLIVE OIL** in a salad dressing, with **GARLIC** and **SOY SAUCE** as a baste or dipping sauce.

SIMPLE WAYS TO ENJOY

HOW HONEY IS MADE

Bees make honey to store as food for the hive in winter when there are not many plants in flower, and so not much nectar around. Honey bees collect nectar from the flowers, store it in their stomachs, then take it back to the hive. Worker bees suck it out and "chew" it to add enzymes that break down the sugars. They then spread it in the wax honeycomb chambers and fan it with their wings to evaporate the water so it thickens. When it's sticky enough, they seal the chambers with wax and it is kept there until they need to eat it.

An average beehive makes more than twice as much honey as it needs, so the rest can be harvested without causing any suffering for the insects.

HONEY BARBECUE SAUCE

Whisk 2 tbsp each clear honey, balsamic vinegar, and tomato purée. Flavour with crushed garlic and Worcestershire sauce. Season. Use as a baste or as a dipping sauce.

HONEY AND PEANUT BITES

Melt 85g (3oz) butter, 3 tbsp set honey, 4 tbsp wholegrain peanut butter, a handful of raisins, and the grated zest and juice of ½ lemon. Bring to the boil. Roughly crush a packet of plain biscuits. Stir in. Press into a small, greased, shallow baking tin. Cool, chill, and cut into fingers.

HONEY AND WALNUT FIGS

Halve fresh figs. Put on squares of buttered foil. Add a little spoonful of set honey sprinkle with toasted pine nuts and a good squeeze of lime juice. Wrap and bake at 180°C (350°F/Gas 4) until tender. Serve with ice cream.

HONEY, LEMON, AND CHOCOLATE CHIP BOMB

Put 1 litre (1¾ pints) soft-scoop vanilla ice cream in a chilled bowl. Mash in 3 tbsp clear honey, the grated zest and juice of 1 lemon, and a good handful of dark chocolate chips. Work quickly. Pack into a pudding basin. Wrap and freeze. Loosen the edges and turn out. Decorate with mint sprigs.

HONEY AND DRIED BLUEBERRY FILO PARCELS

Sweeten some soft white cheese with clear honey and natural vanilla. Add some dried blueberries. Brush sheets of filo pastry with melted butter. Fold in half, brush again. Put spoonfuls of cheese mixture in the centres. Fold into parcels. Put on a buttered baking sheet. Brush again. Bake at 200°C (400°F/Gas 6) until golden.

FISH & SEAFOOD

AN ORGANIC SALMON FARM

ROBBIE RENDALL, WESTRAY SALMON

For Robbie Rendall and his two brothers, home was, and still is, an agricultural farm on the Orkneys. In 1989 they diversified into fish farming. There was a niche market for organic farming, so they became a pilot project in 1999.

There were no Soil Association standards for fish farming at that time, but they stuck by their guidelines and the Soil Association created standards for them. To go organic they had to reduce their stock levels slightly (to meet the guidelines of 10kg of fish per cubic metre), stop using anti-fouling compounds and, obviously, source organic feed. The feed – fishmeal and organic wheat – makes a difference to the fish. "If you buy conventionally farmed salmon, you'll see it is a bright red colour. This is artificial pigment put in the feed because buyers say their customers prefer it. Our fish is paler because the only pigment used is shrimp shells. Our organic fish tastes exactly the same – if not better – and has no artificial additives." Every morning Robbie and his team hand feed the salmon in the low-density nets anchored far out to sea.

The fish are kept in 60-metre circumference pens, which are plastic collars with nets hanging to a depth of six metres. Supermarkets don't like the fish to be too big, so they need "grading" three or four times a year. Years ago people had to catch them and slide them down different-sized pipes. Robbie has a cage in the water with grading bars. The little ones swim through, the big ones can't. It's simple, and stress-free for the fish.

Most of Westray salmon goes to supermarkets, but they also sell about 10–12 tons a year locally. When they started farming organically, they sold around 70 tons a year; last year it was nearly 300 tons. Robbie knows organic fish farming is still in its infancy, but although the future may not be guaranteed, he believes they did the right thing.

Robbie's fish are very healthy, which he puts down to their location. "We're very much out on our own here. Up the West Coast of Scotland there are fish farms right next door to each other, so diseases spread quickly, but as we're remote we avoid this. The nearest farm is on the other part of Orkney mainland, about 20 miles away." Their geographical location, right in the North Sea, helps to keep parasites and debris to a minimum because the strong tide is a natural cleanser, sweeping through in currents 24 hours a day.

See p216 for Robbie's *Salmon Chowder with Whisky.*

OPPOSITE, ABOVE LEFT The salmon pens at Bay of Cleat on a summer's day.

ABOVE RIGHT Keith Kent netting out fish for harvest.

BELOW Robbie Rendall holding an organic salmon.

OILY FISH

Eating oily fish helps prevent heart disease and many other illnesses. A delicious way to stay healthy. We've featured only fish from sustainable stocks around our shores, and we don't recommend buying wild salmon or freshwater eels as stocks are dwindling fast. Choose line- or net-caught fish from stocks certified by the Marine Stewardship Council (see p220), certified organic farmed fish, or hand-line caught. The Marine Conservation Society (MCS) rates fish varieties out of five: the lower the mark, the more sustainable. Fish rated 4/5 should be boughtfrom MCS recommended sources. See *www.fishonline.org* for more information and ratings.

WHAT WHEN AND HOW

WHAT TYPES
Herring: Small and rounded with silvery-blue, scaly skin. MCS rating 3/5.
Mackerel: Smooth, blue-green and silver skin with dark, wavy stripes. MCS rating 3/5.
Salmon: Saltwater fish that swim up rivers to spawn. Speckled, silvery skin. Avoid intensively reared ones. MCS rating for Pacific salmon certified by the Soil Association or the MSC 2/5.
Sardines and pilchards: Little, silvery-scaled fish. Smaller ones are sardines; larger are pilchards. The MSC recommends pilchards, marketed as Cornish sardines, net-caught off the south-west coast. MCS rating 3/5.
Sea trout: Brown trout species that migrate to sea, often mistaken for salmon. MCS rating 3/5.
Brown trout: (Also golden and blue, not featured here.) Rarer, brownish-gold, freshwater fish. MCS rating 3/5.
Rainbow trout: Freshwater fish; green-gold with a pink flash. MCS rating 3/5.

WHEN IN SEASON
Most species should be avoided during spawning, so enjoy fresh in the months below: **Herring:** All year (they spawn at any time so you can't avoid); **Mackerel:** August–February; **Salmon:** Organically farmed all year; **Sardines and pilchards:** September–February; **Sea trout:** Wild, April–October, organically farmed all year; **Brown trout:** Wild, April–September, organically farmed all year; **Rainbow trout:** Wild, January–September, organically farmed all year

HOW TO CHOOSE AND STORE
Buy fish with slippery, shiny, bright-coloured skin and firm flesh. For whole fish, the eyes should be bright and prominent, gills bright red and clean. Best eaten fresh. At most, wrap well and store in the fridge for up to 24 hours.

Cornish sardine (pilchard) Usually cleaned and left whole. Large ones need their scales scraping off like herrings. Best grilled, fried, or baked.

Mackerel A delicious, moist fish with greyish-brown flesh and a rich flavour that, like herring, is good with a sharp sauce to complement it. Best grilled or fried whole, or filleted. Fewer fine bones than herring.

Sea trout Pink flesh. Similar to salmon, but slightly coarser. Sold whole, in fillets, or steaks. Can be poached, steamed, grilled, fried, or baked.

Scrape off the scales before use.

Herring A rich, oily flavour and creamy-coloured flesh. It can be cooked whole or filleted first. Usually fried or grilled, but can be stuffed and baked. Good with a sharp or fruity sauce.

Salmon Pink, succulent flesh that can be grilled, fried, poached, steamed, or baked. Sold whole or in fillets or steaks.

Bright, prominent eyes.

Rainbow trout Delicately flavoured fish with white or pink flesh. Usually sold whole but also available filleted. Cook as for salmon.

Brown trout Similar to rainbow trout, but considered to have a better flavour. Usually sold whole.

PERFECT PAIRINGS

MACKEREL and **HERRING** coated in **OATMEAL** before frying; **MUSTARD**, **HORSERADISH**, **RHUBARB**, or **GOOSEBERRY** sauce offsets the richness. **SARDINES** and **PILCHARDS LEMON** or **LIME** mixed with or squeezed over; **CHOPPED FRESH HERBS** and **OLIVE OIL** to marinate before grilling. **SALMON**, **SEA**, **RAINBOW**, and **BROWN TROUT HOLLANDAISE SAUCE** (see p330) when poached; **MAYONNAISE**, flavoured with chopped **WATERCRESS** when poached and served hot or cold.

SIMPLE WAYS TO ENJOY

TO PREPARE

TO SKIN
For fillets, see Cod Family, p222. For whole fish, it is best to peel off the skin after cooking.

TO CLEAN
Make a slit down the belly, pull out the guts. Rinse and pat dry with kitchen paper. For mackerel, make several slashes on each side, if cooking whole.

TO BONE
Cut off the head and tail. Open out the cleaned fish on a board, skin-side up. Run your thumb down the central backbone several times, quite firmly. Turn the fish over and lift off the backbone. Remove any stray bones. Trim off the fins with scissors.

TO SCALE
Dip your fingers in salt and hold the fish by the tail on a large sheet of newspaper. Scrape away the scales with a knife, working from the tail to the head.

SWEET SOUSED MACKEREL OR HERRING
Bone small mackerels or herrings. Season and sprinkle with thinly sliced onion and a little chopped dill. Roll up, starting from the head end. Place in an ovenproof dish. Mix together equal quantities of white wine vinegar and water, and sweeten to taste with light soft brown sugar. Pour over the fish. Tuck in a bay leaf. Cover with foil and bake at 180°C (350°F/Gas 4) for 45 minutes. Leave to cool, then chill. Lift out of the cooking juices to serve.

GRILLED CORNISH SARDINES WITH CHILLI LIME DRIZZLE
Sweeten the juice of a lime with clear honey and a finely chopped, seeded red or green jalapeno chilli. Clean and scale some Cornish sardines. Grill on oiled foil until golden and sizzling on each side. Serve with the drizzle spooned over, or omit the drizzle and serve with lemon or lime wedges.

PAN-SEARED SALMON OR TROUT WITH BABY LEAVES
Sprinkle salmon or trout fillets with coarsely crushed black peppercorns. Fry in a little unsalted butter on each side until cooked through. Remove from the pan and keep warm. Stir in a splash of brandy and ignite. Shake the pan until the flames die down. Add some crème fraîche; sweeten with honey. Season. Lay each fillet on a good handful of salad leaves. Spoon sauce over.

SIMPLE FISH CAKES
Mix cooked mashed potatoes with half the quantity of flaked, cooked salmon, mackerel, trout, or crab. Add a little chopped parsley, a pinch of cayenne, a squeeze of lemon juice, seasoning, and a beaten egg. Shape into cakes. Dip in flour, fry until golden on both sides. Serve with mayonnaise.

TROUT WITH ALMONDS AND HERBS

SERVES 4 **PREPARATION TIME** 10 minutes **COOKING TIME** 10-12 minutes
VARIATION You could use coriander and parsley, omit the thyme and chives,
and add a pinch of cumin seeds; or try an orange instead of the lemon.
SERVE WITH boiled potatoes and some wilted greens.

1 Rinse the fish and pat dry with kitchen paper. Cut off the heads, if liked. Season inside and out with salt and pepper.

2 Melt half the butter with the oil in a large frying pan. Add the fish and fry gently for 5 minutes on each side until golden and cooked through. Remove from the pan with a fish slice and put on warm plates. Keep warm.

3 Add the remaining butter to the pan. When it has melted, add the almonds and fry quickly until golden. Quickly add the lemon juice and zest, to prevent them cooking further, the herbs, and a little more seasoning. Stir and spoon over the fish. Serve straight away.

INGREDIENTS
4 river trout, cleaned
Salt and freshly ground
  black pepper
60g (2oz) unsalted butter
2 tbsp olive oil
60g (2oz) flaked almonds
Finely grated zest and juice of
  ½ lemon
2 tbsp chopped fresh parsley
1 tbsp chopped fresh thyme
1 tbsp snipped fresh chives

SALMON CHOWDER WITH WHISKY

ROBBIE AT WESTRAY SALMON

Robbie Rendall runs the organic Westray Salmon Farm, Orkney. See pp210–11.

INGREDIENTS
1 onion, chopped
1 leek, sliced
1 large waxy potato, diced
15g (½oz) butter
300g (10oz) salmon, skinned and cut into small chunks
60g (2oz) fresh or frozen sweetcorn
60g (2oz) fresh or frozen peas (optional)
600ml (1 pint) fish or chicken stock
150ml (5fl oz) dry white wine
1 bay leaf
1 large tomato, skinned, seeded, and chopped
Salt and freshly ground black pepper
2 tbsp whisky
4 tbsp double cream
Chopped fresh parsley, to garnish

SERVES 4–5 **PREPARATION TIME** 20 minutes **COOKING TIME** 35 minutes.
Salmon is often thought of as a delicate food, but it makes a hearty, rich soup. If you like a thicker soup, blend 1 tbsp cornflour with the whisky before adding it.

1 Fry the onion and leek gently, stirring until soft but not brown, about 5 minutes. Add the remaining ingredients except the whisky, cream, and parsley. Bring to the boil, reduce the heat, part-cover, and simmer for 30 minutes until the potatoes are tender.

2 Remove the bay leaf. Stir in the whisky and cream, and simmer for 1 minute. Taste and reseason, if necessary. Ladle into warm bowls and garnish with chopped parsley.

GRILLED CORNISH SARDINES WITH SALSA VERDE

SERVES 4 **PREPARATION TIME** 20 minutes **COOKING TIME** 6–8 minutes
VARIATION If you have the barbecue fired up, put the fish in a hinged wire rack and cook them over the coals. You can cook mackerel or herrings in the same way, but they'll need 5–8 minutes each side. The salsa is also good spooned over oysters just before eating.

1 Trim off the feathery stalks from the watercress. Place in a blender with the parsley, marjoram, breadcrumbs, oil, lemon juice, and capers. Run the machine until the mixture is chopped and blended, stopping and scraping down the sides as necessary. Season to taste.

2 Place the Cornish sardines on foil on the grill rack. Grill for 3–4 minutes on each side until sizzling brown and cooked through. Serve with the salsa verde spooned over.

INGREDIENTS
8–12 fresh Cornish sardines,
  cleaned and scaled

FOR THE SALSA VERDE
1 bunch of watercress
3 sprigs of parsley
2 sprigs of marjoram
30g (1oz) breadcrumbs
120ml (4fl oz) olive oil
3 tbsp lemon juice
1 tbsp pickled capers
Salt and freshly ground
  black pepper

MACKEREL WITH RHUBARB SAUCE

SOPHIE GRIGSON

An award-winning food writer and television presenter, Sophie is also a champion of organic and seasonal produce.

SERVES 6 **PREPARATION TIME** 10 minutes **COOKING TIME** 10 minutes for the sauce, 10–15 minutes for the fish **SERVE WITH** parsleyed new potatoes.

A summer classic for those August days when garden rhubarb is still around and mackerel are back on the menu after their spawning period. The tartness of rhubarb offsets the richness of the flesh. Or you could add half a star anise as the fruit cooks, or 1 tsp crushed coriander seeds.

1 Put the rhubarb into a pan with the butter, sugar, and orange juice. Cover and cook gently over a low heat, stirring a couple of times, until the juices begin to run. Remove the lid and raise the heat. Simmer until the rhubarb is tender, about 5 minutes. Stir in the orange zest and salt and pepper to taste. Either keep warm, or reheat when needed.

2 Preheat the grill. Make several diagonal slashes on either side of each mackerel, and season inside and out with salt and pepper. Grill for 5–8 minutes on each side, then serve with the sauce.

INGREDIENTS
6 fine mackerel, cleaned

FOR THE SAUCE
450g (1lb) trimmed garden
  rhubarb, cut into 2cm (¾in)
  lengths, halved or quartered
  lengthways when particularly
  thick and chunky
15g (½oz) butter
2 tbsp sugar
Finely grated zest and juice
  of ½ orange
Salt and freshly ground black
  pepper

COD FAMILY

Here we are looking at the main large, white, round fish. On other pages you will discover flat fish and the more unusual white sea fish and oily fish. The Marine Conservation Society (MCS) recommends we avoid eating some species because of falling stocks. We are, therefore, including only those that can be sustainably fished (see below), with the MCS sustainability rating for each species – the lower the rating out of five, the more sustainable it is. We have an abundance of fabulous seafood surrounding our shores, so although we talk about our ever-popular cod here, you will also discover other sensational fish to try.

Looks a bit like coley but is more delicate, like whiting.

WHAT WHEN AND HOW

WHAT TYPES
Cod: Can weigh up to 5–6kg (11–13lb). It has a long, speckled brown and grey-green body and a barb on its lower jaw. Some are being successfully organically farmed. MCS rating 4/5.
Haddock: Smaller than cod, up to 3kg (6½lb) with a brownish, grey-flecked body. MCS rating 4/5.
Coley (saithe): A blue-grey body. As big as cod, a good substitute. MCS rating 2/5.
Whiting: Small, usually up to 2kg (4½lb), with a rounded belly and silvery-grey skin. MCS rating 4/5.
Pollack: Smaller relative of coley, similar to haddock in weight. It too is underrated, but it is an excellent alternative to both cod and haddock. MCS rating 3/5.

WHEN IN SEASON
Some sources say fish are available all year, but many are frozen to supply the market. Even when actual seasons don't apply, all species should be avoided during their spawning time, so eat fresh only in the months below.
Cod: May–January; **Haddock and whiting:** May–February; **Coley (saithe) and pollack:** May–December

HOW TO CHOOSE AND STORE
Choose firm, moist flesh that smells of the ocean but not too "fishy". Avoid any that look discoloured and drying, or slimy. Best eaten on day of purchase or, if you must, wrap them well and store in the fridge for up to 24 hours.

SUSTAINABLE FISHING

Very simplified, some modern fishing methods mean that tons of unwanted fish are caught and destroyed – as are dolphins, seals, and other sea mammals. Line-fishing is more selective and so preferable for catching some species, and it also prevents damage to the sea bed. Look out for "line-caught" when you buy, but check it is seabird-friendly, too, as unless bird-scaring and other protection methods are in place, they go for the bait, get entangled in the lines, and drown.

The Marine Stewardship Council (MSC) has also developed a worldwide certification scheme. Fisheries who sign up to it are assessed independently against the MSC standards to ensure they are well managed and sustainable. When successfully checked, they can display the blue-tick MSC label. This is the best guide that the fish has been caught responsibly.

The texture is finer than that of some of the bigger fish.

PERFECT PAIRINGS

CHEESE and **BACON** go surprisingly well as a topping, or cheese in a sauce. **CHIPS** – of course (see p124); **TOMATOES** as a sauce or as an accompaniment. **CIDER** or **WHITE WINE** for poaching white fish and then made into a cream sauce. **TARTARE SAUCE** with any grilled or fried fish.

SIMPLE WAYS TO ENJOY

TO PREPARE

To skin fillets: Put on a board, skin-side down. Make a small cut at the tail end between the flesh and skin. Dip your fingers in salt (for a better grip), hold the flap of skin firmly, and ease the flesh away from the skin with a large, sharp knife, pulling the skin as you go.

FISH DIPPERS WITH TOMATO AND CUCUMBER MAYONNAISE

Flavour mayonnaise with tomato ketchup and a splash of Worcestershire sauce. Add finely chopped cucumber. Season to taste. Chill. Cut white fish fillets into finger-length strips and roll in plain flour seasoned with salt and pepper. Dip into beaten egg, then breadcrumbs. Fry in hot oil until golden and cooked. Drain on kitchen paper. Serve with the mayonnaise.

CEVICHE

Cut very fresh cod or haddock loin (or monkfish, turbot, halibut, or salmon) into slices, then narrow strips. Mix with a seeded and finely chopped green jalapeño pepper and some diced red pepper. Squeeze lime juice all over. Season, stir, and chill for 1–2 hours until the fish is opaque. Sprinkle with coriander leaves, drizzle with olive oil, and serve with crusty bread and a tomato and onion salad.

TANDOORI FISH

In a large, shallow baking dish, mix a small carton of plain yogurt with a squeeze of lemon juice, 1 tsp each ground cumin, ground coriander, and ground turmeric, and 2 tsp paprika. Add salt and pepper. Mix well. Lay skinned fillets of any white fish in the marinade and turn to coat. Leave for 2 hours. Turn over the fish again, then bake in the oven at 180°C (350°F/Gas 4) for 20 minutes. Lift out and serve with rice.

FISH PROVENÇAL

Soften some chopped onion and garlic in olive oil. Add a good splash of white wine, some skinned, chopped tomatoes, a little tomato purée, a pinch of caster sugar, and a little chopped fresh oregano. Simmer gently until pulpy. Add some diced, skinned white fish and a handful of sliced olives. Season. Simmer until fish is just tender. Serve with rice.

THAI GREEN FISH CURRY WITH MANGETOUT

SERVES 4 **PREPARATION TIME** 15 minutes **COOKING TIME** 15 minutes
VARIATION This can be cooked with broccoli, French beans, or courgettes instead of the mangetout. The wonderful thing about Thai curries is that although they taste hot when you eat them, the fire dissipates very quickly.
SERVE WITH Thai jasmine rice.

1 Boil the potatoes in lightly salted water for about 5 minutes until almost tender. Steam the mangetout in a metal colander or steamer over the potatoes for 3 minutes. Drain.

2 Mix the coconut milk with the curry paste in a pan. Add the fish and drained potatoes, the chilli strips, and a little seasoning. Bring to the boil, reduce the heat, part-cover and simmer very gently for 10 minutes until the fish and potatoes are tender. Gently stir in the mangetout. Taste and reseason, if necessary. Spoon over Thai jasmine rice in bowls. Garnish with torn basil or coriander leaves.

INGREDIENTS
2 waxy potatoes, scrubbed and
   cut into small chunks
115g (4oz) mangetout
400g (14oz) can coconut milk
2 tbsp Thai green curry paste
550g (1¼lb) cod, coley, or other
   meaty white fish, skinned and
   cut into chunks
1–2 thin green chillies (according
   to taste), seeded and cut into
   thin strips
Salt and freshly ground
   black pepper
A few torn fresh basil or
   coriander leaves, to garnish

FISH AND PUMPKIN CHIPS

DONNA AIR

A TV presenter and actress, Donna is also a champion of organic food, and acts as a spokesperson for the Soil Association.

SERVES 4 **PREPARATION TIME** 25 minutes **COOKING TIME** 35–40 minutes **SERVE WITH** peas steamed with fresh mint, or other seasonal vegetables mashed with a little spoonful of cream. **There is nothing quite like fish and chips on a cold autumn night. It is quick, simple, and very tasty. This is a dish I have always enjoyed and never gets any complaints from my little one either.**

1 Preheat the oven to 240°C (475°F/Gas 9) – or its highest setting.

2 Peel the pumpkin and cut into chips. I normally go for chunky chips, but size is up to you. Put them on a baking sheet, drizzle with a little oil, and pop in the oven for about 30 minutes, turning over halfway through cooking until crisp, but tender inside, and nicely browned. (A quicker option is to pan-fry them.)

3 Meanwhile, sift the flour into a bowl. Make a well in the middle, add the salt with 2 tbsp oil and the ale, or light beer, and whisk until smooth. Whisk the egg white until stiff, then fold into the batter.

4 Heat the oil in a deep-fat fryer or heavy saucepan to 180°C (350°F) or until a cube of day-old bread browns in 30 seconds when dropped in. Coat the fish in a little seasoned flour, then dip it in the batter.

5 Fry the battered fish, one piece at a time, in the oil for about 8 minutes until crisp and golden brown. Carefully remove and drain on kitchen paper. Keep warm whilst cooking the rest. Serve immediately with the pumpkin chips.

INGREDIENTS
1 pumpkin, about 1.25kg (2¾lb)
Olive oil, for drizzling
115g (4oz) plain flour
A pinch of salt
2 tbsp vegetable oil, plus extra for deep-frying
150ml (5fl oz) ale, or any light beer, or milk, if preferred
1 large egg white
4 white fish fillets, such as coley or pollack, about 175g/6oz each, skinned
Seasoned flour

FLAT FISH

These extraordinary creatures start life round but evolve so both eyes of some species are on one side of their head. They are delicious, from little dabs and succulent spotted plaice, up to big and meaty halibut. Unfortunately, wild Atlantic halibut is endangered and should be completely avoided, although efforts are being made to farm it sustainably. Pacific and Greenland varieties are less threatened, but even so, halibut should be treated with caution. Avoid buying immature fish that won't have had a chance to breed. Each species featured has a rating out of five for sustainability.

similar to, but less expensive than, turbot.

Brill Excellent, underrated fish with small flakes and a very good flavour. Sold in fillets or steaks. Can be fried, poached, grilled, baked, or steamed.

WHAT WHEN AND HOW

WHAT TYPES
Brill: Large, flat and round, similar to turbot but less expensive. MCS rating 4/5.
Dab: Smaller relative of flounder, plaice, and sole. Avoid eating fish under 20cm (8in) long. MCS rating 2/5.
Dover sole: Large, oval fish with short fins. Avoid under 28cm (11in) long. Hastings Fleet trammel fish is MSC certified. MCS rating 4/5.
Lemon sole: Rounder than Dover sole, light, brown-flecked skin. Best bought from Cornwall. Avoid under 25cm (10in) long. MCS rating 3/5.
Plaice: Brown or grey skin with orange spots. Avoid under 30cm (12in) long. Choose Irish sea-caught. MCS rating 4/5.
Turbot: Fat, speckled brown body. Short fins. MCS rating 4/5.
Halibut: Largest flat fish, brown with grey spots. Wide, tapering fins. "Chicks" weigh 1–3kg (2¼–6½lb). MCS rating 4/5.
Witch: Near transparent, ugly with reddish brown skin. Megrim is similar. Avoid under 28cm (11in) long. MCS rating 3/5.

Halibut An exceptionally good fish with white, firm flesh. Sold in fillets or steaks. Can be cooked any way, but particularly good poached or baked in a sauce.

WHEN IN SEASON
Like other fish, except when farmed, it is recommended you avoid the spawning season. Eat fresh only in these months:
Brill and witch: October–February; **Dab and Dover sole:** July–March; **Lemon sole:** September–March; **Plaice:** April–December; **Turbot:** September–March, farmed all year; **Halibut:** Organically farmed all year

HOW TO CHOOSE AND STORE
Buy fish with firm flesh, moist but not slimy skin and a fresh smell. Best eaten fresh, but at most, store in the fridge for up to 24 hours, well wrapped.

Witch Great-tasting fish with a really good texture. Cook as sole or plaice.

Cook using any recipe for Dover sole.

Lemon sole Soft, delicate flesh with a pronounced flavour. Good cooked whole or in fillets, needs delicate flavourings.

Plaice Similar to lemon sole, it has lovely, melting flesh and a definite flavour. Serve whole or in fillets with a sauce, or stuffed.

Turbot White, firm, and meaty yet sweet, moist, and delicate. Turbot is the most highly prized of all flat fish. Cut into fillets or steaks. Can be cooked any way and will take stronger, more adventurous flavourings.

Dover sole King of soles. Long, and narrower than others. Superb flavour and texture. One about 450g (1lb) will serve one person generously. Usually fried or grilled.

Plumper than most flat fish, so meatier flesh.

Dab The smallest of the flat fish, with a sweet flavour like young plaice. Good cooked whole.

PERFECT PAIRINGS

MELTED BUTTER to fry whole fish or fillets in, then sprinkle with **PARSLEY** or chopped **MIXED HERBS** and a squeeze of **LEMON JUICE**. **PRAWNS** in cream sauce or melted butter, spooned over cooked, rolled fillets, or steaks. **BACON**, **SPICY SAUSAGES**, and other **CHARCUTERIE** for the meaty ones like halibut. **TOMATOES** and **PEPPERS** for poached or baked fish.

SIMPLE WAYS TO ENJOY

TO PREPARE

FOR COOKING WHOLE
Cut off the fins round the edge with scissors. Trim the tail. Leave the heads intact.

TO SKIN
All have white skin underneath that doesn't need removing before cooking, as it's soft and undetectable. To remove dark skin from a whole fish, trim as above, then make a nick in the skin at the tail end. Lift a flap of skin. With salted fingers, gently pull it back, easing with a knife as you go. When you reach the head end, cut it off with scissors. For fillets, see page 222.

TO FILLET
Trim the fins and tail as above. Cut off the head. Make a slit along the centre of the fish (down the backbone) with a sharp-pointed knife. Slice one fillet away, cutting from the backbone to just between the flesh and the bones, following the lines of the bones and gently pulling the fillet free with your spare hand. Repeat with the other fillet on that side, then turn the fish over and repeat the whole process on the other side. If you buy fish ready-filleted, both top and bottom fillets will be whole.

BUTTER SAUCE FOR WHOLE GRILLED FISH →

Finely chop a small onion. Put in a pan with 2 tbsp water and 2 tbsp cider vinegar. Bring to the boil, reduce the heat, and simmer until the onion is soft and the liquid is reduced by half. Whisk in ½ block of butter, a small piece at a time, until thickened. Add some chopped parsley or tarragon. Season to taste. Spoon over grilled, whole flat fish.

FISH FILLETS WITH MELTED CHEESE AND APPLE CABBAGE

Simmer shredded green cabbage and some sliced apples in a little cider until tender. Season. Put in an ovenproof dish. Top with sliced tomatoes, fillets of turbot, halibut, or brill, and season again. Cover with grated Cheddar cheese. Bake in the oven at 190°C (375°F/Gas 5) until golden and cooked through.

MUSHROOM-STUFFED PLAICE, DAB, OR LEMON SOLE

Soften finely chopped button mushrooms in a knob of butter, stirring. Add enough breadcrumbs to form a moist stuffing. Add some chopped tarragon or thyme. Season to taste. Halve whole fish fillets (or use halves you have filleted yourself). Skin, if dark. Put a little stuffing in the centres of the fillet and fold in three. Put in individual gratin dishes. Spoon a little crème fraîche over each. Season lightly. Bake at 180°C (350°F/Gas 4) for about 20 minutes until cooked through. Garnish with small sprigs of tarragon or thyme.

HALIBUT IN ROSEMARY AND GARLIC CRUST

INGREDIENTS
60g (2oz) couscous
1 tsp ground turmeric
1 tbsp chopped fresh rosemary
1 large garlic clove, very
  finely chopped
60g (2oz) hard sheep's cheese or
  Parmesan, finely grated
Salt and freshly ground
  black pepper
Sunflower oil, for greasing
1 egg, beaten
3 tbsp plain flour, seasoned
4 halibut fillets, about
  150g (5oz) each
200ml (7fl oz) passata
½ tsp clear honey
Small sprigs of fresh rosemary,
  to garnish

SERVES 4 **PREPARATION TIME** 20 minutes **COOKING TIME** 15 minutes
VARIATION Use turbot or any other meaty, white fish, like cod or haddock loin,
or monkfish, instead. **SERVE WITH** baby potatoes and French beans.

1 Stir 5 tbsp boiling water into the couscous in a bowl. Cover for
5 minutes, spread on a plate, and leave to cool. Stir in turmeric,
chopped rosemary, garlic, cheese, and seasoning. Preheat the oven
to 190°C (375°F/Gas 5). Oil a roasting tin and heat in the oven.

2 Put the egg on one plate, and the flour on another. Dip the fish in
the flour, the egg, then the couscous. Put in the hot roasting tin.
Bake for 15 minutes until golden and cooked through, turning once.

3 Heat the passata and honey. Season to taste. Spoon on to 4 warm
plates and top with the halibut. Garnish with sprigs of rosemary.

PLAICE FILLETS WITH EGG SAUCE ON BRUSCHETTA

SERVES 4 or 8 **PREPARATION TIME** 20 minutes **COOKING TIME** 20 minutes **VARIATION** Use sole or dab fillets instead. There's no need to remove the white skin: it's soft when cooked and unnoticeable.

1 Boil the eggs in a pan of water for 7 minutes. Drain, and place in cold water. To make the bruschetta, heat 60g (2oz) of the butter with the oil in a frying pan, and brown the bread slices on both sides. Drain on kitchen paper.

2 Butter a large dinner plate. Squeeze the lemon juice over the skin side of the fish and season lightly. Roll up and put on the plate. Add 2 tbsp of the milk. Cover with a lid or another plate and steam over a pan of simmering water for about 15 minutes or until tender and cooked through.

3 Meanwhile, shell and chop the eggs. Put the flour in a small saucepan. Whisk in the remaining milk. Add the remaining butter and the bay leaf. Bring to the boil and cook for 2 minutes, whisking all the time. Discard the bay leaf. Blend in the fish cooking milk and the cream. Reserve a little of the egg for garnish, then stir in the remainder with the chopped parsley. Season to taste.

4 Put the bruschetta on warm plates. Top each with a plaice roll and spoon the sauce over. Garnish with the reserved egg and the sprigs of parsley.

INGREDIENTS
2 eggs
75g (2½oz) butter, plus extra
   for greasing
2 tbsp olive oil
8 diagonal slices French bread
Juice of ½ lemon
2 plaice, each filleted into four,
   black skin removed
Salt and freshly ground
   black pepper
150ml (5fl oz) milk
15g (½oz) plain flour
1 bay leaf
3 tbsp single cream
1 tbsp chopped fresh parsley
8 small sprigs of fresh parsley,
   to garnish

SPECIALITY SEA FISH

Here we feature the more exotic-looking white fish species caught in British waters. Marvel at how the grotesque monkfish can produce such tasty, meaty flesh; or how the golden John Dory, with its spiny back and distinctive black spot, can yield only tiny, sweet fillets because of its huge head. There are beautiful species, too, like the colourful and delicate red mullet. Choose line- or net-caught fish where possible, and don't buy undersized fish. Each variety of fish has been given a sustainability rating by the Marine Conservation Society (MCS), which we've included below. The lower the rating out of five, the more sustainable the fish.

Monkfish White, thick, meaty flesh that can be cooked conventionally, but is also good for kebabs or roasting.

WHAT WHEN AND HOW

WHAT TYPES
Sea bream: Several small-scaled varieties. Avoid buying under 23cm (9in). MCS rating 2/5.
Sea bass: Small-scaled, silver-black, 350–675g (12oz–1½lb). For wild, choose MSC-certified from Holderness coast. MCS rating 3/5.
John Dory: Named after its golden-yellow colour (*jaune doré*, in French), with large spines and a black spot on its side. Avoid under 25cm (10in). Caught off the south coast. MCS rating 3/5.
Monkfish (anglerfish): Huge head with long barb on lip and long tail – the edible part. Buy mature fish over 70cm (28in). MCS rating 4/5.
Grey mullet: Similar to sea bass with larger scales. Don't buy under 35cm (14in). No relation to red mullet. MCS rating 4/5.
Red mullet: Smallish with shimmering red, pink, and orange skin. Don't buy under 22cm (8½in). MCS rating 3/5.
Red gurnard: Bony with a long body and wedge-shaped head. Avoid under 20cm (8in). MCS rating 2/5.

WHEN IN SEASON
Sea bream: June–March, organically farmed all year **Sea bass:** July–February, organically farmed all year **John Dory and grey mullet:** September–May **Monkfish:** August–January **Red mullet:** August–April **Red gurnard:** October–May

HOW TO CHOOSE AND STORE
If whole, they should be firm with bright, prominent eyes and red gills. Fillets should be fresh-smelling and moist. Best eaten on the day of purchase.

Red gurnard Not so widely used here, but excellent for soups and stews, and good fried.

Tricky to fillet: ask the fishmonger to do it.

Grey mullet Delicious if
caught out at sea, can taste
muddy if caught near land.
Cook whole, or in fillets.

Like sea bass, but
with smaller scales.

The tail is
the part
that's eaten.

Red mullet A pretty fish
with delicately textured
and flavoured flesh. Good
cooked whole, or in fillets.

The head
takes up
a third of
the body.

Sea bass Distinctive, sweet-flavoured fish that
can be stuffed and baked whole. Fillets are best
pan-fried or grilled, but can be cooked any way.

There are different
varieties available in
a range of colours.

John Dory Small, dense-fleshed
fillets. Good grilled or pan-fried,
and can take strong flavours
like chilli or garlic.

sea bream
Delicately flavoured
fish. Can be cooked whole or filleted.
Poach, fry, grill, bake, or steam.

PERFECT PAIRINGS

Mediterranean flavours of **TOMATOES**, **GARLIC**, **ONIONS**, and **OLIVES**, sautéed, stewed, or baked. Spicy rub of **CHILLI**, **CUMIN**, **PAPRIKA**, and seasoning before grilling or frying. **MELTED BUTTER** with chopped **FRESH HERBS** for grilling, frying, or baking. **CRUSHED POTATOES** and/or **CELERIAC** as a bed for the cooked fillets.

SIMPLE WAYS TO ENJOY

TO PREPARE

Best to buy in fillets or ready-cleaned to cook whole. To scale, see p214. Usually cooked with the skin on and often served skin-side up to reveal crispy golden skin flecked with the colour of the fish.

TO STUFF

Trim off the fins or spines, if necessary. Gently open the body cavity and fill with your chosen stuffing.

BAKED FISH PARCELS WTH TOMATOES, LEMON, AND THYME

For each fish, cut a large double-thickness oval of greaseproof paper. Spread liberally with unsalted butter, but not to the edges. Lay a few slices of tomato on one half, then a small whole fish (like red mullet) or a meaty fish fillet. Lay a thyme sprig over. Sprinkle with lemon juice. Season. Fold the paper over the fish and pleat the edges to seal. Put on a baking sheet. Bake at 180°C (350°F/Gas 4) for 20 minutes. Transfer to plates, open at the table.

PAN-FRIED FILLETS WITH RED CHILLI PASTE

Mix some ground cumin and smoked paprika. Add a little sweet paprika and some crushed garlic. Make into a paste with tomato purée, red wine vinegar, and olive oil. Sweeten with honey. Add chilli powder to taste. Smear over fish fillets, cut in half lengthways. Fry in a little olive oil. Arrange at angles on lightly wilted spinach, and spoon the pan juices over.

MONKFISH AND BACON KEBABS

Stretch some streaky bacon rashers. Cut in half. Wrap round monkfish cubes. Thread, interspersed with small bay leaves, on soaked wooden skewers. Brush with olive oil and season with black pepper. Grill on foil until golden and cooked through. Garnish with lemon wedges.

PAN-ROASTED FILLETS, BABY POTATOES, AND SHALLOTS

Fry some scrubbed baby potatoes and peeled whole shallots in a little butter and olive oil until turning golden. Cover, turn down heat, cook gently until tender. Season fish fillets and sprinkle with lemon juice. Fry in a separate pan in butter and olive oil, skin-side down, until golden. Cover and cook gently until opaque; don't turn over. Scatter with chopped chervil and chives. Serve with the vegetables and the pan juices poured over.

FILO-TOPPED MONKFISH BLUSH

SERVES 4–6 **PREPARATION TIME** 15 minutes **COOKING TIME** 30–35 minutes
VARIATION You can use any fish you like, and this recipe is a lovely way to try
lesser known, but more sustainable, varieties such as pollack or red mullet.
SERVE WITH boiled potatoes and a green salad.

1 Heat the butter and half the oil in a flameproof casserole. Add the
onion, and cook gently for 3–4 minutes. Then add the leek, garlic,
and bacon, and fry, stirring, for 4–5 minutes until soft.

2 Add the tomatoes, wine, mushrooms, and sugar. Bring to the boil,
reduce the heat, cover, and simmer for 10–15 minutes until pulpy,
stirring occasionally.

3 Add the monkfish and plenty of seasoning. Simmer very gently for
8–10 minutes until the fish is cooked but still holds its shape. Stir in
the crème fraîche and parsley. Taste and reseason, if necessary.

4 Meanwhile, preheat the oven to 190°C (375°F/Gas 5). Brush the
sheets of filo pastry with the remaining oil. Crumple gently like
sheets of paper and place on an oiled baking sheet. Bake in the oven
for 5 minutes until crisp and browned.

5 Spoon the fish mixture on to warm plates, top with the crisp filo
pastry and serve immediately.

INGREDIENTS
30g (1oz) butter
4 tbsp olive oil
1 small onion, chopped
1 small leek, sliced
1 garlic clove, crushed
2 streaky bacon rashers, diced
450g (1lb) tomatoes, skinned
  and chopped
150ml (5fl oz) rosé wine
115g (4oz) baby white button
  mushrooms
A good pinch of caster sugar
675g (1½lb) monkfish, cut
  into chunks
Salt and freshly ground
  black pepper
4 tbsp crème fraîche
1 tbsp chopped fresh parsley
4–6 sheets filo pastry

GRILLED RED BREAM WITH SPICE RUB

ATUL KOCHHAR

A critically acclaimed chef and restaurateur, Atul is chef-patron of Benares restaurant in London. His was the first Indian restaurant in Britain to win a Michelin star.

SERVES 4 **PREPARATION TIME** 15 minutes **COOKING TIME** 6–8 minutes

This is very much my kind of dish when I want to entertain, but also to sit and chat with my friends. I love coming up with new combinations of spices, and the spice rub here is a particular favourite. Try sea bass or John Dory as an alternative fish.

1 Mix all the ingredients for the spice rub together and season with salt.

2 Line a baking sheet with foil and place the fish fillets on it, skin-side down. Brush the spice rub over the fish. Place under a hot grill for 6–8 minutes, until cooked through and lightly golden. Remove from the heat and keep warm.

3 Meanwhile, mix together all the ingredients for the tomato salad. Serve the fish with the salad and some lemon wedges.

INGREDIENTS
4 red bream fillets, about 150g
  (5½oz) each
Lemon wedges, to serve

FOR THE SPICE RUB
3 tbsp walnut or olive oil
4 tbsp chopped coriander leaves
2 garlic cloves, crushed
1 tsp coriander seeds, crushed
1 tsp lemon juice
1 small green chilli, very
  finely chopped

FOR THE TOMATO SALAD
4 plum tomatoes, chopped
1 tbsp chopped coriander leaves
1½ tsp walnut or olive oil
1 tbsp walnuts, toasted in
  a dry frying pan and then
  lightly crushed
Sea salt and freshly ground
  black pepper

Recipe from *Fish Indian Style* by Atul Kochhar, published by Absolute Press, with photography by David Loftus

SMOKED FISH

Fish were first smoked to preserve them. Picture a row of herrings hanging up over a smoking fire in the open air to dry out. Traditional smoking methods are still similar today but the fish aren't desiccated. Smoking adds an exciting dimension in texture and flavour and gives us a whole new range of fish to enjoy. Different woods give different flavours. Whether you're tempted by a deep golden kipper or some meltingly soft, thinly sliced smoked salmon, there are fish for breakfast, fish for dinner, and plenty to tempt the taste buds for light meals in between.

WHAT WHEN AND HOW

WHAT TYPES
Cold smoked: The fish are prepared, salted or brined, then smoked at around 25°C (77°F), not hot enough to cook them, so they're still raw after smoking, like cod, haddock, finnan haddies, whiting, bloaters and kippers (herrings), salmon and trout. Salmon and trout can be eaten raw, the others should be cooked first. Look for traditionally smoked, undyed varieties.
Hot smoked: Similar, but the fish are smoked at a higher temperature, so they cook at the same time. They can be eaten as they are, grilled, or used in cooked dishes. They include buckling (herring), mackerel, some trout and salmon, and Arbroath smokies.

WHEN IN SEASON
All year

HOW TO CHOOSE AND STORE
All fish should look and smell fresh with bright, firm flesh. Avoid if the surface is dry and discoloured. Best used on the day of purchase or, at most, kept well wrapped in the fridge for up to 24 hours. Can be frozen for up to 2 months, if not using immediately. Smoked salmon, trout, and mackerel are often vacuum-packed for a longer shelf life.

Haddock The most famous of the smoked white fish, with a sweet, lightly smoked flavour. Cod (below), whiting, and some pollack are also available. Best poached.

sold commercially as bloater paste, popular in the 20th century.

Bloaters Herrings smoked whole, with their innards intact. Strong fish taste but mild smoky flavour. Usually grilled.

Mackerel Hot smoked whole or fillets, good hot or cold, and also for pâté.

Kippers Traditionally herrings that are split open, cleaned, salted, and smoked. Also sold as fillets. Best "jugged" (see p241), poached, or grilled.

Kippers are traditionally sold in pairs.

Try cooked and flaked, cold in a salad.

smoked trout Whole hot smoked fish. Serve whole or fillet first.

salmon Whole fillets (sides) are hot or cold smoked. Cold smoked is thinly sliced for salads, starters, and sandwiches; hot smoked is served in fillets, like mackerel.

Colour ranges from pale pink to orangey red, depending on the fish and the style of smoking.

Cod Whole fillets or loins, with a pale creamy colour and plump succulent flesh. Best poached.

If dyed, the flesh will be bright yellow.

Finnan haddie Named after the village of Findon, Aberdeen, were they were first produced. Whole haddock, headed and gutted, split, salted, and smoked whole. Best poached or grilled.

Buckling (herring) Whole gutted herrings, hot smoked. Good grilled, or cold in salad.

Arbroath smokies small whole haddock, split, salted, and hot smoked.

SMOKED FISH **239**

PERFECT PAIRINGS

EGGS, scrambled with smoked salmon, trout, or kippers; poached with smoked white fish; hard-boiled, chopped, or quartered; in rice dishes or a salad. **CREAM CHEESE** with smoked salmon, trout, or mackerel for pâté or sandwiches. **CHEDDAR CHEESE** melted on or as a sauce for smoked white fish. **SPINACH**, lightly wilted and served as a bed for any poached or grilled fillets, or raw in a salad. **HORSERADISH CREAM** with smoked mackerel, buckling, salmon, or trout. **POTATOES**, boiled waxy ones, in cold or warm salads with all.

SIMPLE WAYS TO ENJOY

TO PREPARE

Very little needed. Smoked white fish fillets can be skinned before cooking (see p222). Arbroath smokies and bloaters: remove the bone before cooking. Buckling, to serve cold: remove skin and lift the fish off the bones in two fillets.

←SMOKED FISH KEDGEREE

Boil some rice. Mix with cooked, flaked smoked fish (use smoked white fish, kipper, salmon, or mackerel, or a mixture for added colour and flavour), and cooked peas. Flavour with ground cumin, grated nutmeg, salt and pepper. Add some chopped fresh parsley, moisten with single cream. Stir gently over a low heat until piping hot. Top with hard- or soft-boiled egg wedges. Garnish with more parsley.

JUGGED KIPPERS

Put a pair of kippers in a tall jug. Pour on boiling water, cover, leave to stand for 5 minutes. Drain and serve topped with pats of butter and a sprinkling of chopped fresh parsley.

ARBROATH SMOKIES OR BLOATERS

Remove the bone, spread the inside of the fish with butter, add some pepper, and close again. Grill on both sides until the butter melts and the fish is piping hot.

SMOKED MACKEREL OR BUCKLING WITH ROOT REMOULADE

Cut celeriac, raw beetroot, and carrots into thin matchsticks. Blend some mayonnaise with a little grated horseradish and a splash of white balsamic condiment. Mix with the vegetables. Season to taste. Place a little pile on small plates and lay a mackerel or buckling fillet to one side of each. Garnish with parsley and lemon wedges. Serve with crusty bread.

CRUSTACEANS

Tucking into a freshly cooked, pot-caught Devon crab or Cornish lobster, or peeling a pint of little, pink prawns, is a delight. Here you'll discover how to prepare and enjoy these and other glorious crustaceans from all around our coast, as well as freshwater crayfish, which are available caught, wild, or farmed. Sadly, our native, white-clawed species (pictured right) is in decline in some areas since the introduction of American signal crayfish in the 1970s. They've aggressively taken over rivers and lakes. Each crustacean has a MCS sustainability rating, which we've included below.

small amount of meat in claws. ↗

spider crab sweet, white meat; doesn't yield as much as the brown crab, but worth tackling.

WHAT WHEN AND HOW

WHAT TYPES
Brown crabs: Fat, squat. Most sustainably caught in the Devon Inshore Potting Agreement area. MCS rating 3/5.
Spider crabs: Spiny, spider-like. Often net-caught. Avoid small. MCS rating 3/5.
Lobster: Blue-black, with a fat tail, and large front claws. Choose pot-caught. MCS rating 4/5.
Langoustines: Tiny lobster relative; also called scampi, Dublin Bay prawns, Norway lobsters. Many are exported. Look for Scottish creel-caught; trawled often die or are injured when caught, and a huge by-catch is destroyed, too. MCS rating 3/5.
Brown shrimp: Transparent when alive. Average size 3cm (1½in). MCS rating 3/5.
Northern (cold-water) prawns: Buy from fisheries using sorting grids to reduce by-catch. Search for common prawns, too, in rock pools. MCS rating 3/5.
Freshwater crayfish: Like mini lobsters. Buy farmed or wild-caught signals. MCS rating 4/5.

Brown crab Cocks have more sweet, white meat than hens. The brown meat is prepared separately when it is dressed. Best bought freshly boiled.

WHEN IN SEASON
As with other fish, avoid in the spawning season, but enjoy fresh in the months below:
Crabs: July–March **Lobster:** October–June
Langoustines: December–August **Prawns:** November–May **Shrimp:** All year **Crayfish:** Farmed all year

HOW TO CHOOSE AND STORE
Choose fresh-smelling, undamaged specimens, live or cooked. Crabs and lobsters should feel heavy for their size. If live, keep covered with a damp cloth or seaweed to prevent dehydration. Cook as soon as possible (see To Prepare, p244.) Keep cooked crustaceans on a tray covered with foil. Use on the day of purchase.

Langoustine The sweet, tender tail meat is used as scampi, but they can be boiled, then split and grilled briefly. Fiddly to eat, but delicious.

Pink when raw or cooked.

Bright orangey-red when cooked.

Brick red when cooked.

Freshwater crayfish Very sweet, succulent flesh. Usually sold ready-cooked. If raw, see To Prepare, p244. Treat like lobster.

Lobster Our native lobsters are considered some of the best in the world; sweet and succulent.

Bright pink when cooked.

Brownish-pink when cooked.

There is some meat in each of the legs as well as the large claws.

Brown shrimp Tiny morsels of the sweetest flesh. Fiddly to prepare, but worth it. If raw, plunge in boiling, salted water.

Northern (cold-water) prawns Sweet, juicy flesh. Sold raw or cooked, peeled or unpeeled.

PERFECT PAIRINGS

CRAB, **LOBSTER**, and **CRAYFISH** can take on stronger flavours like **CHILLI**, **BRANDY**, or **CHEESES**. **LANGOUSTINE** (scampi) tails, egged and crumbed, deep-fried, and served with **TARTARE SAUCE**. **FOR ALL** **MAYONNAISE** as a dip, plain or flavoured with chopped watercress, cucumber, saffron, or garlic; **GARLIC BUTTER** drizzled over or used as a dip; **LOVAGE** to flavour seafood chowders.

SIMPLE WAYS TO ENJOY

TO PREPARE

RAW LOBSTER AND CRAYFISH
To kill humanely, freeze crayfish for 45 minutes, lobsters 2 hours, plunge in boiling salted water and cook: 5 minutes for crayfish; lobsters 10 minutes/500g (1lb 2oz). Add 5 minutes per extra 250g (9oz). Or, buy freshly boiled.

COOKED LOBSTER AND CRAYFISH
Twist off legs and claws. Crack open, remove meat. Split lobster in half down back with a sharp knife. Remove gills behind head, and black intestine. Leave the red coral and green tomalley – it's edible – or remove to mix with meat if not using the shells. Loosen the flesh in the tail, cut in pieces, and put back in the tail.

CRAB
Twist off large claws. Pull off legs. Pull body away from top shell. Remove intestines and scrape to remove any dark meat, then discard. Scoop out dark meat from shell. Discard the gills from body. Crack claws and legs and remove meat. Pick white meat from body.

COOKED PRAWNS, SHRIMP, AND LANGOUSTINE
Pull off head and tail. Turn upside down, peel off legs and shell. Remove the dark intestine.

POTTED PRAWNS, SHRIMP, OR CRAB
Melt 85g (3oz) unsalted butter. Add 450g (1lb) peeled prawns, shrimp, or the dark and white meat from a large cooked crab, ¼ tsp ground mace, a few drops of Tabasco, finely grated zest of ½ lemon, and seasoning. Heat, tossing gently, for 2 minutes only. Pack into pots. Melt more unsalted butter to pour over. Leave to cool, then chill. Turn out and serve with wholegrain bread.

GRILLED LOBSTER OR CRAYFISH GRATIN
Prepare lobster or crayfish (see left) and return the meat to the shells. Blend some crème fraîche with a splash of brandy and grated Cheddar cheese. Season. Spoon the cream mixture over the meat in the shells. Put on a grill rack under a moderate grill until bubbling and turning golden and the meat is hot through.

PIRI PIRI PRAWNS
Mix a little chopped garlic and fresh root ginger with a chopped piri piri chilli, some paprika, a couple of spoonfuls of olive oil, and enough lime juice to make a runny marinade. Season well. Add whole, unshelled (preferably raw) prawns. Toss well and marinate for 2 hours. Griddle until sizzling on both sides and cooked through. Serve with finger bowls.

SEAFOOD WITH MARIE ROSE SAUCE

Shred some lettuce and put in wine goblets. Add a good handful of cooked peeled prawns, shrimp, white crab meat, or chopped crayfish tails to each. Mix equal quantities of mayonnaise and crème fraîche. Flavour with tomato ketchup, a squeeze of lemon, a few drops of Tabasco, and seasoning. Spoon over the shellfish and sprinkle with paprika. Garnish with a slice of lemon and cucumber.

GRILLED LANGOUSTINES OR PRAWNS WITH TARRAGON BUTTER

Split cooked langoustines in half or use raw prawns. Lay on foil in the grill pan. Mash some softened butter with chopped tarragon and a good grinding of pepper. Smear over the crustaceans. Grill as near to the heat source as possible for 2–3 minutes until turning golden in places and sizzling. Serve with the melted butter.

LOBSTER OR CRAB THERMIDOR

Prepare as on p244, and return the white meat to the shell. Soften a finely chopped onion in a knob of butter. Add 4 tbsp dry vermouth and 450ml (15fl oz) fish stock. Boil until syrupy. Add 5 tbsp double cream, ½ tsp Dijon mustard, and 1 tsp each chopped chervil and parsley. Stir in the dark meat or green tomalley. Spike with lemon juice. Season. Spoon the mixture over the meat in the shells. Sprinkle with finely grated Cheddar or Parmesan cheese. Grill until golden and bubbling.

DRESSED CRAB

Prepare a large crab as on p244, keeping dark and white meat separate. Mix the dark meat with 1 tbsp brown breadcrumbs, a good squeeze of lemon juice, ½ tsp Dijon mustard, and a few drops of Tabasco. Season. Season the white meat lightly. Wash the crab shell, and pack the white meat in either side of the shell, leaving the centre free. Spoon the dark meat into the centre. Put a row of chopped parsley down the two dividing lines. Place on a bed of shredded lettuce and surround with sliced cucumber, tomatoes, and lemon wedges.

CRAB AND LEEK BISQUE

SERVES 4–6 **PREPARATION TIME** 30 minutes **COOKING TIME** 50–55 minutes
VARIATION Use lobster, if you can afford it. **SERVE WITH** crusty bread, followed
by a salad or cheese with some crisp celery and oatcakes.

1 Remove all the meat from the crab, keeping the dark and light
meat separate. Put the crab shell in a pan with the stock and half
the dark crab meat. Bring to the boil, reduce the heat, cover, and
simmer gently for 45 minutes. Strain.

2 Make the crab butter by mashing the remaining dark meat with
45g (1½oz) of the butter and the parsley. Shape into a sausage using
greaseproof paper and chill.

3 Fry the leek gently in the remaining butter until softened, but not
browned. Add the vermouth and simmer for 5 minutes. Flame the
brandy and stir in.

4 Blend the flour with the milk and stir in. Add half the strained
stock, bring to the boil, and cook for 2 minutes, stirring. Tip into
a blender and purée with the white crab meat. Return to the pan,
stir in the remaining stock and the cream. Season to taste. Heat
through. Ladle into warm bowls and top each with a slice of the
crab butter. Serve immediately.

INGREDIENTS
1 large fresh cooked crab
1 litre (1¾ pints) fish or
  chicken stock
75g (2½oz) butter
1 tbsp chopped fresh parsley
1 large leek, chopped
5 tbsp dry vermouth
2 tbsp brandy
3 tbsp plain flour
5 tbsp milk
150ml (5fl oz) single cream
Salt and freshly ground
  black pepper

MOLLUSCS

From humble winkles to imperial oysters, all are a delight. Only a few native oysters are harvested wild now; most are responsibly farmed in independent fisheries along with Pacific oysters, introduced here in the 1970s (see below). For scallops, choose diver-caught or from responsibly managed farms. Mussels are farmed, usually rope-grown all year, or wild in season. If possible, choose hand-gathered molluscs as dredging destroys the eco-system. The Soil Association is now certifying oysters and mussels as organic. We've also included squid, technically a mollusc, though very different. Buy from Scottish waters; it's not targeted there, but is a by-catch of white fish.

Clams several varieties. Classically served in a white wine or tomato sauce with pasta, or in a chowder. Good with saffron, too.

WHAT WHEN AND HOW

WHAT TYPES

Bivalves: Shellfish in two shells joined by a hinge – such as mussels, oysters, clams, razor clams, cockles, and king scallops.

Gastropods: Snail-like creatures that clamp on to rocks with a sucker. Winkles (periwinkles) and whelks are most popular.

Cephalopods: Soft bodied with an internal shell. Squid is most popular for cooking, although cuttlefish are in the same family.

See *www.fishonline.org* for individual sustainability ratings.

WHEN IN SEASON

Cockles: September–February; **Clams, Razor clams:** October–April; **Mussels:** Wild, October–March; farmed all year; **Oysters:** Native, September–April, rock (Pacific), farmed all year; **King scallops:** October–March, farmed all year; **Whelks:** January–September; **Winkles:** July–January; **Squid:** June–November

HOW TO CHOOSE AND STORE

Shells should be undamaged, bivalves shut. Avoid if broken, the shells are open or don't close when sharply tapped. Avoid razor clams under 10cm (4in). All should smell pleasantly of the sea. Keep oysters rounded-side down. Scallops should look creamy white and moist. Squid should be sweet-smelling and slippery. Keep wrapped in a biodegradable plastic bag in the fridge (or see p250). Eat on the day of purchase.

shell resembles a cut-throat razor.

Razor clams Pale, creamy-coloured, soft flesh that firms on cooking. Good served in the shells with flavoured butter or a sauce.

King scallops Creamy, tender flesh with bright orange coral. Don't overcook – just a minute or two is enough. Can be poached and served in its shell in a sauce, pan-fried, or grilled.

sold with or without the shell and coral.

Distinctive, blue-black shells.

Whelks Large, snail-like creatures, usually boiled, with juicy but chewy flesh and a strong flavour.

Often sold ready-cooked.

Winkles small, black, snail-like mollusc with tasty, slightly rubbery, flesh.

Cockles Like baby clams, tiny little nuggets that taste of the sea. Often sold ready-cooked and shelled, but can be cooked as clams in soups or with pasta.

Squid Firm, pure white flesh and a sweet, fishy flavour, often sold ready-cleaned. Ink is sometimes used. Can be stuffed whole or cut into rings and fried, grilled, or gently stewed in olive oil and garlic.

Mussels Glorious steamed in a variety of sauces or in soups, or rice or pasta dishes.

THE WORLD OF OYSTERS

Natives are indigenous but are depleted from over-fishing, pollution and disease, so are now also farmed. Wild ones are the property of the Crown and cannot be harvested without a licence. The Solent has one of the largest wild native oyster beds left in UK but Whitstable has one of the most famous. Pacifics are farmed all round our shores from Cornwall to Scotland. Organic oysters are grown in Poole, Dorset.

The quality and flavour of all oysters depends on their habitat. Some are sweet, others are salty, some have a mineral aftertaste, others are more fruity or even taste of cucumber. The texture can vary, too, depending on the season and the weather. Natives are more expensive, with a stronger flavour, and take up to five years to grow. An ancient law prevents them being fished in their spawning season, May to August. That's why they're eaten only when there's an "r" in the month. Pacifics are bigger, cheaper and take only three years to grow.

Natives take their names from their area. Most fisheries supply Pacific oysters too. Some of the best known are:
Whitstable: Famous ancient wild oyster bed of the Free Fishery. Smooth texture, delicate meat.
Falmouth Bay: Harvested from rowing and sailing boats from ancient wild beds in the estuary. Full, sweet flavour.
Colchester: Famous for native oysters since Roman times, now farmed. Robust, earthy flavour.
Galway bay: Renowned Irish wild Clarinbridge oysters, and also farmed. Succulent flavour.
Loch Ryan: Once wild, now farmed in the West Coast sea loch. Firm texture, slightly sweet taste.
Duchy of Cornwall: Farmed in the Helford estuary. Sweet flavour.

Variable shape, usually elongated and sometimes very rough.

Pacific (rock or gigas) oysters Widely farmed all over Britain. Serve like native oysters.

Round, flat, crinkly shells.

Native (European flat) oysters They were poor man's food once, used to pad out beef pies as meat was too dear! Serve shucked (opened) raw or briefly grilled.

PERFECT PAIRINGS

MUSSELS and **CLAMS** **DRY CIDER**, **VERMOUTH**, **PERNOD**, or **WINE** when cooking. **FENNEL** added when cooking, **DILL** or **CHERVIL** as garnish. **SCALLOPS** poached in milk and made into **BÉCHAMEL** or **LIGHT CHEESE SAUCE**, spooned over or glazed; **CHILLI**, fresh chopped or dried flakes, when pan-searing. **OYSTERS** **FRESH LEMON/LIME JUICE** and **PEPPER/TABASCO** or finely chopped **SHALLOTS** in **RED WINE VINEGAR**, spooned over. **COCKLES**, **WINKLES**, and **WHELKS** **MALT VINEGAR** and **BLACK PEPPER** sprinkled over; **MELTED BUTTER** with **GARLIC** and **HERBS**, as for snails.

SIMPLE WAYS TO ENJOY

TO PREPARE

If time, put mussels, clams, cockles, winkles, or whelks (if raw) in a bowl of water. Sprinkle with oats (they clean these filter feeders inside). Leave for 2 hours. Discard broken ones and bivalves that stay open when tapped. Scrub. Remove any barnacles. Gastropods need no more prep.

MUSSELS
Pull off any beards.

OYSTERS
To shuck, hold firmly, flat-side up, hand protected by a cloth. Push a knife between the shells, near the hinge. Twist, pushing towards hinge until it breaks. Lift off top shell; don't spill juices. Loosen oyster from shell with a knife.

SCALLOPS
Open as above, but they have no juice. Cut under where attached to shell. Peel off membrane. Rinse. Remove black intestine.

SQUID
Pull out head and ink sac. Cut tentacles off; reserve. Discard head. Pull out clear quill from body. Pull skin off body. Pull or cut off side flaps to cook too. Rinse, slice or leave whole.

COCKLE SOFTIES

Buy ready-cooked cockles or boil fresh ones in salted water for 5 minutes. Drain, and remove from their shells. Mix with some thinly sliced cucumber, malt vinegar, and black pepper to taste. Stir, leave for 5 minutes, then drain. Cut a slice off the top of some soft wholemeal rolls. Pull out most of the insides. Butter inside the shells and lids. Spoon in the cockle mixture, and top with the lids.

SPAGHETTI WITH CLAMS

Make some tomato sauce (see p144). Steam the clams in a little dry white wine in a covered pan for 5 minutes, shaking occasionally, until they open. Drain, reserving the liquor. Discard any that are still shut. Remove the clams from their shells. Cook some spaghetti according to the packet instructions. Drain and return to the pan. Add the tomato sauce, the clams, and their cooking liquor to taste. Toss over a gentle heat until hot. Season. Garnish with chopped parsley.

RAZOR CLAMS WITH CHIVE BUTTER

Steam razor clams as cockles (see p251). Drain. Meanwhile, melt some unsalted butter with crushed garlic. Stir in snipped chives and a little finely grated lemon zest. Remove the top shells from the clams. Lay them in their bottom shells on plates. Spoon the chive butter over and add a good grinding of black pepper.

TO BOIL WINKLES OR WHELKS

Put 1 quartered onion, 1 bay leaf, 6 peppercorns, and a good pinch of salt in a pan half-full of water. Bring to the boil. Add the winkles or whelks – boil for 5 minutes for winkles, 8 minutes for whelks. Drain, discarding the flavourings, and leave to cool slightly. To eat, pick off the sucker and pull out meat with a winkle-picker or pin.

TO STEAM BIVALVES

Put in a pan with about 1cm (½in) water, wine, or half and half. Bring to the boil, cover, and steam for 5 minutes. Drain. Remove from the shells, if necessary.

ANGELS ON HORSEBACK

Stretch streaky bacon rashers with the back of a knife. Halve. Wrap each half round a shucked oyster or ½ scallop. Grill until bacon is golden, turning once. (For cherubs on horseback, replace oyster with a button mushroom.)

MOULES MARINIÈRE

Prepare 1.8kg (4lb) mussels. Soften a finely chopped onion and celery stick with a crushed garlic clove in a good knob of butter without browning. Add a glass each of dry white wine and water, the mussels, and a good grinding of pepper. Bring to the boil, cover, and steam for 5 minutes, shaking the pan occasionally, until the mussels open. Discard any still closed. Ladle the mussels and liquor into warm bowls. Garnish with chopped parsley.

GRILLED OYSTERS WITH CRÈME FRAÎCHE AND SHEEP'S CHEESE

Shuck some oysters. Carefully place on the grill rack; don't spill the juice. Add a few drops of Tabasco and a sprinkling of snipped fresh chives to each. Top each with 1 tsp crème fraîche and 1 tsp finely grated hard sheep's cheese or Parmesan. Season. Grill for 1 minute until the cheese is bubbling.

WINKLES OR WHELKS WITH BLACK BUTTER

Cook some winkles or whelks. Put in bowls. Meanwhile, melt some butter in a pan. As soon as it foams, smells nutty, and begins to turn brown, add a splash of red wine vinegar and some chopped fresh thyme. Boil for 30 seconds. Spoon into little dishes. Pick out the meat and dip in the sauce.

CRISPY SALT, PEPPER, AND SMOKED PAPRIKA SQUID

Prepare a squid and cut into thick rings. Rinse and dry on kitchen paper. Season some cornflour with a little smoked paprika, coarsely ground black pepper, and garlic salt. Use to coat the squid. Deep-fry in hot oil in small batches for barely 1 minute until lightly golden. Don't overcook. Drain on kitchen paper. Keep warm while you cook the rest. Serve with lime wedges.

SIZZLING SCALLOPS WITH CHILLIES

Melt some unsalted butter with olive oil. Add chopped spring onions and finely chopped red chilli. Stir-fry for 2 minutes. Add some king scallops, preferably with their corals (allow 4–5 per person), and sprinkle with paprika, seasoning, and lime juice. Fry for 1 minute, turn them over, and fry for 1–2 minutes more. Garnish with a few whole chive stalks.

MUSSELS WITH FENNEL, GARLIC, AND TOMATOES

SERVES 4 **PREPARATION TIME** 25 minutes **COOKING TIME** 8 minutes
VARIATION If you like chillies, add a finely chopped red or green one (as hot as you dare) to the fennel mixture before adding the mussels. A splash of Pernod enhances the flavour of the fennel, but you can omit it if you prefer.
SERVE WITH crusty bread.

1 Melt the butter in a large pan. Add the onion, fennel, and garlic and fry gently, stirring, for 3 minutes until softened but not browned. Add the wine, tomatoes, Pernod (if using), and tomato purée. Stir well.

2 Add the mussels and a good grinding of black pepper. Bring to the boil, cover, reduce the heat, and cook gently for 5 minutes until the mussels open, shaking the pan occasionally. Discard any that remain closed.

3 Ladle into warm bowls, including all the lovely juices.

INGREDIENTS
30g (1oz) unsalted butter
1 onion, chopped
1 fennel bulb, chopped
1 large garlic clove, chopped
150ml (5fl oz) dry white wine
4 tomatoes, skinned, seeded, and chopped
1 tbsp Pernod (optional)
2 tsp tomato purée
1.8kg (4lb) mussels, prepared (see p250)
Freshly ground black pepper

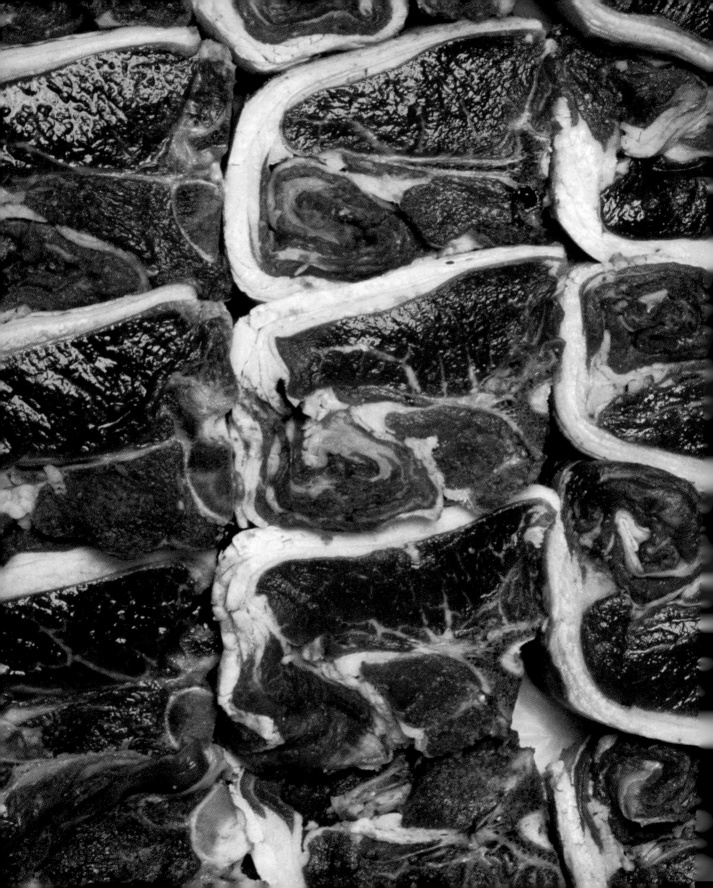

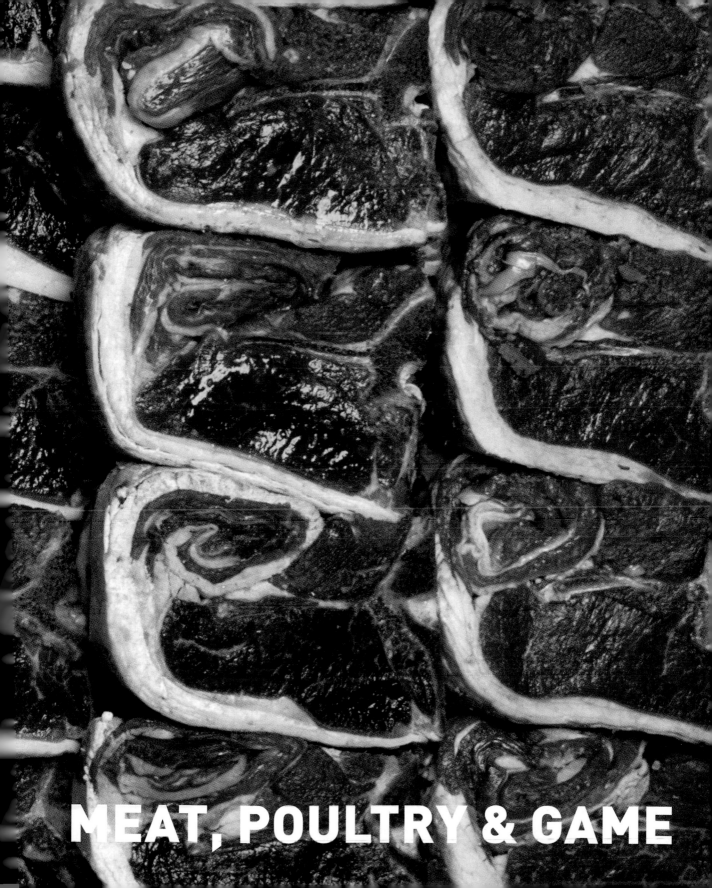

MEAT, POULTRY & GAME

BREEDS

Organic beef cattle can be kept outside in winter (with shelter, food, and water provided) so they need to be hardy. Here are some favourite breeds, selected for their superb meat.

HEREFORD
Famous for its red coat and white face, it's good for milk but produces succulent, marbled beef. The animals are known for their good temperament; they get less stressed, enhancing the quality of the meat. An adaptable, native breed.

BEEF SHORTHORN
A popular breed for organic and other farming systems, they can be red, red and white, white, or roan, with or without horns. They are docile animals and produce excellent quality, tender beef with good marbling.

BELTED GALLOWAY
Black, dun, or red, with a thick wide band round its belly and no horns. It is a large, ancient, Scottish breed, well able to withstand extreme weather conditions, and produces sweet, tender, juicy meat.

ABERDEEN ANGUS
One of the most well-known breeds, originating in Scotland. It is traditionally black, but sometimes red from breeding the black animals with red European stock. The meat has superb eating qualities with a good marbling of fat. Bred all over Britain.

WELSH BLACK
One of the oldest British rare breeds, a stocky Welsh mountain beef strain and southern Welsh dairy have intermingled to produce a hardy dual breed. Mostly black and horned, though some are red. Beef quality is excellent: good marbling.

SOUTH DEVON
Beautiful, brown animals with a docile nature, so easy to manage. They are extremely good at converting forage into a meat that is highly sought after for its good marbling, excellent flavour, tenderness, and succulence.

PINK (ROSE) VEAL
Male dairy calves humanely reared for meat instead of being destroyed (see above right).

BEEF AND VEAL

Organic British beef is among the best in the world. Calves suckle their mothers until around nine months old, and all cattle graze pasture for most of their life. The Soil Association is encouraging dairy farmers to rear dual breeds — cows for milk, steers for beef. Male dairy calves are reared for British pink veal (see below) — if more people ate it, demand would increase, saving more from a miserable fate.

PINK (ROSE) VEAL

The Soil Association and other organic campaigners (including Sophie Grigson) are promoting high-welfare pink (rose) veal. The calves are reared with plenty of space, light, and clean bedding; outside in pastures, but indoors in winter. They have a proper diet, and are encouraged to suckle from their own or a foster mum. They have a happy six months of life. Their meat is pink, tender, and tasty, and produced from stress-free animals.

HOW TO CHOOSE AND STORE

For beef, choose well-hung meat for best texture and flavour. It should be deep red with a marbling of fat; moist, not wet. Avoid if dry, greyish-tinged, or with gristle. The fat should be creamy white and smell fresh. Pink veal should be hung for a week for best flavour. Remove from its wrapping, freshly wrap, keep on the lowest fridge shelf. Eat offal, minced beef, and small veal cuts on day of purchase. Store joints and chops for 2–3 days in the fridge.

STEWING

Shin of beef cut from the fore leg, needs careful trimming. Usually diced and used for stews and casseroles.

Diced braising steak usually lean chuck, blade, or flank. Often sold minced. Braise, casserole, or stew.

JOINTS

Topside Lean joint with little fat (sometimes has fat tied round it to keep it moist during cooking.) Roast or pot roast. Silverside is best pot roasted. Also sold salted.

Sirloin Boned and rolled (also available on the bone with the fillet intact), and sliced as steaks. Large joint from just in front of the rump with a good outer fat layer. Excellent for roasting. Steaks: grill or fry.

Rib on the bone (Also available boned and rolled.) Excellent roasting cut. Small joints are good, but a large joint with several ribs cooks best.

Brisket Cut from the underside behind the front leg. Brisket has a great flavour but needs long, slow cooking.

STEAKS

Rump steak Thick, juicy.

Fillet steak (or tenderloin) Cut from the eye of the sirloin, meltingly tender. Served as here in steaks, to grill or fry, or whole, to roast. Chateaubriand is a thick steak cut from centre of fillet, for two people. Tornedos or filet mignon are small, trimmed fillets.

T-bone steak (also called Porterhouse) Thick slice of sirloin, cut down through the bone (hence the "T" shape), with sirloin steak one side, fillet the other.

Sirloin steak Cut from the sirloin without the fillet. Thin ones are called "minute steaks". Grill or fry.

OFFAL

Ribeye steak Cut from the fore ribs. Originally an American cut, now popular here. Grill or fry.

Veal escalope Leg of veal, cut into thin steaks and usually beaten flat. Best fried plain, or egged and crumbed.

Veal chop Also known as bone-in veal steak. Cut from the rib. Best grilled or fried, but can be roasted.

Oxtail The meaty tail, sold in chunks. Needs long, slow cooking. Stew, braise, or use in soup. Try ox kidney, liver, heart, tongue, tripe, and calf's liver, kidneys, and sweetbreads.

BEEF AND VEAL **257**

PERFECT PAIRINGS

YORKSHIRE PUDDING and **HORSERADISH SAUCE** with roasts. **ENGLISH MUSTARD,** **MUSHROOMS**, and **FRIED ONIONS** are traditional British accompaniments with steaks. **RED WINE** or **BEER** on its own or with stock as a sauce, or for braising and casseroling. **PARSNIPS** roasted with joints or in casseroles and stews. **MELTING CHEESE** and **HAM** to sandwich veal escalopes together before egg and crumbing. **BAY LEAVES** are a favourite herb for beef, **SAGE** for veal. Mediterranean flavours like **OLIVES**, **TOMATOES**, **GARLIC**, and **BASIL** with all.

SIMPLE WAYS TO ENJOY

TO PREPARE

TO FLATTEN ESCALOPES
Put in a biodegradable plastic bag and beat with a meat mallet or rolling pin.

TO MAKE MINCE AT HOME
Select lean braising steak. Pass through a mincer or finely chop in a food processor.

SHIN OF BEEF, FOR STEWING
Trim excess fat and cut out any thick gristle. Cut into cubes.

JOINTS
Season the fat only with salt; sprinkle the whole joint with pepper and herbs, if using.

STEAKS
Marinate before grilling, if liked, or just brush with oil.

RARE OR WELL DONE?

To test steaks are cooked to your liking, press the surface of the cooked meat gently with a finger:

Wobbly – very rare
Firmer with a little "give" – medium rare
Firm – well done
Hard – ruined!

BOLOGNESE SAUCE

Brown minced steak, chopped onion, and garlic, stirring until the meat is lump-free. Add canned chopped tomatoes, a splash of wine, a bay leaf, a slice of lemon, some tomato purée, and a pinch of sugar. Season. Simmer until tender. Discard the bay leaf and lemon. Add some chopped oregano.

BEEF, BEER, AND PARSNIP CASSEROLE

Brown diced stewing beef with some onions in oil. Add diced parsnips, brown beer, and stock. Bring to the boil, and thicken with flour and water. Season, and add a bouquet garni. Cover and cook in the oven at 160°C (325°F/Gas 3) until rich and tender.

OXTAIL STEW

Brown oxtail pieces in oil in a flameproof casserole. Remove. Brown some sliced carrots, celery, and onions. Return the oxtail; sprinkle in some flour. Cover with half stock, half red wine. Add a bay leaf, a pinch of ground cloves, and a chopped tomato. Cover and cook at 150°C (300°F/Gas 2) for 4 hours. Discard the bay leaf, and reseason.

VEAL ESCALOPES WITH LEMON AND CUMIN

Flavour fresh breadcrumbs with cumin seeds and grated lemon zest. Season well. Dip flattened veal escalopes in beaten egg, then in the breadcrumbs. Fry in hot oil and butter.

CALF'S (OR LAMB'S) LIVER WITH CRISPY BACON AND APPLE

Fry thin, streaky bacon until crisp. Remove. Fry apple slices in butter until golden. Remove. Lightly fry seasoned, thinly sliced liver. Serve together.

FILLET STEAKS ON PÂTÉ CROÛTES WITH RED WINE GLAZE

SERVES 4 **PREPARATION TIME** 10 minutes **COOKING TIME** 4–16 minutes
SERVE WITH sautéed potatoes and mangetout. When thyme is in flower, use sprigs with flower heads for garnish.

1 Melt 15g (½oz) of the butter with the oil in a frying pan. Fry the bread on both sides until golden but still soft. Drain on kitchen paper.

2 Heat the remaining butter in the pan and fry the steaks until cooked to your liking (2–8 minutes each side for rare through to well done). Wrap in foil and leave to rest while you make the sauce.

3 Add the brandy to the pan and ignite. Shake the pan until the flames subside. Add the wine, tomato purée, chopped thyme, and sugar. Bring to the boil and cook, stirring, until thickened and reduced. Season to taste. Add the juices from the steaks.

4 Quickly spread the pâté on the croûtes and put on warm plates. Top each with a steak, then spoon the hot glaze over. Garnish with tiny sprigs of thyme.

INGREDIENTS
30g (1oz) butter
2 tbsp olive oil
4 thin slices of French bread
4 small fillet steaks, trimmed
1 tbsp brandy
120ml (4fl oz) red wine
1 tbsp tomato purée
2 tsp chopped fresh thyme
A good pinch of caster sugar
Salt and freshly ground
  black pepper
60g (2oz) smooth chicken
  liver pâté
Tiny sprigs of fresh thyme,
  to garnish

BRAISED BRISKET

JULIET KINDERSLEY

Juliet Kindersley and her husband own the award-winning Sheepdrove Organic Farm in Berkshire, which rears and produces organic meat for its nationwide home-delivery meat-hamper scheme.

SERVES 6–8 **PREPARATION TIME** 10 minutes **COOKING TIME** 4 hours 5 minutes **SERVE WITH** creamy mashed potatoes, steamed greens or beans, and horseradish sauce. **A really full-flavoured cut, brisket is excellent for braising, pot-roasting, and boiling; this recipe is our family version of the French country classic, pot-au-feu. It can be served at once or prepared a day ahead.**

1 Preheat the oven to 160°C (325°F/Gas 3).

2 Put the beef, garlic, bay leaf, thyme, Worcestershire sauce, pepper, and stout in a casserole; add enough of the stock to come no more than halfway up the meat. Bring just to the boil, cover tightly with foil, put on the lid and oven-braise until fork-tender, about 4 hours, turning the meat halfway through cooking.

3 Let the meat rest on a warmed platter, covered loosely with foil, while you boil down the sauce until reduced by half, then season to taste. Slice the meat and return to the sauce.

4 If cooking in advance, cool the whole joint in the casserole, and refrigerate overnight. When you are ready, preheat the oven to 180°C (350°F/Gas 4). Slice the meat and reheat it in the sauce in the oven for 30 minutes.

INGREDIENTS
1.5kg (3lb 3oz) rolled brisket
  of beef
1 garlic clove, crushed
1 bay leaf
1 tbsp fresh thyme leaves
2 tsp Worcestershire sauce
½ tsp freshly ground black
  pepper
300ml (10fl oz) stout
360ml (12fl oz) chicken or
  beef stock
Salt, to taste

BREEDS

Pigs for pork are usually killed when they reach 80kg; for bacon and ham, over 85kg. Here are the favoured organic breeds, many of which are revived rare ones.

TAMWORTH
Famous rare breed. Lively, ginger pig with long legs and pricked-up ears. Popular organic breed as it is excellent for pork and bacon. With the longest snout, it's great for clearing overgrown land.

SADDLEBACK
Rare breed. Cross between Essex and Wessex pigs. Black head and rump, lop ears, and a white band round its shoulders. A heavy, hardy animal; good for outdoor rearing as excellent at grazing.

GLOUCESTER OLD SPOT
Originally known as "the orchard pig" as it loves grazing in apple orchards, enjoying the windfalls in autumn. It's happy outdoors all year with good winter shelter. Very hardy; excellent meat.

BERKSHIRE
Black with white socks, tail tip and a flash on the face. Very popular with Queen Victoria, but lost favour in the trend for eating less fat. It's making a comeback. Gives superior-quality, white meat.

LARGE WHITE
Traditional British pink pig. It is hardy, active, good outdoors and very adaptable. It is excellent for cross-breeding to improve other breeds, and popular with organic farmers. Gives lean, white meat.

HOW TO CHOOSE AND STORE

Fresh pork should be a good, pink colour with pure white fat. It should smell fresh – not unpleasant. Avoid if wet, slimy, or the fat is discoloured. For roasting, choose meat with a layer of fat under the skin – it makes better crackling and adds succulence. Always store on a plate, loosely wrapped, on the bottom shelf of the fridge. Store well away from cooked food. Mince and offal should be eaten on the day of purchase or within 24 hours. Other cuts can be stored for up to 2–3 days.

PORK

Organic and free-range pig farming is a pleasurable sight; those little, tin huts dotted across some land with clusters of happy-looking pigs lying on straw in their doorways, or grubbing around in the earth, are a far cry from intensive rearing. When treated properly, pigs are trouble-free to rear, and fairly easy to feed. The Soil Association says, "A well looked-after pig tends to be a healthy pig, and healthy pigs tend to be robust, relatively disease-free and, at the end of the day, extremely tasty!" Here we feature five of the most popular breeds and their delicious meat.

STEAKS AND FILLETS

Spare rib steak sometimes called shoulder steak. Boneless. Not as tender as leg steaks, with a more pronounced pork flavour.

Tenderloin The fillet cut from the hind loin. Tender, versatile cut that is cooked whole, cubed, sliced, or beaten flat for escalopes.

Leg steak Cut from the fillet end of the leg. The traditional escalope when beaten flat.

ROASTING JOINTS

Loin roast The hind loin is prime for roasting, with or without crackling.

Leg Can be sold whole, but often cut from the fillet end with or without the bone. Also sold diced.

Spare rib roast Cut from the shoulder, extending to the neck end and first couple of ribs. A large joint. Sold on the bone, or boned and rolled.

CHOPS

Shoulder chop More economical cut from the shoulder. Also known as spare rib chops. Shoulder also sold diced.

Belly rashers Underrated cut, sold as slices or in a joint for roasting, with or without bone. Can be fatty. Takes on strong flavours well. Good for Asian recipes, terrines, and mixing with other meats.

Spare ribs Trimmed ribs sold as a rack or individually cut.

Chump chop A boneless chop, more like pork rump steak, cut between the loin and top of the leg.

BRAISING CUTS

Hock The bottom end of the foreleg. If large it can be quite meaty.

Trotter The foot. Again, underrated. Not a lot of meat, but if simmered it makes great gelatinous stock.

OFFAL

Liver Strong, distinctive flavour. Don't overcook if frying. Try kidneys.

ROAST PORK BELLY WITH CARAMELIZED APPLE SAUCE

OLIVER ROWE

Urban chef and restaurateur Oliver runs Konstam, a London restaurant that sources its seasonal ingredients from local producers within the M25.

SERVES 6 **PREPARATION TIME** 1 hour **COOKING TIME** 1 hour 20 minutes–1 hour 45 minutes **SERVE WITH** crispy salad. **All the flavours go beautifully together and everything can all be done while the pork is being prepped and cooked.**

1 Crush the first five marinade ingredients in a pestle and mortar to make a smooth paste, then add the mustard. Score the skin and underside of the pork belly, and trim the excess fat and sinew. Rub the paste all over. Rub the skin side with salt. Leave to stand for 30 minutes, then wipe off the liquid and any excess salt. Arrange the onions in a roasting tray, cut-side down, with the pork on top, skin-side up.

2 Preheat the oven to 240°C (475°F/Gas 9), or its highest setting. Pour 1cm (½in) water in the roasting tray and place in the oven. Cook for 40–45 minutes. When the pork skin is crispy and bubbly, turn the oven down to 150°C (300°F/Gas 2) and cook for another 30–45 minutes. Top up the water, if necessary, but try to open the oven as little as possible. Remove from the oven and leave to rest, uncovered.

3 Cut the quartered apples into slices. In a large, hot frying pan, melt the butter and add the apples. Sprinkle over the sugar. Cook the apples so they are coloured on both sides. Deglaze the pan with a squeeze of lemon, a little cider, cider vinegar, white wine, sparkling wine, ale, lager, water, or stock, to create a sauce.

4 On a carving board, slice the pork into fingers, and place in a warm serving dish. Pour off any fat from the roasting tray, leaving the onions, cooked-on bits, and liquid. Over a high heat, deglaze with sherry, white wine, cider, or beer. Simmer, then strain into a jug.

5 Serve the pork with a drizzle of gravy and a few spoonfuls of the caramelized apple sauce.

INGREDIENTS
FOR THE MARINADE
6 garlic cloves, peeled
½ tsp fine sea salt
½ tsp fennel or dill seed
5 juniper berries
8 white or black peppercorns
1 tsp wholegrain mustard

FOR THE PORK
½ good, organic, free range, fatty
  pork belly, about 900g (2lb)
3 onions, cut in half
Sherry, white wine, cider, or beer,
  for the gravy

FOR THE CARAMELIZED
APPLE SAUCE
4 apples, peeled, quartered,
  and tossed in lemon juice
75g (3oz) butter
3 tbsp golden caster sugar
A little lemon juice, cider, cider
  vinegar, white wine, sparkling
  wine, ale, lager, water, or stock,
  for the sauce

ORGANIC PORK FROM LINCOLNSHIRE

SALLY AND ANDREW JACKSON, PINK PIG ORGANICS

A thriving and buzzing farm, 304-hectare (750-acre) Holme Hall in Lincolnshire, near Scunthorpe, is the home of Pink Pig Organics, run by husband-and-wife team Sally and Andrew Jackson. The Jacksons started converting part of their farm to organic production in the late 1990s, selling their organic produce to the supermarkets. After heavy losses, they happily abandoned the supermarkets and all their produce is now sold through the farm shop, farmers' markets, and their restaurant. "The increase in wildlife on the farm," says Andrew, "and the contentment of our animals, make it all worthwhile."

With a Gloucester Old Spot from Sally's mum, and a Cotswold Gold, they began breeding, crossing the two sows with a Duroc boar. After years of experimentation, Sally and Andrew have found that crossing old-fashioned varieties, to create "Heinz 57" crossbreeds, results in the best balance of fat and flavour, and lots of dotty and spotty pigs! Another advantage of traditional breeds is that the sows are naturally brilliant mothers, unlike some modern mixed breeds that roll and risk squashing their young. However, traditional breeds can be fatty, so the Jacksons plan to create leaner meat by introducing a modern boar breed.

Farming around 70 pigs at a time, Sally and Andrew send three or four off to their local abattoir every Monday morning, which returns the meat the next day. Their farm-shop butcher —

The Pink Pig sign.

Matthew Barrowcliff — makes all their sausages and cures the hams and bacon. Their pigs are reared outdoors from the moment of birth. Born in corrugated-iron "arcs", the piglets are weaned for six weeks then moved outside, where all the pigs, in various stages of growth, share paddocks. The sandy soil of the Scunthorpe area is naturally free-draining, so it's ideal for outdoor pig production (you can guarantee the muddiest of fields when pigs are involved!), and provides perfect growing conditions for the Jacksons' organic root vegetables. Their pigs' manure helps maintain fertile organic soil.

With locals showing an interest in their produce, one Saturday in 1999, Sally sold chickens, eggs, sausages, and vegetables at the end of the drive. Selling their produce direct to the consumer proved a success from the outset. They opened a little shop and 24-seater restaurant, and in 2001 "The Pink Pig" was born. They now have a 90-seater restaurant, an online shop, a shop on site selling their own and other local farmers' produce, and local deliveries. A fun, friendly, family-run enterprise, they also run several Pink Pig Adventure Days, when over 1,500 children a year come to learn about food and farming. The service is free and open all year — provided by fund-raising and a little help from the Soil Association-led Food for Life Partnership.

See p273 for Sally's *Pink Pig Cowboy Casserole*.

OPPOSITE, ABOVE LEFT Sally and Andrew in the paddock.
ABOVE RIGHT One of their spotty pigs outside its shelter "arc".
BELOW Just some of the many mixed breeds they farm.

CURED MEATS AND SAUSAGES

Haggis and the banger are both great British institutions; our bacon is second to none, and our black and white puddings rival any continental ones. Here we've concentrated on some of our traditional favourites, but there are numerous other British-made delicacies, such as salt beef, smoked meats, poultry and game, pâtés, brawn, and also even charcuterie such as salami and pancetta. In organic sausages, not only must the meat be organic, but also any cereals or other ingredients. The Soil Association has strict guidelines on which additives can be used, those being only natural flavours that have been extracted by physical means.

WHAT WHEN AND HOW

WHAT TYPES
Meat sausages: Choose at least 70 per cent meat in natural casings. Often flavoured with herbs, wine, chillies, or fruit, and made in different shapes and sizes.
Pudding sausages: Black pudding (blood sausage) is pork fat, oatmeal, onions, herbs, spices, and blood – usually pigs'. White pudding is beef suet, oatmeal, onions, spices, and seasoning. Haggis is made from the lungs, heart, and liver of sheep or lamb, mixed with meat and fat, oatmeal, onion, spices, and seasoning encased in a sheep's stomach, boiled. Haslet is minced pork, bread, onions, sage, and seasoning, in a pig's caul (stomach lining), roasted.
Raw cured meats: Streaky (belly) and back (loin) bacon, and gammon (hind-leg). There are also bacon joints, cut from other parts of the pig. Either dry-cured by hand-rubbing with a sea-salt mix, or wet-cured by immersing in brine. Brown sugar, honey, or maple syrup are added for sweet cures. Other flavourings, like juniper berries, may be used. They may also be traditionally smoked in a smokehouse, or artificial smoke flavour may be added. When cooked, gammon becomes ham, cooked to traditional recipes such as Wiltshire and York.

HOW TO CHOOSE AND STORE
Choose plump sausages with a high meat content – avoid any that are cheap and uniformly pale pink, as they will contain mostly fat, rusk, and water. Bacon and gammon should be moist, not wet or slimy. There should be little smell. Pudding sausages should not smell. Avoid cooked meats if drying out; buy freshly sliced, if possible. Store wrapped in the fridge and use within a few days – vacuum-packed will keep longer.

RAW CURED MEATS

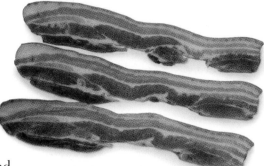

Streaky bacon Smoked or unsmoked. Use for wrapping other foods to keep them moist when grilling, frying, roasting, or baking; or use diced in stews, casseroles, and pies.

Back bacon The one to grill or fry for a traditional breakfast, sandwiches, or to accompany other meats, like liver.

Gammon joint Cut from the top of the leg. Sold with or without bone. Boil or roast.

Gammon steak. Thick slice from the top of the hind leg. Best grilled or fried.

MEAT SAUSAGES

Traditional pork sausages Thick, meaty sausages sold in strings. You usually get 6-8 for 450g (1lb). Grill, fry, casserole, or roast.

Traditional pork chipolatas Thinner, meaty sausages usually sold 12-16 to 450g (1lb). Grill, fry, casserole, or roast. Often cut into short lengths for sausages on sticks.

Cumberland sausage Originated in Cumbria and was traditionally made from the now-extinct Cumberland pig. There is a campaign to give it Protected Geographical Indication status. Usually sold in a flat coil by weight. Grill, fry, or roast.

Lincolnshire sausages Another traditional sausage, made only with Lincolnshire pork, with a chunky texture and flavoured with sage. Grill, fry, or roast.

PUDDING SAUSAGES

Haslet Usually bought sliced. Delicious served cold with salad or pickles, particularly beetroot.

Haggis Boil and serve with mashed potatoes and swede (neeps), and a good gravy, or scoop out and fry or microwave to serve for breakfast.

White pudding Savoury flavour, and softer texture than black pudding. Grill or fry for breakfast, or dice and add to other savoury mixtures.

Black pudding Delicious, slightly spicy, peppery flavour, and dryish texture. Slice and grill or fry for breakfast, or dice and add to casseroles or braises.

PERFECT PAIRINGS

PARSLEY SAUCE with hot-boiled ham joints; **BROWN SUGAR** or **HONEY** and **MUSTARD** to glaze them. **CHEESE** with **HAM** as partners to poultry, veal, chicory, or celery. **MASHED CELERIAC** as an alternative to swede with haggis. **EGGS**, **TOMATOES**, and **MUSHROOMS** with bacon, black or white pudding, or haggis for a traditional northern British breakfast. **BARBECUE SAUCE** to brush sausages, ham, or gammon steaks before grilling. **BRAISED RED CABBAGE** with sausages, gammon, or ham. **ENGLISH**, **GRAINY**, or any **FLAVOURED MUSTARD** with all.

SIMPLE WAYS TO ENJOY

TO PREPARE

SAUSAGES
Separate the links, if necessary. Don't prick sausages – you'll release all their lovely flavour and juices.

BLACK AND WHITE PUDDING
Remove the skin, if necessary, then slice or dice, as required.

HAGGIS
No preparation needed if boiling. Alternatively, split, scoop out of the case and microwave or fry.

BACON
Remove the rind from rashers with scissors, if necessary.

GAMMON AND BACON STEAKS
Snip the edge with scissors to stop these curling up when grilling or frying.

GAMMON AND BACON JOINTS
If they are salty, either soak for a few hours in cold water, or put in a pan, cover with water, bring to the boil and throw away the water, then proceed to cook as required.

SAUSAGE TOAD

Put some sausages and roughly chopped onion in a baking dish with a little oil. Cook at 220°C (425°F/Gas 7) until sizzling. Make a batter with 115g (4oz) seasoned flour, 2 eggs, and 300ml (10fl oz) milk and water mixed. Beat well. Pour over the sizzling sausages. Bake until risen and crisp.

BRAISED BROAD BEANS WITH BLACK OR WHITE PUDDING

Soak a handful of raisins in a splash of red wine. Cook some baby broad beans. Pop them out of their skins. Soften a thinly sliced onion in oil. Add a handful of pine nuts; brown. Just cover with chicken stock. Add the raisins, beans, some diced red apple, crushed garlic, skinned diced black or white pudding, and chopped fresh rosemary and parsley. Cover. Simmer gently until apple is tender and a little juice is left. Season. Drizzle with olive oil.

SPAGHETTI WITH HAM AND MINTED PEAS

Soften a chopped onion in butter and oil. Add some diced ham, peas, and chopped mint. Cover. Cook gently until tender. Add cooked, drained spaghetti, cream and seasoning. Toss until hot.

BLT WITH A KICK

Toast bread on one side. Spread soft sides with mayonnaise. Sandwich with grilled bacon, sliced tomatoes, lettuce, black pepper, and chopped chilli.

HAGGIS AND SWEDE MOUSSAKA

Split a haggis; crumble. Layer in a buttered ovenproof dish with cooked sliced swede and chopped tomatoes. Cover with béchamel sauce (p324). Bake at 190°C (375°F/Gas 5) until hot through and lightly browned.

PINK PIG COWBOY CASSEROLE

SALLY AT PINK PIG ORGANICS

Sally Jackson and her husband Andrew run Pink Pig Organics in Scunthorpe. See pp268–9.

INGREDIENTS
6 good-quality organic
 pork sausages
1 onion, chopped
2 garlic cloves, crushed
1 red pepper, seeded, and
 cut into thin strips
1 tsp paprika
1 tsp red wine vinegar
400g (14oz) can chopped
 tomatoes
150ml (5fl oz) water
1 tbsp tomato purée
1 tbsp black treacle
1 tbsp dark soft brown sugar
1 bay leaf
Salt and freshly ground
 black pepper
435g (15½oz) can baked beans

SERVES 3 (or 2 adults, 2 children) **PREPARATION TIME** 10 minutes **COOKING TIME** 50 minutes. **This is a hearty casserole that young and old alike will enjoy. Serve with chunks of organic bread to sop up the juices and say "yee ha" a lot while eating!**

1 Heat a flameproof casserole, add the sausages, and cook until lightly browned. Add the onion, garlic, and red pepper, and fry, stirring, until browned. Add the paprika and red wine vinegar, stir well, and cook for a minute.

2 Add the tomatoes, water, tomato purée, treacle, sugar, and bay leaf. Season with salt and pepper. Bring to the boil, reduce the heat, and simmer for about 20 minutes until everything is tender.

3 Add the beans and continue to simmer gently for 10 minutes. Ladle into warm bowls and serve straight away.

A DEVON SHEEP FARMER

DUNCAN HOLTON, FORD BARTON FARM

Ford Barton Farm, just north of Tiverton, Devon, is Duncan Holton's 105-hectare (260-acre) mixed farm, with a pedigree herd of Beef Shorthorns and a flock of Wensleydale sheep – both rare breeds. The farmland runs either side of a valley, with gently sloping fields and native hedgerows. Duncan has always farmed traditionally, so going organic, in 2008, wasn't far removed from how he had worked before.

Duncan's Beef Shorthorns are mostly used for pedigree breeding, so his main food stock is the sheep. When they first started keeping Wensleydale sheep they were on the endangered species list, and virtually extinct. They now have over 260 breeding ewes that live outdoors all year (apart from lambing time), extensively grazing. In the past they have mostly been reared for wool, rather than meat. They used to be known as "the monks' larder", because they provided wool for clothing, mutton for meat, tallow for lighting, and milk. Their meat is lean, with a good flavour, and the wool is the finest of the lustre longwools. Duncan's mother used to send the wool off to be processed, then dye it with natural dyes. Duncan would like to revive the practice: "We're hoping we will be able to market our wool as organic, as it's naturally dyed, too."

Spring is lambing season, and the busiest time of year for the Holtons. After a week indoors, the lambs are turned out onto the grass with their mothers. Over the summer months the ewes are sheared, and the grass fields reseeded, and – as autumn leaves begin to fall – the lambs are sheared. In September the lambs, now between 7 and 10 months old, are slaughtered, with the best being kept for breeding the next generation.

Duncan grows all his own organic corn, oats, and barley for feed. All they have to buy in is the organic molasses. He has also changed the grassland, switching from high rye grass content to high clover and more traditional varieties, to put nitrogen back in. They also include herbage and chicory, which brings up minerals and trace elements as it's much deeper rooting than grasses. Worms can be a big problem for all sheep farmers, and Duncan believes strongly in prevention rather than relying on chemical wormers as treatment. To keep his sheep healthy he uses a clean grazing system. "The sheep graze in one field and then I move them on and put the cows in the original field. They have different worms so it breaks the cycle."

Duncan is in conversion until 2010, and he's glad he's taken the step. "I've always believed in what we were doing and it will be nice to have the official recognition, when we get it!"

See p279 for Duncan's *Lamb Casserole with Cider*.

OPPOSITE, ABOVE LEFT Moving the flock to fresh grass.

ABOVE RIGHT Duncan with a young Wensleydale ram.

BELOW A small treat makes keeping a close eye on the flock easier!

BREEDS

This is a selection of the most popular organic breeds of both animals chosen for their manageability, superb meat, milk, and – in some cases – wool.

SHEEP

TEXEL
Bred for exceptional carcasses and because it is relatively hardy. It is very adaptable and is regularly used to sire ewes of all breeds.

LLEYN
Originating in Wales, it is now a popular breed throughout Britain, being quiet, adaptable, and good in all weathers.

SUFFOLK
Originally from near Bury St Edmunds, a cross between a Southdown ram and a Norfolk horn ewe. Once bred for mutton, now sold for lamb too. Hardy, it is also found in Ireland, Scotland, and Wales.

SCOTTISH BLACKFACE
Native to the highlands, this breed can cope with the most inhospitable terrain and climate. Although found all over Britain, the majority are farmed in Scotland.

GOATS

BRITISH SAANEN
White breed, sometimes with freckles. It's largely reared for milk but often in bigger herds, so there are many male kids (often called cabrito or chevon) for meat. Some are kept for breeding.

ANGLO NUBIAN
Pretty breed with long, floppy ears and glossy coat. Bred for meat as well as milk. Often crossed with other breeds, particularly Boer goats from South Africa, bred purely for meat.

TOGGENBURG
Another popular, medium-brown, dairy breed that's very strong. The male kids make good meat.

LAMB AND GOAT

Most sheep, organic or not, are free-range, grazing on hillsides or in fields. Disease control is the main difference. Non-organic animals, for instance, are often wormed by drenching every few weeks, and they're dipped in organophosphates to prevent scab, a practice prohibited under Soil Association standards. Organic farmers apply a more holistic approach, using worm-free or low-infestation fields, double fencing to prevent scab spreading, and generally avoiding causing stress to the animals. Goats have a good life too. They are often a by-product of a dairy herd but some are bred purely for their delicious, low-fat meat.

HOW TO CHOOSE AND STORE

The meats are interchangeable. Lamb develops flavour as it grows, with mutton being least tender but with the richest flavour. Lambs, or kids (cabrito) are animals up to a year old; hoggets are lambs 1–2 years; chevons are goats over 1 year; mutton refers to sheep (and sometimes goats) over 2 years. All meat should smell and look fresh. It should be moist, not wet, and the fat should be white and firm. Put on a plate and wrap loosely in a biodegradable plastic bag. Keep away from cooked foods. Can be stored in the fridge, on the lowest shelf, for up to 3 days.

BRAISING

Diced meat (Lamb shown here.) Cut from the shoulder or leg for stews, casseroles, and curries. Also sold minced.

Shanks (Lamb shown here.) Cut from the base of the leg. Needs long, slow cooking. Excellent flavour.

ROASTING JOINTS

Leg (Lamb shown here.) Top-quality joint can be fast- or slow-roasted. Mutton may be boiled.

Shoulder (Mutton shown here.) Inexpensive joint, good roasted, or can be diced and casseroled. Sold whole or in halves.

Rack Usually lamb. A whole side of best end of neck, often sold ready-trimmed. Good roasted, or can be cut into chops and fried or grilled. Also good braised.

CHOPS AND STEAKS

Chump chops (Lamb shown here.) Meaty chop. Best grilled or fried.

Neck fillet Usually lamb. Tender eye of the neck muscles. Can be stuffed and roasted whole, cubed for kebabs or curries, or sliced, beaten flat, and sautéed as escalopes.

Loin chops (Lamb shown here.) Boneless steaks cut from the loin. Grill or fry. Also sold as a whole piece for roasting.

Leg steaks (Goat shown here.) Cut from the top of the leg of a lamb or goat. Grill or fry.

Cutlets (Mutton shown here.) Cut from the ribs. Grill, fry, or casserole.

OFFAL

Look out, too, for lamb's sweetbreads and tongue.

Liver (Lamb shown here.) Best sliced and fried. Don't overcook or it becomes tough.

Heart (Lamb shown here.) Can be cut into chunks, or stuffed whole. Needs long, slow cooking to tenderize.

Kidney (Lamb shown here.) Best fried, or can be brushed with butter or a baste and grilled. Also good casseroled.

PERFECT PAIRINGS

MINT SAUCE for lamb. **REDCURRANT JELLY** with all. **CAPER SAUCE** with boiled mutton or lamb. **LEEKS** and **ONIONS** roasted or braised with, or in a sauce. Fresh or dried **APRICOTS** or **PLUMS** with **SWEET SPICES** for tagines and curries. **PLAIN YOGURT** as the base of a curry sauce, or as a relish with **CHOPPED MINT** and **CUCUMBER**, or chopped **APPLE** or **PEAR**. **CAPERS** in a sauce or salsa, or to spike stews and casseroles.

SIMPLE WAYS TO ENJOY

TO PREPARE

Trim off excess fat before cooking, if necessary.

FOR KIDNEYS
Remove the skin, if necessary, halve, and snip out the central cores with scissors. Cut in chunks, if desired.

FOR RACKS AND CUTLETS
Scrape off the last 2cm (¾in) of the meat from the ends of bones, if liked. Cut racks into portions or leave whole, as desired.

FOR LIVER AND HEART
Trim off any tubes or pipes. Slice or cut into chunks or strips, as required. Hearts can be stuffed whole.

LAMB, MUTTON, OR GOAT CURRY
Brown some diced meat with chopped onions and garlic in oil. Add mild curry paste and a pinch of ground allspice. Add coconut milk, one or two chopped tomatoes, and a chopped mild chilli. Season. Cover and simmer gently until rich and tender. Add chopped coriander.

CHOPS OR STEAKS WITH GARLIC AND ROSEMARY
Season chops or steaks and brown in butter and oil. Remove. Add some crushed garlic, chopped rosemary, and a little stock. Return the meat to the pan. Cover. Cook very gently for 8–10 minutes, turning once.

DEVILLED KIDNEYS
Sauté prepared kidneys in butter and oil until brown but still soft. Add a little curry paste, tomato ketchup, Worcestershire sauce, and English mustard. Season. Stir until coated, adding a splash of water if necessary.

PEPPERED LAMB'S LIVER OR FILLETS
Thinly slice liver, or beat sliced neck fillets flat. Coat in coarsely crushed black peppercorns. Quickly brown on one side in butter and oil. Flip over, fry just until beads of blood or juices appear. Remove the meat, and keep warm. Deglaze the pan with a little stock and wine. Stir in a little redcurrant jelly. Season. Spoon the sauce over the meat.

HARICOT MUTTON SHANKS OR HEART
Brown some mutton chops, shanks, or chunks of heart with sliced onions in butter. Put in a casserole with diced carrots, turnips, and drained canned haricot beans. Blend some stock with tomato purée. Add to meat with a bay leaf. Season. Cover, cook at 160°C (325°F/Gas 3) until really tender.

LAMB CASSEROLE WITH CIDER

DUNCAN AT FORD BARTON FARM

A Devonshire rare-breeds farmer in conversion, Duncan Holton produces wool as well as meat from his sheep, and also rears pedigree cattle. See pp274–5.

SERVES 4–6 **PREPARATION TIME** 20 minutes **COOKING TIME** 1¾ hours. If it's more convenient, this casserole can cooked on the hob, stirred occasionally, and will need only about 1 hour (but it will only benefit if left longer!). It can be made in advance as it reheats very well.

1 Preheat the oven to 160°C (325°F/Gas 3). Place the meat in a bowl, sprinkle over the flour, and toss until well coated.

2 Heat the butter and oil in a flameproof casserole and fry the meat for about 5 minutes to brown it all over. Remove with a slotted spoon and set aside. Add the onions and garlic (if using) and fry, stirring, for 2 minutes until softened. Add the parsley, stock and cider to the casserole and bring to the boil, stirring. Add the Worcestershire sauce and seasoning and cook for a further 5 minutes.

3 Return the meat to the casserole and cover, then cook in the oven for 1½ hours, stirring halfway through. Serve with either boiled potatoes, spaghetti or noodles, and any vegetable that's in season.

INGREDIENTS
900g (2lb) lean, boneless lamb
  leg or shoulder, cubed
2 tbsp plain flour
60g (2oz) butter
1 tsp olive oil
2 small onions, chopped
½ garlic clove, chopped
  (optional)
2 tbsp chopped fresh parsley
300ml (10fl oz) stock
300ml (10fl oz) dry cider
1 tbsp Worcestershire sauce
1 tsp salt
½ tsp pepper

POT-ROASTED LEG OF LAMB WITH GOOSEBERRY, MINT, AND SAGE JELLY

TRUDIE STYLER

A film producer and founder of Lake House Organics, Trudie is Vice President of the Soil Association.

SERVES 8–10 **PREPARATION TIME** 15 minutes **COOKING TIME** 6 hours.
A great Sunday lunch dish when you have a table full of family and friends; you can stick it on in the morning, go out for a lovely, long walk, and come back starving hungry. All you need do is serve up, pour yourself some wine, and enjoy. Serve with mashed potatoes or bulgar wheat and a steamed green vegetable.

1 Preheat the oven to 110°C (225°F/Gas ¼). Heat the olive oil in a large flameproof casserole over a moderate heat. Season the lamb, add to the casserole, and brown on all sides for 8–10 minutes.

2 Add the onions and red wine. Spoon the jelly over the lamb and sprinkle with the herbs. Cover tightly with a lid or foil, and slow-cook in the oven for about 6 hours, or until very tender and falling off the bone. Do make sure you baste the lamb with the cooking juices at least once halfway though cooking.

INGREDIENTS
2 tbsp good-quality olive oil
2 kg (4½lb) leg of lamb
4 red onions, quartered
250ml (8fl oz) red wine
113g (4oz) jar Lake House
  organics Gooseberry, Mint and
  Sage Jelly (or a good-quality
  mint jelly)
1 tbsp chopped fresh mint
1 tbsp chopped fresh sage

These are three favourite breeds for organic farmers. All of them have good temperaments and produce excellent-quality meat.

SASSO
Originally from France, a brown-and-white bird that's popular with organic farmers as it's slow-growing, so has time to develop really good meat. Naturally resistant to disease, hardy, and easy to rear.

LIGHT SUSSEX
Predominantly white with a black tail and black-and-white-striped neck. Popular, dual-purpose breed that's good and meaty, but a productive egg-layer too. Alert but docile, hardy, and very adaptable.

INDIAN/CORNISH GAME
Popular organic variety that needs space to roam. It's big-breasted so makes great eating; also thick legged and likes a milder climate. Mahogany brown, tinged with black (the cock is more black) and a greenish sheen.

HOW TO CHOOSE AND STORE

Choose a bird with a firm, plump breast and tight skin. It should look and smell fresh. Corn-fed chicken will have yellow skin and a rich flavour. Hygiene is very important when handling raw chicken. If the bird has giblets, remove immediately. Store in a separate container, or on a plate to catch any drips. Wrap loosely but thoroughly. Put on the bottom shelf of the fridge away from any cooked food. Wash your hands thoroughly after handling. Cook within 2 days.

CHICKEN

Chicken used to be a luxury, then with intensive farming it became a cheap, everyday food with the birds paying a very high price – their quality of life. Up to 40,000 live in a windowless hut, with no space to move or behave naturally, and constant light. They are susceptible to lameness and heart problems and are permanently distressed. Defra regulations say free-range birds must have continuous daytime access to the open air for at least half their life. Soil Association standards are even higher; laying birds must have daytime access outside all their lives; two-thirds for meat birds. Laying birds must have 10 square metres of space, meat birds four – at least double the Defra regulation for free-range farming.

CASSEROLE OR BRAISE

Thigh sometimes sold attached to the drumstick as a leg portion. Often cheaper than drumsticks. Not as tender as breast, but less likely to dry out.

Diced casserole meat usually dark meat cut from the thigh.

ROAST

Oven-ready bird As it says, usually sold trussed and ready to cook. Remove the giblets, if they come in the bird, and use for stock.

GRILL OR FRY

Drumstick The leg of the bird. Good hot or cold. Popular with children.

Wing The end of the wing without the breast. The inedible flat wing tip is trimmed off.

Boneless breast The most popular but also most expensive cut. The breast is cut off the bone before being sold. Take care when cooking so as not to dry it out. Sometimes available already skinned.

OFFAL

Liver Delicious, tender morsels, rich in iron. Surprisingly inexpensive. Take care not to overcook: they should look brown on the outside, pink inside.

Wing and breast portion More popular than leg and thigh portions, as most people prefer breast.

PERFECT PAIRINGS

BREAD SAUCE and **STUFFING** are the traditional accompaniments to a plain roast; **GARLIC** and **LEMON** are excellent to flavour a chicken before roasting; try smearing the breast with **HONEY**, too, for a golden glaze; **SAGE**, **THYME**, and **ROSEMARY** are popular herbs. All spices from **CHILLI** to **CUMIN**, **TURMERIC** to **SAFFRON** go well in curries, casseroles, and as rubs for grilling and barbecuing. **SWEETCORN**, **LEEKS**, and **MUSHROOMS** are favourite vegetables for soups and as accompaniments.

SIMPLE WAYS TO ENJOY

TO PREPARE

Wipe with kitchen paper. Always use a separate board and wash well in hot, soapy water afterwards. Remove the skin from breasts before cooking, if liked. When roasting, take off the wing tips or tuck under, and stuff the neck end, not the body cavity.

To joint a bird: Gently pull the leg away from the body. Cut down through the skin and flesh to the joint. Break the leg joint, cut through it and flesh and skin. Repeat on the other side. Cut down one side of the breast bone, easing the flesh away. Cut through the wing joint, cut away remaining skin and remove. Repeat on other side. Use carcass for stock or soup (see below).

CHICKEN STOCK

Break up a raw or cooked carcass. Put in a pan with an onion, bits of raw vegetables, and bouquet garni. Cover with water. Season. Bring to the boil, skim surface. Reduce heat, cover and simmer for 1 hour. Strain, cool, store in fridge. For cream of chicken soup, pick off meat, return it to stock, thicken with flour, mixed to a paste with water, enrich with cream. Simmer for 5 minutes.

OVEN-FRIED CHICKEN

Dip portions, drumsticks or thighs in milk, then in seasoned flour. Leave for 30 minutes. Dip in milk again. Coat in breadcrumbs. Heat some butter and olive oil in a roasting tin at 190°C (375°F/Gas 5). When it is sizzling, add chicken. Baste. Bake until tender and golden, about 1 hour. Serve with bacon rolls and corn cobs.

SIMPLE CHICKEN CASSEROLE

Soften a chopped onion in oil in a flameproof casserole. Brown some diced chicken. Add some chopped large tomatoes (or a can), a slug of sherry, some button mushrooms, chopped rosemary and seasoning. Bring to the boil, then cook in the oven at 180°C (350°F/Gas 4) for 1 hour until tender. Taste and reseason. Serve with rice or fluffy mash.

SPICY BUFFALO WINGS

Flavour some passata with honey, Worcestershire and sweet chilli sauce. Season. Add trimmed chicken wings, and toss. Marinate for 2 hours. Thread on skewers. Grill or barbecue for about 20 minutes, turning occasionally, until cooked through.

CHICKEN LIVER PÂTÉ

Soften an onion and some garlic in ½ block of butter. Add 450g (1lb) trimmed chicken livers and chopped thyme. Cook gently until just cooked but still soft. Purée with a good splash of brandy. Season. Pack in a small pot. Cover with a layer of melted butter. Cool, then chill.

SLOW-ROAST CHICKEN

JONATHAN DIMBLEBY

Jonathan Dimbleby, writer, broadcaster and film-maker, was President of the Soil Association from 1996 to 2008.

SERVES 4–6 **PREPARATION TIME** 15 minutes **COOKING TIME** 8–10 hours

This recipe can be used for any free-range organic meat. The secret is that the oven has to be at its lowest setting so that the meat can evenly slow-cook over a long period: 8–10 hours, depending on the size of your bird. It's actually very difficult to overcook it!

1 Preheat the oven to 60°C (140°F/Gas ⅛) – or its lowest setting. Wash the chicken inside and out and pat dry with kitchen paper. Place the chicken in a roasting tin and pour over a generous glug of olive oil. Use your hands to ensure that the oil covers the whole bird, including the breast and legs. Add a couple of grinds of freshly milled black pepper and, if you wish, a little salt.

2 Cover loosely with foil and put in the oven. Check every 2–3 hours to ensure the meat is not drying out (you can take the foil off). Cook for 5 hours per kilo (2¼lb) – take an hour off the total cooking time if your lowest oven setting is 110°C (225°F/Gas ¼).

3 Check if the chicken is cooked through by inserting a skewer into the thickest part of the meat – the juices should run clear. When the chicken is cooked, remove it from the oven and ensure your foil lid fits snugly over the bird, so that the heat is retained inside.

4 Turn the oven up to 200°C (400°F/Gas 6). Place your prepared vegetables, evenly cut, in a roasting tin. Add a splash of olive oil and a sprig of thyme, and toss. Roast for about 45–50 minutes or until golden brown, turning frequently to ensure even cooking.

5 Return the chicken to the oven, uncovered, for the last 20 minutes to brown. I don't think this recipe needs gravy, as the meat is always wonderfully succulent and moist. However, you can add a splash of white wine to the pan juices and simmer until they have thickened and reduced.

INGREDIENTS
1 oven-ready chicken, about 1.8kg (4lb)
Olive oil
Salt (optional) and freshly ground black pepper
Seasonal vegetables to roast (such as garlic, red onions, carrots, parsnips, and potatoes), chopped
A sprig of fresh thyme

STIR-FRIED CHICKEN WITH NOODLES

SERVES 4 **PREPARATION TIME** 10–15 minutes **COOKING TIME** 6–7 minutes
VARIATION Use ordinary sliced chestnut or cup mushrooms instead of oyster mushrooms, and add a handful or two of sprouted beans for extra crunch.

1 Trim the spring onions and cut in short, diagonal lengths. Heat the oil and stir-fry the spring onions, garlic, ginger, peppers, and chicken for 4 minutes, or until the chicken is cooked.

2 Add the cucumber, mushrooms, and pak choi and stir-fry for 1–2 minutes. Add the oyster and soy sauces and stock. Stir-fry for a further 30 seconds, then stir in the noodles. Toss well until the noodles are piping hot.

3 Serve in warm bowls, with extra soy sauce to sprinkle over. If using, peel thin strips of carrot lengthwise with a potato peeler, and arrange a cluster on top of each bowl of stir fry as a garnish.

INGREDIENTS
1 bunch of spring onions
1 garlic clove, finely chopped
1 tbsp sunflower oil
1 tsp grated fresh root ginger
1 green pepper, seeded and
  thinly sliced
1 red pepper, seeded and
  thinly sliced
350g (12oz) skinless chicken
  breasts, cut into thin strips
¼ cucumber, cut into
  matchsticks
115g (4oz) oyster mushrooms,
  sliced
2 heads pak choi, shredded
1 tbsp oyster sauce
1 tbsp soy sauce
120ml (4fl oz) chicken stock
250g (9oz) fresh egg noodles
1 carrot, peeled (optional)

STUFFED CHICKEN UNDER A BRICK

ARTHUR POTTS DAWSON

Arthur is executive chef and co-owner of the eco-friendly restaurant Acorn House, in London.

INGREDIENTS
4 tbsp cream cheese, goat's cheese, or Stilton
Grated zest and juice of 1 lemon
Sea salt and cracked black pepper
2 thin slices York (or other dry-cured) ham
1 small, oven-ready chicken, about 1.5kg (3lb 3oz), boned, with bones also out of the legs, or two chicken breasts with skin
8 fresh sage leaves
A knob of butter

SERVES 2 **PREPARATION TIME** 15 minutes **COOKING TIME** 15 minutes.
This method, using hot weights, keeps the meat really moist and tender.

1 Preheat oven to 180°C (350°F/Gas 4). Put a heavy ovenproof frying pan (smaller than the one used to cook the chicken) in the oven to heat. Add to the cheese a little lemon juice, half the zest, and season. Spread the cheese on the centre of each ham slice, keeping the rest for the sauce. Fold over the sides to make a parcel. Slide your thumb between the breast and skin of the chicken to create two cavities. Put a parcel and sage leaf inside each cavity. Pull skin back in place.

2 Melt the butter in a large, ovenproof frying pan. Pan-fry the chicken, breast-side down, for 8 minutes, then add the remaining sage. Lay buttered foil on the chicken. Put the hot pan from the oven on top. Weigh down with a brick, heavy pan, or weights. Transfer to the oven for 7 minutes. Halve the chicken, place on warm serving plates, skin-side up. Melt the rest of the cheese in the pan with the remaining lemon juice and zest, and season to taste. Drizzle over the chicken.

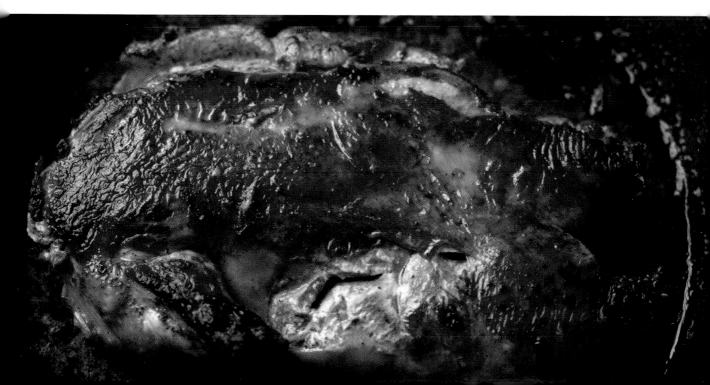

These are some of the most common birds chosen by organic and free-range farmers for their excellent eating qualities.

TURKEY

WHITE
The most common of the turkeys with a wide breast and short, stubby legs. It's liked by many as, when plucked, the skin is very white.

NORFOLK BRONZE
Beautiful plumage with metallic-tinged back feathers and white flecks, favoured by free-range and organic producers.

FARMED DUCK

BARBARY (MUSKOVY)
Brought to England from America in the 15th century. They come in white, blue, black, and chocolate. They're quite quiet; they don't quack much!

AYLESBURY
Originated in the Buckinghamshire town, they're a fast-growing breed with a gentle, friendly temperament.

FARMED GOOSE

WHITE
The most common white-feathered birds, of which there are many breeds, such as Wessex, Norfolk, and Embden, from Germany.

BRECON BUFF
Hardy, plump-breasted breed first reared in Wales in the 20th century. White and brownish-buff feathers. Distinctive, bright pink beak and feet. Good at foraging.

TURKEY, DUCK, AND GOOSE

Millions of British birds are intensively reared, turkeys often fattened in sheds of up to 25,000. These birds don't roost in trees or forage outside like wild ones; they are kept totally indoors and often have their beaks trimmed to stop them pecking each other out of boredom. The males are bred with such large breasts they can't mate, only reproducing by artificial insemination. Geese and ducks are aquatic but they're kept in similar conditions with no access to water to dabble in either. However, organic and free-range birds spend most of their days outdoors in peace with all they need to behave naturally.

WHEN IN SEASON

Turkey: All year, but many to be sold whole are bred for the Christmas market, so best in December. Some are bred for Easter, too.
Duck: All year.
Goose: September–December. Some are reared for Michaelmas in September (a tradition since Elizabeth I was dining on one when she heard of the Spanish Armada's defeat), but most for Christmas.

HOW TO CHOOSE AND STORE

Buy fresh birds from a reliable source. Always remove the giblets before wrapping and storing on a dish on the bottom shelf of the fridge. Keep according to the supplier's instructions. Portions and whole birds will keep several days in the fridge. Note: Goose fat is the new olive oil – considered by many foodies as the best medium for roasting potatoes – but a lot is imported. Ideally, buy artisan goose fat produced here.

Boneless rolled turkey joint The dark meat and breast tied in a neat joint for easy roasting and carving. More succulent and better flavoured than breast joints.

BONELESS ROASTS

Boneless turkey breast joint Pure white meat joint for those who prefer it. Make sure it's basted well or covered with bacon to keep it moist. Don't overcook. A turkey bone-in crown is also available.

WHOLE BIRDS

Goose Fatty bird, rich and succulent, with a superb flavour. To get tender results it needs longer cooking than most books tell you. Roast as duck. It has lots of bone, so allow 550g (1¼lb) per person. Keep the fat and store in the fridge (up to 3 months), and use for roasting potatoes.

Turkey Whole birds can be very large. Bronze have the superior flavour. Fast- or slow-roast. Best to start cooking breast-down to keep it moist, and cover with foil. Turn over halfway through cooking. Remove the foil for the last 30 minutes. Allow 350g (12oz) per person.

Duck Fatty bird with an excellent, rich, slightly gamey flavour. Can be braised. Cook on a rack, so the fat collects underneath, in a very hot oven at first, then in a moderate oven to tenderize the meat. One good-sized bird will serve 4 people. You can use duck fat like goose fat (see left) to roast potatoes (but it's not as good!).

PORTIONS

Turkey wing Sold with or without the first wing tip. Quite meaty. Best casseroled but can be grilled or roasted. Turkey thighs and diced thigh meat also available.

Turkey drumstick Meaty, inexpensive cut. If large, one can be carved, once cooked, to serve 2–3 people. Roast, grill, or casserole.

Turkey steak A thick slice of breast meat. Marinate, then grill or fry; beat flat for an escalope, cut into strips for stir-fries, or dice for kebabs, quick curries, or braises.

Duck breast Sold with or without skin. Delicious, tender meat. Don't overcook, best served pink. Fry or grill.

Duck leg The leg and thigh portion. Delicious flavour. Grill, fry, or casserole. Also used for French confit de canard, salted, gently poached in oil until meltingly tender, then preserved in goose fat.

TURKEY, DUCK, AND GOOSE 289

PERFECT PAIRINGS

BREAD SAUCE and **CRANBERRY SAUCE** for turkey. **APPLE** or **GOOSEBERRY SAUCE** with duck or goose. Stone fruits such as **PLUMS, APRICOTS, CHERRIES**, and **GREENGAGES** in a sauce, in stuffing or cooked in a casserole. Sweet spices such as **NUTMEG, MACE, CINNAMON, STAR ANISE**, and **CHINESE FIVE-SPICE** in marinades, stir-fries, or casseroles. **GREEN TEA LEAVES** mixed with **DRY RICE, ORANGE**, and **SUGAR** and used to smoke duck or goose in a wok over a low heat before roasting until crispy.

SIMPLE WAYS TO ENJOY

TO PREPARE

For general preparations and how to joint a bird, see To Prepare on p284. When roasting, smear the turkey breast with butter or oil, then season with salt. For duck or goose, prick all over with a fork and season with salt. Roast duck or goose on a rack over the tin, to collect the excess fat.

CHESTNUT AND ORANGE STUFFING

Soften chopped onions and mushrooms in butter. Add some chopped cooked chestnuts, breadcrumbs, the grated zest and juice of an orange, and lots of chopped thyme and parsley. Season well. Bind with beaten egg. Stuff the neck end of the bird. Roll the remainder into balls and roast separately.

TURKEY AND REDCURRANT POT

Brown turkey thighs, wings, or diced meat in oil. Remove. Brown some sliced onions. Add flour and blend in chicken stock. Boil to thicken. Stir in some redcurrant jelly and soy sauce. Add a few sliced mushrooms. Return the turkey to the pan. Add a bouquet garni and season. Cover and simmer until tender. Discard the bouquet garni. Serve with mash and salad.

CHINESE-STYLE TURKEY OR DUCK

Make a dipping sauce. Heat some orange juice, tomato ketchup, red wine vinegar, soy sauce, and garlic. Sweeten with honey. Slightly thicken with a little cornflour and water. Cool. Flatten skinned turkey or duck breasts and cut into large pieces. Toss in soy sauce. Make a batter with flour, a pinch of salt and mustard, a splash of wine vinegar, and enough water to form a cream. Dip the meat in batter. Deep-fry until golden and cooked. Eat with the dip.

DUCK WITH APPLE, PEAS, AND SPINACH

Brown duck portions in a pan. Remove. Brown quartered onions. Return the duck and moisten with stock. Season. Cover; simmer until tender. Spoon off the fat. Add some sliced dessert apple, peas, baby spinach, and chopped mint. Reseason. Cover and simmer until apple is tender and spinach has texture.

MUSTARD-, CHEESE-, AND HAM-TOPPED TURKEY STEAKS

SERVES 4 **PREPARATION TIME** 10 minutes **COOKING TIME** 10–15 minutes
VARIATION You can use beaten-out chicken breasts or pork fillets instead if you prefer. **SERVE WITH** pan-roasted vine tomatoes (see p144) with the spinach, or with chips or new potatoes and a tomato salad.

1 Preheat the grill. Put the steaks one at a time in a biodegradable plastic bag and beat with a meat mallet or rolling pin to flatten. Brush on both sides with oil, season lightly, and place on the grill rack. Grill under a moderate heat for 5 minutes each side.

2 Add a scraping of mustard to each steak. Lay the ham slices on top. Cover with the cheese. Grill for a further 4 minutes until the cheese melts and bubbles.

3 Meanwhile, wash the spinach well. Shake off the excess water. Place in a large pan or wok and cook, tossing and stirring, for a few minutes until wilted but still with some texture. Drain thoroughly. Pile the spinach on to plates. Top each portion with a turkey steak. Arrange a few slices of tomato in a cluster on one corner of each steak and garnish with a tiny sprig of parsley.

INGREDIENTS
4 turkey steaks, about 150g
  (5½oz) each
2 tbsp olive oil
Salt and freshly ground
  black pepper
2 tsp English mustard
4 slices ham
115g (4oz) Cheddar cheese,
  grated
450g (1lb) spinach
2 tomatoes, thinly sliced, and
  tiny, fresh parsley sprigs,
  to garnish

WARM DUCK BREAST SALAD WITH BLUEBERRIES

SERVES 4 **PREPARATION TIME** 20 minutes **COOKING TIME** 15–20 minutes
VARIATION This is equally delicious served with fresh raspberries and raspberry juice, in place of the blueberries, in the dressing.

1 Boil the potatoes in lightly salted water until just tender, about 10 minutes. Drain.

2 Put the salad leaves in a large bowl with the tomatoes, cucumber, and onion rings.

3 Use a sharp knife to remove the sinew that runs from the pointed end of the duck breasts on the flesh side (to stop them curling during cooking). Sprinkle the skin with salt and celery seeds.

4 Heat a large, non-stick frying pan. Add the duck breasts, skin-side down, and fry over a moderate heat for 6 minutes until the fat runs and the skin is browned. Turn over and cook the other side for a further 6–8 minutes until just cooked but still slightly pink inside. Remove from the pan, wrap in foil and keep warm.

5 Spoon off all but 1 tbsp of the duck fat in the frying pan. Add the remaining dressing ingredients, except the blueberries and herbs. Bring to the boil, stirring. Taste and reseason, if necessary. Throw in the blueberries and rosemary, and stir gently.

6 Add the potatoes to the salad and toss gently. Pile in the centre of four large plates. Cut the duck breasts into diagonal slices and arrange attractively on top of the salad. Spoon the dressing over. Sprinkle with chopped parsley. Serve straight away.

INGREDIENTS
350g (12oz) unpeeled salad
  potatoes, cut into
  bite-sized pieces
115g (4oz) mixed salad leaves
8 cherry tomatoes, quartered
¼ cucumber, diced
1 small red onion, thinly sliced
  and separated into rings
4 duck breasts
Salt
1 tsp celery seeds

FOR THE DRESSING
3 tbsp olive oil
3 tbsp blueberry juice
1½ tbsp red wine vinegar
½ tsp Dijon mustard
115g (4oz) blueberries
½ tsp chopped fresh rosemary
A little chopped fresh parsley

GAME BIRDS

Game bird shooting is a properly managed system. Modern gamekeepers prevent poaching and maintain the natural habitat of the birds, protecting them and other wildlife. They may also rear pheasant and partridge chicks to boost wild stock. Young poults are kept in enclosed land (release pens), so they're safe from predators, but live a relatively wild existence. When they mature, they're released. Those that survive the shooting season continue to live wild. Here we look at the most common game birds and how to enjoy them. We've not featured quail as they're protected in the wild and not organically farmed.

WHAT WHEN AND HOW

WHAT TYPES

Wild duck: We're featuring Mallard, the most common of the wild ducks. The males have the distinctive, green head and the females brown speckles. Sold individually or as a brace (a pair). Look out for teal, too, much smaller with a rusty head and green eye patches.

Grouse: Red grouse is native to Britain, feeding on heather on moorlands. There are also black game (black grouse; not Northern Ireland (NI)), ptarmigan (white grouse), and capercaillie (great grouse; both S only).

Partridge: Small birds. Two types, grey (considered the better of the two), indigenous to Britain, and red leg, brought here from France.

Wild goose: There are several species, that fall into two types, "grey" (like greylag) and "black" (like barnacle and, also, Canada, introduced here from USA).

Pheasant: Quite large birds; cocks have beautiful plumage, while hens are brown-flecked. Long tail feathers on both.

Wood pigeon: The smallest – and probably the most prolific – of wild birds, and an agricultural pest.

Woodcock: Wading bird with a long bill that lives in moist woodland throughout Britain. Highly prized.

Guinea fowl: Although originally a wild species, they're not technically classed as game as they're good foragers and are often farmed free-range or organically. They are good pest controllers. Treat like chicken.

WHEN IN SEASON

Shooting seasons
Pheasant: 1 October–1 February (31 January, S); **Partridge:** 1 September –1 February (31 January, S); **Grouse:** 12 August–10 December; **Woodcock:** October–January (E,W,NI); September–January (S); **Wild duck and goose:** September–January; **Wood pigeon:** All year (best February–May); **Guinea fowl:** Organically farmed all year.

HOW TO CHOOSE AND STORE

Buy from reliable sources and don't accept any that are illegally shot. They may have a strong smell but it shouldn't be rancid. The flesh should be firm and the skin taut. In the old days, they were considered good to eat when the maggots had got in: it meant they had been well hung for at least 10 days. We don't recommend that now, but they should have been hung for a few days to enhance the flavour and tenderize the flesh. Remove any giblets and wrap separately. Store, well wrapped in a biodegradable plastic bag, on a plate on the bottom shelf of the fridge for up to 2–3 days.

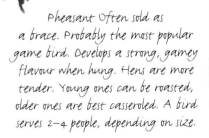

Pheasant Often sold as a brace. Probably the most popular game bird. Develops a strong, gamey flavour when hung. Hens are more tender. Young ones can be roasted, older ones are best casseroled. A bird serves 2–4 people, depending on size.

Wood pigeon small birds with a strong flavour. The breasts are the meaty part. They need very quick cooking. If using whole birds, best cook long and slow to tenderize them. Often then the meat is taken off the bones and put in a pie with the thickened cooking juices.

Wild duck (Mallard) They have an earthy, slightly gamey flavour and are not fatty like domestic birds. Roast or casserole. One bird serves 2–4 people (depending on appetite).

Grouse Red grouse is the most highly prized, with a good, gamey flavour, and succulent flesh. One bird feeds 1–2 people. Roast, casserole, or braise.

Partridge Mild, delicate, subtle flavour. Small birds, each serves 1 person. Roast, casserole, braise, or grill.

Woodcock Traditionally cooked whole, undrawn, with the beaked head pushed into the body to truss it. Can be drawn, if preferred. Often roasted and served on fried bread or toast.

PERFECT PAIRINGS

BREAD SAUCE, **CRISPY BUTTERED BREADCRUMBS**, and **GAME CHIPS** (hot crisps) with roast birds. **JERUSALEM ARTICHOKES** or **BEETROOT** as a purée or roasted in chunks with roast pheasant and other game birds. **QUINCE JELLY** with any roasted bird. **APPLES**, **PEARS**, **PLUMS**, and **BERRIES** all offset the richness of the meat. **CAJUN SPICES** (a mixture of **SMOKED** and **SWEET PAPRIKA**, **PEPPER**, **CAYENNE**, **DRIED OREGANO**, and **THYME** with **GARLIC** and **ONION**) as a rub before roasting, grilling, or frying.

SIMPLE WAYS TO ENJOY

TO PREPARE

Remove any giblets (boil separately to use for stock, sauce, or gravy). Cover the breasts of small game birds in streaky bacon before roasting to keep them moist. Pull out any fat just inside the rim of the body cavity.

To halve
Using poultry shears or a large sharp knife, start at centre of neck end and cut through the breastbone all along the body. Pull the two halves of the bird apart, then cut all along the backbone to divide completely.

To quarter
Cut through the natural division between breast and leg, then cut through the thigh joint.

PHEASANT, GUINEA FOWL, OR GROUSE, AND APPLE CASSEROLE

Brown quartered birds in butter and oil in a casserole. Remove. Brown some button onions. Add sliced pippin apples and toss in the juices. Put the bird portions on top. Pour on some cider and stock. Season. Cover and cook in the oven at 180°C (350°F/Gas 4) until tender. Remove the birds, onions, and apples. Boil the juices until well reduced. Stir in some crème fraîche and a splash of brandy. Pour over, and garnish with parsley.

ROAST GAME BIRDS WITH BLACKBERRY AND ORANGE SAUCE

Push ½ an onion and some sage inside each of a brace of wild ducks or a wild goose. Put in a roasting tin. Rub breasts with butter. Season. Roast in the oven at 230°C (450°F/Gas 8) for 20 minutes. Lower to 180°C (350°F/Gas 4) and roast until tender. Remove, keep warm. Spoon off fat. Add some stock and zest of 1 orange, and juice of 2. Boil until reduced and thickened. Add ripe blackberries, simmer until softened. Sweeten and season to taste.

SAUTÉED PIGEON BREASTS WITH BEETROOT SALSA

Grate some raw beetroot and carrot. Finely chop some spring onions. Toss in a splash of white balsamic condiment and olive oil. Season. Sautée the pigeon breasts in butter and olive oil a few minutes only, until just cooked and tender. Wrap in foil; rest for 5 minutes. Slice, arrange on plates with the salsa.

SIMPLE ROAST WOODCOCK OR PARTRIDGE

Season the birds and stuff with thyme. Sprinkle with lemon zest. Wrap in bacon rashers. Smear with butter. Roast at 200°C (400°F/Gas 6) until tender. Halve. Put on fried bread. Spoon over thin gravy made from juices.

POT-ROASTED PHEASANT WITH BEETROOT AND SHALLOTS

SERVES 4 **PREPARATION TIME** 30 minutes **COOKING TIME** 1 hour
VARIATION You can use guinea fowl instead, or even hare tastes good this way but you'll need to cook it for longer to make it meltingly tender. **SERVE WITH** celeriac and potato mash and a green salad.

1 Preheat the oven to 180°C (350°F/Gas 4).

2 Heat the butter in a flameproof casserole. Add the shallots and lardons and cook, stirring, for 3 minutes until lightly golden. Remove with a slotted spoon.

3 Add the pheasant and brown all over. Remove from the casserole. Add the beetroot, mushrooms, shallots and lardons. Mix well, then top with the pheasant. Blend the wine, stock, tomato purée, and sugar together and pour over. Bring to the boil. Season well. Tuck in the bay leaf. Cover and cook in the oven for about 1 hour, or until really tender.

4 Discard the bay leaf. Taste and reseason, if necessary. Sprinkle with a little chopped parsley and serve hot.

INGREDIENTS
15g (½oz) butter
12 shallots, peeled and
  left whole
60g (2oz) smoked bacon lardons
1 oven-ready cock pheasant,
  quartered
4 freshly boiled beetroot, peeled
  and cut in chunks
85g (3oz) baby button
  mushrooms
150ml (5fl oz) red wine
150ml (5fl oz) chicken stock
1 tsp tomato purée
A good pinch of caster sugar
Salt and freshly ground
  black pepper
1 bay leaf
Chopped fresh parsley,
  to garnish

PARTRIDGE WITH ROASTED PEARS, KOHL RABI, AND WALNUTS

SERVES 4 **PREPARATION TIME** 15 minutes **COOKING TIME** 50 minutes
VARIATION You can replace the partridge with a quarter of pheasant, guinea fowl, or chicken, per person. We've left the skin on the pears, but you can peel them if you prefer. Try the recipe with dessert apples, or use turnips instead of kohl rabi. **SERVE WITH** fluffy mashed potatoes and a green vegetable.

1 Push a sprig of thyme inside each bird. Secure their legs to their bodies using cocktail sticks. Smear half the butter over. Season lightly and lay the bacon over the breasts.

2 Preheat the oven to 200°C (400°F/Gas 6). Boil the kohl rabi in the stock for 2 minutes. Drain, reserving the stock.

3 Melt the remaining butter in a large roasting tin. Add the onions, kohl rabi, and pears, and turn over in the butter. Push to one side. Put the walnuts in the base of the tin and place the partridges on top. Roast in the oven for 45 minutes until everything is golden and cooked through, turning over the fruit and vegetables once during cooking.

4 Lift the birds and the fruit and vegetables out of the tin. Keep warm. Add the cider and reserved stock to the tin. Boil on a high heat, stirring and scraping up the sediment, for about 3 minutes until well reduced and slightly thickened. Taste and reseason.

5 Transfer the partridges, pears, and vegetables to warm serving plates. Remove the cocktail sticks from the birds and spoon the gravy over.

INGREDIENTS
4 sprigs of fresh thyme
4 oven-ready partridges
85g (3oz) butter
Salt and freshly ground
 black pepper
8 rashers streaky bacon,
 cut into thirds
2 kohl rabi, cut into eighths
200ml (7fl oz) chicken stock
2 onions, cut into eighths
4 firm small pears, quartered
 and cored
30g (1oz) walnuts
150ml (5fl oz) pear or apple cider

BREEDS

All furred game is lean, dark, close-textured, and low in saturated fat. Venison is deer meat. Loin, fillet, saddle, shoulder, and haunch can all be roasted; loin, leg steaks, and medallions are good grilled or fried. Also available diced for stewing and casseroling, or minced. We've featured three main breeds. For rabbit and hare meat, see below.

VENISON

RED DEER
Roaming free and feeding on Highland or farmed on woodland vegetation, red deer venison has a rich, gamey flavour, ideal for roasting, grilling, stews, and casseroles.

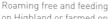

ROE DEER
Substantially smaller than the red deer. Paler-fleshed than red deer venison, and less widely available, it is considered by some to have a more delicate flavour and texture.

FALLOW DEER
Small, parkland-grazing deer, with a milder flavour and finer texture than gamey red deer.

RABBIT AND HARE

WILD RABBIT
Stronger flavour than farmed rabbit, rather like a slightly gamey chicken. Usually casseroled or stewed, but can be roasted, wrapped in bacon or buttered foil.

HARE
Strong, gamey flesh, highly prized amongst connoisseurs. Best jointed and casseroled. Saddles can be roasted after marinating.

FURRED GAME

Rabbits are everywhere. You might also see a hare dashing through a field or a majestic stag on a hillside. It is necessary that their numbers are managed as they destroy crops. That doesn't mean we support inhumane killing or using chemical warfare to destroy them, but rather properly organized control by experts. Venison is also organically and responsibly farmed in this country to meet public demand. Rabbits are farmed too, but not to such high welfare standards, so we recommend you eat wild ones.

WHAT WHEN AND HOW

WHAT TYPES
Hare (brown): Scarce in some areas, due to loss of natural habitat and illegal killing. Farmers are actively encouraged to provide a natural habitat for them (like grassy leys on organic farmland). There is no closed season but they cannot be sold between March and July, and the Game and Wildlife Conservation Trust says avoid February – when they are breeding. They're thriving in game-keepered areas, where they are properly managed.
Wild rabbit: Now prolific after a decline because of myxomatosis, they have many natural predators but have always been culled by farmers protecting their crops.
Venison: We've featured the most common deer, fallow, red, and roe. Some are also organically farmed or kept in free-range park herds. You may also get sika, Chinese water (E), and muntjac (E, W, S). Look out, too, for wild boar, not featured here.

WHEN IN SEASON
Hare: No closed season in E, S, or W, but buy only August–January. In Northern Ireland (NI) 12 August–31 January; **Wild rabbit:** All year (best July–December); **Red and Fallow deer, bucks:** In E, W, NI, August–April. In S 1 July–20 October; **Red and Fallow deer, hinds:** In E, W November–March. In NI 1 November–28 February. In S 21 October–15 February. Organically farmed all year; **Roe deer, bucks:** In E, W April–October. In S 1 April–20 October. **Roe deer, hinds:** In E, W November–March, In S 21 October–31 March. Not found in NI.

HOW TO CHOOSE AND STORE
Always buy from a traceable and reliable source. Do not accept unlawfully killed game. Always store on a plate, loosely wrapped, on the bottom shelf of the fridge to make absolutely sure no drips can fall on other foods. Use within 2–3 days.

PERFECT PAIRINGS

REDCURRANT JELLY in sauces and to serve with roast game; **FRAGRANT HERBS** such as **ROSEMARY**, **SAGE**, **THYME**, and **BAY** to flavour casseroles and for stuffings; **FORTIFIED WINES**, **BEERS**, **GIN**, and **BRANDY** to enhance sauces; try serving **POLENTA** instead of mash with saucy game dishes; **CHESTNUTS**, **BEETROOT**, and **DRIED FRUITS** such as **PRUNES**, **APRICOTS**, and **RAISINS** are favourite additions to braises.

SIMPLE WAYS TO ENJOY

TO PREPARE

Hare and rabbit may be whole or ready-jointed. Wipe the meat with damp kitchen paper. Hare may need rinsing and patting dry. Hare used traditionally to have the blood sold with it to enrich the sauce. If it does, stir it into the gravy to thicken it just before serving, but don't boil.

Venison needs little preparation. If cooking a saddle, make sure it has a layer of fat wrapped round it. If it does not, wrap it in fat bacon, or smear liberally with butter, and wrap in foil.

JUGGED HARE OR RABBIT

Marinate jointed hare or rabbit overnight in sliced onion, carrot, celery, juniper berries, a bouquet garni, a splash of red wine vinegar and olive oil, and a glass each of red wine and water. Brown bacon lardons and chopped onions. Put in a casserole with the marinated meat. Blend some flour into the pan, strain in the marinade and add stock. Boil to thicken. Add 1 tbsp redcurrant jelly. Pour over the meat. Season. Cover, cook at 160°C (325°F/Gas 3) until tender.

GRILLED VENISON WITH CARAMELIZED ONIONS

Soften plenty of sliced onions in a little oil and butter. Add a sprinkling of sugar and a good splash of balsamic vinegar. Cook, stirring, until soft and richly golden. Season. Set aside. Brush venison steaks with oil. Cook under a hot grill, about 4 minutes a side for medium rare (don't overcook or they go tough). Serve topped with the caramelized onions.

ROAST SADDLE OF VENISON WITH GRAINY MUSTARD

Brown venison in oil. Smear with butter and grainy mustard. Add a splash of red wine. Season. Wrap tightly in foil. Roast in the oven at 200°C (400°F/Gas 6) for 20 minutes per 450g (1lb), plus 20 minutes. Remove from oven and rest. Pour juices into a pan, boil, and reduce. Carve meat and spoon juices over.

RABBIT AND BUTTER BEAN STEW

Soak and boil some butter beans. Drain. Put a jointed rabbit in a pan with a sliced onion, some quartered tomatoes, diced potatoes and carrots, chopped red and green pepper, baby corn cobs, the beans, some diced white pudding, and chicken stock. Season. Add a bay leaf. Cover, and simmer until really tender. Discard the bay leaf before serving.

FILLET OF VENISON WITH JUNIPER AND PEPPER SAUCE

THANE PRINCE

Thane was a regular food writer with *The Telegraph* for 10 years. She now runs *The Aldeburgh Cookery School* in Suffolk.

SERVES 2 **PREPARATION TIME** 5 minutes **COOKING TIME** 10 minutes
SERVE WITH creamy mashed potatoes and brussels sprouts.

This is a wonderfully quick dish to prepare, and delicious to eat. Venison is very low in fat, so adding crème fraiche to the sauce gives it a touch of richness.

1 Crush half the juniper berries with the peppercorns until fine. Press them into both sides of the venison steaks and leave to sit at room temperature while you start the sauce.

2 Heat the oil in a frying pan and cook the shallot over a low to medium heat until soft. Add the crushed garlic, and fry until they begin to colour. Scrape onto a side plate and reserve.

3 Place the pan back on a medium heat and, when hot, put in the venison steaks. Cook for 3–5 minutes without moving the steaks, before turning and cooking the other side, again for 3–5 minutes.

4 Take the steaks from the pan and put on a warmed plate to rest while you finish the sauce.

5 Put the shallots and garlic back into the pan, add the sherry, and stir well to de-glaze the pan. Bring to the boil, crush the remaining juniper berries, and add to the pan with the honey and the crème frâiche. Simmer for about 1 minute, seasoning to taste with salt and freshly ground black pepper. Serve the venison with the sauce spooned on top.

INGREDIENTS
2 x 150g (5oz) venison steaks cut from the loin fillet
1 medium shallot, finely chopped
1 clove garlic, peeled and crushed
2 tbsp olive oil
12 juniper berries
8 black peppercorns
50ml (2fl oz) dry sherry
  or white wine
½ tsp honey or brown sugar
2 tbsp full fat crème frâiche
Salt and freshly ground black
  pepper, to taste

VENISON RAGOUT WITH GUINNESS AND PRUNES

SERVES 4 **PREPARATION TIME** 20 minutes **COOKING TIME** 2 hours
SERVE WITH jacket potatoes and lightly cooked Brussels sprouts.

1 Preheat the oven to 160°C (325°F/Gas 3).

2 Mix 1 tbsp of the flour with a little salt and pepper and the allspice. Use to coat the venison. Heat half the oil and butter in a flameproof casserole and brown the venison. Remove with a slotted spoon. Heat the remaining oil and butter and fry the leek and carrot for 2 minutes, stirring. Add the rest of the flour, the Guinness, and crumbled stock cube. Bring to the boil, stirring. Add the black pudding.

3 Return the venison to the casserole, then add the mushrooms, prunes, and bouquet garni. Season. Cover and cook in the oven for 2 hours until meltingly tender. Discard the bouquet garni, thin with a little water, if necessary, taste, and reseason if necessary.

INGREDIENTS
3 tbsp plain flour
Salt and freshly ground
  black pepper
A good pinch of ground allspice
675g (1½lb) diced venison
2 tbsp sunflower oil
A good knob of butter
1 leek, thinly sliced
1 carrot, sliced
330ml (11fl oz) can Guinness
1 beef stock cube
115g (4oz) black pudding,
  skinned and chopped
115g (4oz) crimini mushrooms
115g (4oz) ready-to-eat
  prunes, halved
1 bouquet garni

RABBIT AND SWEETCORN PIE WITH A HERB CRUST

SERVES 4 **PREPARATION TIME** 1½ hours **COOKING TIME** 30 minutes
VARIATION Wild rabbit tastes like free-range organic chicken, which you
could use instead.

1 Sift the flour and salt into a bowl. Add 60g (2oz) of the
butter and rub in with the fingertips. Stir in the herbs. Add the
remaining butter and the iced water. Mix with a round-bladed
knife to form a lumpy dough. Knead gently on a lightly floured
surface and roll out to an oblong. Fold the bottom third up and
the top third down over it. Press the edges with the rolling pin.
Quarter-turn the dough. Roll, fold, and turn twice more. Wrap
in foil and chill.

2 Put the rabbit in a pan with the lardons and all the vegetables.
Add the stock, the bay leaf, and seasoning to taste. Bring to the
boil, reduce the heat, part-cover, and simmer gently for about an
hour, until the rabbit is tender. Lift out the rabbit. Remove the
meat, and cut into pieces. Put in a 1.7-litre (3-pint) pie dish on a
baking sheet. Discard the bay leaf.

3 Blend the sherry with the flour and 1 tbsp water. Stir into the
vegetables and stock, then bring to the boil, stirring. Add the
cream and season to taste. Stir into the rabbit. Allow to cool.

4 Preheat the oven to 220°C (425°F/Gas 7). Roll and fold the
pastry once more. Roll out to slightly bigger than the pie dish.
Cut off a strip all round. Dampen the rim of the dish and lay the
strip on top. Dampen the strip. Lay the pastry on top. Press the
edges together to seal. Trim, knock up, and flute with the back of
a knife. Make leaves out of the trimmings. Arrange on top. Make
a slit in the top to allow steam to escape. Glaze with cream. Bake
for 30 minutes until risen and golden. Serve hot.

INGREDIENTS
FOR THE FLAKY PASTRY
225g (8oz) plain flour
¼ tsp salt
175g (6oz) cold butter, diced
2 tbsp chopped fresh parsley
1 tbsp chopped fresh thyme
About 8 tbsp iced water, to mix

FOR THE FILLING
1 oven-ready wild rabbit, jointed
60g (2oz) smoked bacon lardons
1 onion, chopped
2 carrots, sliced
1 potato, diced
4 tomatoes, skinned and
    chopped
Kernels from 2 sweetcorn
    cobs, or 175g (6oz) canned
    or frozen sweetcorn
600ml (1 pint) chicken stock
1 bay leaf
Salt and freshly ground black
    pepper
3 tbsp dry sherry
4 tbsp plain flour
4 tbsp double cream, plus a little
    for glazing

CHEESE, DAIRY & EGGS

ORGANIC CHEESEMAKING IN WALES

CARWYN ADAMS, CAWS CENARTH CHEESE

Glyneithinog Dairy Farm in Pembrokeshire, West Wales, started producing Caws Cenarth Caerphilly (Caerfilli in Welsh) in the 1980s. In 1999, Carwyn and his wife Susanna decided, with his parents Gwynfor and Thelma Adams, to make the enterprise organic. By 2001 the dairy farm was totally organic.

Their first organic cheese, Perl Wen — a cross between Brie and Caerphilly, with a mould-ripened crust — was a great success, and won a Silver World Cheese Award in 2000. Spurred on by this success, Carwyn took on the challenge of trying to make a blue cheese, knowing that another company in Wales had already tried and failed to do so. Perseverence proved worthwhile: the blue Perl Las has won several accolades, including a Gold British Cheese Award in 2005. That same year they sold their herd to a local dairy farm, which agreed to supply them with organic milk for their cheesemaking. Organic milk comes from cattle that graze in nutrient-rich fields, making the milk creamier than non-organic alternatives. Up until 2005 they had been making pasteurized cheese, but Carwyn found it took out quite a lot of residual flavours, so they switched to unpasteurized milk.

All Carwyn's cheeses are made by hand, then stored in a temperature-controlled store room to mature.

Carwyn Adams in the store room.

Carwyn employs three cheesemakers and two people turning, maturing, and packing the cheeses, but it is still a family operation. Carwyn himself does a bit of everything, but is the creative mind behind the operation, while his wife Susanna looks after their two young children, Lucas and Alisa, and his aunt Betty manages the onsite shop.

Carwyn continues to experiment: his latest cheese, Golden Cenarth (a washed rind, continental-style soft cheese), is proving to be an instant hit, and his next experiment is creating a two-year-old, mature, hard-pressed cheese — a venture that brings with it a whole new set of challenges. "The cheeses we make at the moment mature quickly, so there is a fast turnover. Making a mature variety means the money is tied up in the milk for a long time."

For now, continuing to supply customers with his range of award-winning cheeses, the production of Golden Cenarth being in full swing, and preparing to supply supermarkets with whole, mini wax-coated Caerphilly cheeses for Christmas, Carwyn has his hands full.

See p313 for Carwyn's *Deep-fried Caerphilly with Apple and Lemon Marmalade*.

OPPOSITE Carwyn's Caerphilly maturing on shelves in his store room.

HARD CHEESES

Cheddar is the quintessential British cheese. When mature, it's nutty and full-flavoured, with quite a kick. It originated in Somerset, but it doesn't have to be made there now. Some commercial brands shouldn't be dignified by the name – so best go for an organic farmhouse cheese with an acknowledged reputation. Here you'll find a whole selection of organically made hard cheeses with wonderful flavours and textures, but look out, too, for other exciting artisan cheeses traditionally made around the country, many only in their county or town of origin.

WHAT WHEN AND HOW

WHAT TYPES
Hard and semi-hard cheeses: They start out the same way – milk is separated, the curds drained and cut. They're sometimes cooked to remove more whey, then salted, pressed, and left to ripen. But within that are all the intricacies that create the complex flavours and textures that make each one a unique, mouthwatering delight. The main difference between them is the pressing. Hard cheeses, like Cheddar, are pressed firmly to produce a close, smooth texture, but cheeses like Caerphilly are only lightly pressed or, like Ringwell, not at all, to achieve an open, moist consistency.

WHEN IN SEASON
All year, but some vary over the months, depending on the animals' diet.

HOW TO CHOOSE AND STORE
They should never look sweaty. Avoid any that look different in the centre from around the edge and have cracks running from the rind inwards – they are drying out. All should have a pleasant smell. Try to buy wedges cut to order, in quantities you need; no cheese keeps well once cut. Store in a sealed container in the fridge and remove an hour before serving.

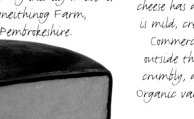

Caerphilly A moist, pale yellow, crumbly cow's milk cheese with a mild, buttery flavour and hint of citrus. Organically made at Glyneithinog Farm, Pembrokeshire.

Lancashire The traditional cheese has an open texture, but is mild, creamy, and buttery. Commercial versions made outside the county are mild, crumbly, and slightly acidic. Organic varieties are available.

Godminster Cheddar A real, organic Somerset Cheddar, made near Bruton, with a taste-tingling flavour.

Dunlop Likened to a sweet, fruity Cheddar, Dunlop was said to have been developed in Scotland by an Irish-born farmer's wife, Barbara Gilmour, in the 17th century.

Hand-covered in local, edible nettles.

Cornish Yarg A firm, fresh-tasting, white, cow's milk cheese with a definite tang. It becomes more creamy and less tangy with age.

Swaledale Traditionally made in Richmond, Yorkshire, for centuries. Firm, white paste with salty-sweet, goaty flavour. Swaledale Cheese Company also makes sheep's and organic cow's milk varieties.

Creamy coloured with natural or waxed rind.

Double Gloucester A rich, whole-milk cheese. Mellow and creamy when young, crumbly with some bite as it matures. Used for the famous Cooper's Hill cheese-rolling contest.

St Egwin Yellow, moist, and pliable with a nutty sweetness and white-dusted, golden rind. Made by Gorsehill Abbey Cheese with milk from its own Freisian and Montbeliarde cows.

Red Leicester Slightly crumbly and creamy, this cheese has a tangy aftertaste. Organic varieties are available.

Moulded in colanders, so distinctive shape.

Ringwell A firm, creamy-sweet, golden-yellow cheese with a rough natural rind. From locally sourced Jersey milk at Wooton Organic Dairy, Somerset.

Wyfe of Bath Made in Somerset at Park Farm, Kelston, this is a hand-made, organic, single-herd, cow's milk cheese with a rich flavour and Gouda-like texture.

Ribblesdale This mild, firm, goat's and sheep's cheese has a nutty, mild flavour. A delicious, less-salty alternative to Parmesan. There is also a cow's milk version.

Coated in wax to give it a longer shelf life.

Daylesford Cheddar A traditionally made, award-winning, organic Cheddar. Made in Gloucestershire, not Somerset.

Cheshire Silky yet crumbly, Britain's oldest named cheese (mentioned in the Doomsday Book) gets its flavour from the salt deposits that permeate the pastures.

Wensleydale A lightly pressed, mild cheese with a honeyed finish. The real deal is made from the milk of cows that graze the limestone pastures around Wensleydale.

PERFECT PAIRINGS

CRUSTY BREAD and **CHUTNEY** for a ploughman's lunch; **TOMATOES**, underneath, on top, beside or cooked with them; **APPLES**, **CELERY**, and **NUTS** for a snack, to round off a meal or in salads; **JACKET POTATOES** topped with them, grated or crumbled; **BEETROOT** and **ONIONS** add sweetness, raw, cooked, or pickled as a garnish or accompaniment.

SIMPLE WAYS TO ENJOY

TO PREPARE

Cut off any inedible rind. Slice, dice, crumble, or grate, as required.

CHEDDAR RAREBIT

Mix 1 tbsp plain flour with 2 tbsp beer or cider in a pan. Add a knob of butter, a large handful grated Cheddar cheese, a pinch of salt, cayenne, and a dash of English mustard. Heat gently, stirring until thick and bubbling. Toast 2 bread slices on one side. Spoon the mixture over untoasted sides. Grill until golden.

TOASTED CHEESE AND ONION SANDWICHES

Butter bread slices on one side. Sandwich butter-side out with slices of hard cheese, chopped sage, and sliced onions. Grill or fry on both sides until golden, pressing down firmly during cooking (or use a sandwich maker).

WHITE CHEESE SALAD WITH BEETROOT AND CAPERS

Shred some lettuce and put on a serving platter. Top with diced cucumber, halved cherry tomatoes, red onion rings, and cubed, cooked beetroot. Scatter a few pickled capers over, drizzle with olive oil and a sprinkling of red wine vinegar. Top with a handful of crumbled white hard cheese and season well with freshly ground black pepper.

MACARONI CHEESE WITH ROASTED PEPPERS

Make a béchamel sauce (p324). Season. Add a large handful of grated well-flavoured hard cheese and a dash of Dijon mustard. Season well. Stir in cooked macaroni and diced, roasted red and green pepper. Put in a flameproof dish. Sprinkle with more grated cheese. Grill until golden and hot.

CHEESE FONDUE

Rub a cut garlic clove round a small pan. Blend 2 tsp cornflour with a splash of kirsch. Add a glass of white wine or cider, 2 large handfuls each grated Cheddar, and any other melting cheese. Heat gently, stirring, until thick. Simmer for a few minutes. Season. Serve with cubes of bread.

DEEP-FRIED CAERPHILLY WITH APPLE AND LEMON MARMALADE

CARWYN AT CAWS CENARTH CHEESE

Carwyn Adams and his family run Caws Cenarth Cheese in Wales, and make all their prize-winning organic cheeses by hand. See pp308-9.

SERVES 4 **PREPARATION TIME** 10 minutes **COOKING TIME** 18 minutes for the marmalade, 3–4 minutes for the cheese. **Caerphilly is lovely cooked like this, or in cheese puddings and omelettes, or even crumbled on a pizza. If you don't like chunky marmalade, coarsely grate the lemon zest, peel off the pith, and chop the flesh.**

1 Quarter the lemon lengthways and remove the pips. Cut crossways in thin slices. Put in a pan with the water and cloves. Bring to the boil, cover, reduce the heat, and simmer for about 15 minutes or until the lemon is very soft (once you add sugar, it stops softening).

2 Meanwhile, peel, core, and quarter the apple. Cut into dice and add to the lemon with the sugar. Stir gently until the sugar dissolves. Boil for 2–3 minutes until the apple is tender but still has a little texture, stirring once or twice. Leave to cool.

3 Trim any rind off the Caerphilly and cut it into four equal wedges. Coat in the flour. Beat the egg on a plate. Put the breadcrumbs on a separate plate. Dip the cheese in the egg, then the breadcrumbs. Repeat until the wedges are well covered. Chill until ready to cook.

4 Heat about 1cm (½in) oil in a frying pan until a cube of day-old bread browns in 30 seconds. Drop in the sage leaves and fry for about 20 seconds until bright green and crisp. As soon as they stop sizzling, remove with a slotted spoon. Drain on kitchen paper.

5 Reheat the oil. Fry the cheese for 1½–2 minutes on each side until golden brown. Drain on kitchen paper. Put the cheese on small serving plates with a spoonful of the marmalade to one side. Garnish with the fried sage.

INGREDIENTS
250g (9oz) wedge Caerphilly cheese
2 tbsp plain flour
1 egg, beaten
60g (2oz) fresh breadcrumbs
Oil, for deep-frying
A handful fresh sage leaves

FOR THE MARMALADE
1 small lemon
6 tbsp water
2 cloves
1 pippin-type dessert apple
75g (2½oz) caster sugar

SOFT CHEESES

These include the clean-tasting, white, delicate, fresh ones, gorgeous on crackers or used in cooking. Then there are the ripened cheeses with unmistakable, soft-bloomed rinds. When immature, they are firm and grainy, but as they mature they ooze into a glorious, melting unctuousness. Lastly, there are the washed-rind cheeses that smell strong but taste sublime. You can buy some organic varieties in supermarkets, including fresh ones to cook with, but if you love cheese, try our tiny selection, then seek out the artisan cheesemakers around the country who create masterpieces to grace your table and delight your palate.

Pant ys Gawn A creamy, soft, organic goat's cheese from Abergavenny Fine Foods.

WHAT WHEN AND HOW

WHAT TYPES

Fresh soft: Once separated, the curds are cut and drained as basic curd cheese. For fromage frais, they are stirred for a smooth texture. For cottage cheese, they are washed after draining. Cream or other flavourings are sometimes added.
Ripe soft and semi-soft: The curds are not cut but drained whole, then usually put into moulds and drained further. They are then removed, salted, inoculated with penicillin, and left to ripen and develop the bloomy rind. Some semi-soft cheeses are washed in brine, wine, cider, or perry during ripening, giving a strong aroma and coloured rind.

WHEN IN SEASON

All year, but will vary in texture and flavour, according to the diet of the animals.

HOW TO CHOOSE AND STORE

Fresh soft: Buy only what you need – they don't keep well. Store in a sealed container in the fridge.
Ripe soft: White-rinded cheeses should "give" slightly when pressed. Avoid if they are discoloured or smell of ammonia. Washed-rind cheeses can smell strong and may have a sticky rind, but should not be wet or slimy. Keep well-wrapped in the fridge in a sealed container with room to "breathe". Take out a while before eating; be careful in hot weather, though, as they'll run quickly.

Rich, creamy texture.

Black-eyed Susan A version of Goldilocks, lightly rolled in black peppercorns when young, from Daisy and Co. Dairy. There is also Vipers Grass with herbs, and smoked Indian Blanket.

Very spreadable texture.

Perl Wen Welsh, Caws Cenarth, organic, pale yellow cheese with soft, bloomed rind. It becomes richer and sweeter as it matures, with a slightly salty aftertaste.

Cowslip Organic, soft, cow's milk cheese, here with chives, from High Weald Dairy, Sussex.

St Tola Soft organic goat's cheese with whorled pale gold rind and white paste as it matures. Made by Inagh Farmhouse Cheese, Co. Clare.

Mild, creamy cheese.

Bath Soft A soft organic Brie-style cheese made to an original 19th-century recipe at Park Farm, Bath from the milk of the farm's own herd.

Finn A semi-soft, organic, cow's milk cheese enriched by the addition of cream. Made at Caeperthy Farm, Herefordshire.

Densely textured, with a mild flavour.

Distinctive, yellow colour.

Goldilocks An organic, Camembert-style cheese made from Jersey milk from Daisy and Co. Dairy, Somerset.

Stinking Bishop A soft cheese with a sticky, orange rind and pungent aroma. A delicious example of a soft, washed-rind cheese.

The bloom on the rind is often flecked with green.

Sussex Slipcote Made from organic sheep's milk at the High Weald Dairy, West Sussex, it's soft and creamy with a slight lemon tang. Available plain, with garlic and herbs (pictured here), peppercorns, mint, and basil.

Little Ryding Sweet, rich-flavoured, creamy, organic, sheep's milk cheese from Wootton Organic Dairy, Somerset.

Penyston A smooth, creamy-centred cheese, with a brine-washed rind and a distinctive aroma and flavour. Made by Daylesford Organic Dairy, Gloucestershire.

PERFECT PAIRINGS

FRESH SOFT CHEESES **SMOKED FISH** and **CAVIAR** to offset their richness; **CHOPPED WALNUTS** or **HAZELNUTS** add a delicious texture to spread on crackers; **SPINACH** combined as a stuffing for pasta, in pies and flans or as a topping on pizza; **FRESH SOFT FRUITS** mashed, folded in and sweetened for a dessert; **RIPE SOFT CHEESES** **GRAPES**, **RED**, or **WHITE CURRANTS** served with them as an alternative to dessert, or **REDCURRANT JELLY** as an accompaniment; **GRILLED BACON** teamed with grilled potato wedges or slices.

SIMPLE WAYS TO ENJOY

TO PREPARE

They can all be used as they are as part of a cheese board. Soft cheeses can be mixed with other sweet and savoury ingredients for many cooked dishes.

Ripe soft cheeses can be cut into wedges for grilling or frying, or cut into cubes for adding to salads, or can be thrown into stir-fries at the last minute.

GRILLED GOAT'S CHEESE, WALNUT, AND BEETROOT SALAD →

Mix some salad leaves with diced beetroot, chopped cucumber, and spring onion. Toss in a little French dressing with a dash of walnut oil added. Grill a couple of slices of soft goat's cheese on oiled foil until just beginning to melt. Slide on top of the salad and scatter with a few chopped walnuts.

CURD CHEESE TARTS

Line 10 sections of a tartlet tin with sweet shortcrust pastry. Beat 60g (2oz) unsalted butter with 60g (2oz) caster sugar, 1 egg, 225g (8oz) curd cheese, the finely grated zest of ½ lemon and 3 tbsp currants. Spoon into the cases. Bake at 190°C (375°F/Gas 5) for about 20 minutes, until golden and set.

CRUNCHY GOLDEN CHEESE WEDGES

Cut portion-sized wedges of any not-too-ripe white-bloomed cheese. Dip in seasoned flour, then beaten egg, then sage-and-onion stuffing mix. Repeat if necessary, to coat. Chill. Fry in hot oil until golden on both sides. Drain on kitchen paper. Serve on salad leaves with redcurrant jelly.

SMELLY CHEESE BRUSCHETTA

Brush slices of French bread with olive oil and toast on both sides. Top with some chopped sun-dried tomatoes and stoned black olives and a few torn sage leaves. Cover with slices of semi-soft, washed-rind, smelly cheese, such as Stinking Bishop. Grill until melted and bubbling. Serve hot.

BLUE CHEESES

Hard and crumbly or soft and creamy, they all have a distinct tang that sets them apart. In Britain we now make numerous types to rival those of other nations. The king has to be Stilton, with its crumbly yet surprisingly spreadable texture and lingering aftertaste. Only seven dairies across Leicestershire, Nottinghamshire, and Derbyshire are certified to make it – it's not from the village of Stilton at all. Here we've chosen a cross-section of taste-tingling organic and artisan cheeses from around Britain, all made from different milks with different attributes. Seek out other local specialities too; you'll not be disappointed.

Perl Las Award-winning, organic, Welsh cheese from Glyneithinog Farm, Pembrokeshire. When young, light and salty; when mature, golden and stronger.

WHAT WHEN AND HOW

WHAT TYPES

Blue cheeses are usually categorized by the milk they are made from — that is, cow's, sheep's, or goat's — rather than by hard or soft (although they do come in different styles and textures). To make the blue, nowadays most have blue cheese mould added to the milk. Then, when the cheese has been made, it is pierced with stainless-steel needles, which allows air in and causes the blue mould to grow. For soft Brie-types, the mould is injected as they are too soft to take the rods.

WHEN IN SEASON

All year, though some cheeses vary according to the animals' diet.

HOW TO CHOOSE AND STORE

They should look fresh and moist but not wet. Avoid any which are discoloured or drying. The smell should be strong, but pleasant. Store thoroughly wrapped individually in waxed paper, or they will mould any other cheeses. Then put them in a sealable box or bag (but with room to "breathe", so they don't dry out), and keep in the bottom of the fridge. Unless using for cooking, take out of the fridge an hour before serving, so they come to room temperature.

Lanark Blue
A Scottish sheep's cheese from Humphrey Errington, Strathclyde. Creamy in spring, full-bodied with real bite in the winter.

Shropshire Blue Creamy-textured cross between Stilton and Blue Cheshire, revived by Colston Bassett and Long Clawson Dairies; both certified to make Stilton.

Dorset Blue Vinney Close to extinction, but revived by Woodbridge Farm, Dorset, and made from skimmed milk, so it is lower in fat than most cheeses.

soft taste and low in fat.

Nanny Bloo slightly acidic, blue goat's cheese with a mild, goaty flavour and a little kick.

Golden, streaked with blue.

Blissful Buffalo Blue Mild with rich, creamy texture and sweet flavour; made by the Exmoor Cheese Company.

slightly grainy texture.

Blue Cheshire Enjoying a revival; rich and crumbly, but not as strong as Stilton.

Organic Stichelton Named after the original name of Stilton village, it has a strong, lingering flavour. Made at Stichelton Dairy, Collingthwaite Farm, Nottinghamshire.

Made with traditional animal rennet.

Distinctive crusty rind.

Blue-green veining and a distinctive, grey rind.

Old Sarum Award-winning, sweet, and moist, made by Loosehanger Farmhouse Cheeses, near Basingstoke.

Organic Stilton A stronger flavour than standard Stilton, with an excellent texture. Available from Cropwell Bishop (pictured), Lye Cross Farm, and Long Clawson Dairy.

Cornish Blue An award-winning, hand-made cheese from The Cornish Cheese Company, with a creamy texture and delicious tang.

BLUE CHEESES **319**

PERFECT PAIRINGS

PEARS are delicious, sliced with one, instead of dessert, or with a blue cheese dressing or potted cheese (see below); **CELERY** and **FENNEL** spread the cheese along the grooves as a snack or eat with the cheeses at the end of a meal; **WALNUTS** nibble with blue cheese or chop and mix into dressings or dips (see below); **BUTTERNUT SQUASH** and **BEETROOT** roasted with crumbled blue cheese on top.

SIMPLE WAYS TO ENJOY

TO PREPARE

Cut off any inedible rind before crumbling, slicing, or cutting into dice, as required.

SOFT BLUE CHEESE MOUSSE →

Dissolve a sachet of powdered gelatine in 2 tbsp water. Purée 115g (4oz) soft blue cheese with a small carton plain yogurt and 2 egg yolks. Stir in the dissolved gelatine. Fold in 150ml (5fl oz) whipped cream and 2 stiffly beaten egg whites. Put in four oiled moulds and chill. Turn out. Garnish with watercress.

BLUE CHEESE DRESSING

Dice a chunk of any blue cheese. Put in a blender or food processor with a squeeze of lemon, a splash of milk, and a small spoonful of honey. Blend with enough sunflower oil to make a smooth cream. Season to taste. Serve with pears (see above), or toss in a green, potato, or pasta salad.

BLUE CHEESE DIP

Dice and crush a wedge of blue cheese. Gradually mash in some mayonnaise and thick plain yogurt. Season, sharpen with lemon juice, and stir in some chopped fresh parsley or snipped chives. Serve with crudités or crackers.

POTTED STILTON WITH PORT

Mash together equal quantities of ripe Stilton cheese and butter. Add a good grating of nutmeg, some freshly ground black pepper and a dash of English mustard. Flavour with port to taste. Pack into a small pot. Melt extra butter and pour over the surface. Chill until firm. Serve with hot toast, or oatcakes.

SPAGHETTI WITH BLUE CHEESE AND LEEKS

Soften a thinly sliced leek in butter. Stir in crumbled blue cheese until melted. Add a little crème fraîche and white wine. Simmer until creamy. Meanwhile, cook spaghetti, drain, return to pan. Add the sauce, and toss gently.

BREEDS

These are the preferred organic breeds of cow, goat, and sheep specifically suited to local conditions, with naturally high milk yields and least prone to disease.

HOLSTEIN FRIESIAN
A small Friesian crossed with a larger Holstein to make the world's highest-yielding dairy cow; produces 80 per cent of British milk. Good for milk, males good for beef. Usually white and black, can be white and red.

DAIRY SHORTHORN
Popular, hardy, organic breed; can be red, white, red and white, or roan. Bred for beef and milk, but now specialist strains for each. Excellent milk producer. High protein/fat ratio, so milk is good for making cheese.

GUERNSEY
Probably developed from two French breeds. Grass-fed, it yields highly nutritious, golden-yellow, creamy milk. Red or yellow with white patches, it produces more milk for less feed than bigger breeds.

JERSEY
From the Channel Island. A pretty, small, usually light brown cow (can be black or grey) with a black nose and white muzzle. It's hardy and produces more rich milk for less feed than any other breed.

SAANEN GOAT
Originally from the Saanen Valley, Switzerland, it's a "pretty" goat with short white hair and a longish body. It has a high milk yield and is very placid.

BRITISH TOGGENBERG GOAT
Another Swiss goat, it can be fawn, grey, or brown with white markings. The females have a shorter coat than males. They have a good milk yield/feed ratio and a good temperament.

ANGLO-NUBIAN GOAT
Distinctive Roman nose, big floppy ears, long body and silky coat in colours from chestnut to cream and lots of mixtures. The milk has a high fat and protein content, making it excellent for cheesemaking.

FRIESLAND SHEEP
The only pure dairy breed of sheep in the UK. It has a big frame and pure white, high-quality fleece. It's highly adaptable with a good, calm temperament.

DAIRY

When you spread butter on your toast, or drink a glass of milk, do you consider the animals it came from? Animal welfare isn't just about the meat you eat; organic dairy farming is a holistic approach. Cows, sheep, and goats bred for milk are fed on a natural, grass-based diet, that includes clover and other organic matter. No pesticides or other agrochemicals are used on the fields. The animals spend plenty of time grazing outdoors (coming inside to comfortable, spacious shelter only in bad weather). They don't yield as much milk as when fed a concentrated feed so they are therefore milked less, which is less stressful and better for their health. Calves are weaned at three months (in conventional farming they're removed after 48 hours — highly stressful for cow and calf). There are different breeds of cows, sheep, and goats reared specifically for their milk, or for milk and meat. The milk can be made into cream, butter, and yogurt, featured here (cheeses are covered separately on pages 308–21). Many people find organic cow's milk tastes better because of the animals' natural diet, and research now shows that, although the nutrients are much the same, it does contain 68 per cent more omega 3 fatty acids — essential for a healthy heart and mind.

HOW TO CHOOSE AND STORE

Always buy dairy products as fresh as possible. Avoid buying from market stalls where they've been exposed to heat and sunlight for a long time; they will deteriorate very quickly. They should be put in the fridge as soon as possible after purchase. Always keep chilled until ready to use. Butter benefits from being taken out of the fridge a short while before use to soften slightly. Always keep in sealed containers or well wrapped, as appropriate, as they can easily take on the flavour of other foods.

Cow's milk Highly nutritious, available whole, semi-skimmed, skimmed, and Channel Island. You can also buy "Raw" (unpasteurized) and UHT (longlife) milk. Most is pasteurized (heated to $71.7\,°C/161\,°F$) to reduce bacteria so it keeps better.

Goat's milk similar to cow's milk but with more easily digestible fat, and lower in lactose and folic acid. Sheep's milk is the most nutritious of all. They are interchangeable.

Buttermilk Traditionally the liquid left from churning butter, but now commercially made from milk soured with lactic acid. Very low in fat.

Clotted cream Cream is slowly heated until it forms a crust. It is then cooled and the crust skimmed off. It contains at least 55 per cent butterfat.

Pouring cream, single cream, whipping, and double cream, (shown here), for whipping or cooking. Crème fraîche and soured cream are soured with lactic acid.

Cow's milk yogurt Fermented with a live culture, which gives it the distinctive taste and texture. Available with no fat, low-fat, or full-fat; set, stirred, or strained (Greek-style).

Butter Churned from cream to separate it into the fatty solids for butter, and buttermilk, which is used to make margarine and other spreads. It's available unsalted (bottom left), lightly salted, or salted. Farmhouse butter (top left) is traditionally made just from churned unpasteurized cream. It has a shorter shelf life, more intense flavour, and a rich, golden colour.

Sheep's milk yogurt Higher in milk solids than cows', so naturally richer and thicker. A good substitute for cream or crème fraîche. Goat's milk yogurt is thinner with a clean, light taste.

PERFECT PAIRINGS

MILK or **CREAM** blended with **EGGS** for quiches, desserts, or sauces; **CREAM** or **YOGURT** with **FRESH** or **COOKED FRUIT**, **CHOCOLATE**, and **COFFEE** for desserts; **BUTTER** with **HERBS**, **GARLIC**, and **SPICES** as a garnish, baked in **BREAD**, or melted for a sauce for **FISH**, **MEAT**, **POULTRY**, and **VEGETABLES**; **YOGURT**, **SOURED CREAM**, or **BUTTERMILK** for **QUICK BREADS** and **SCONES** with great texture and flavour.

SIMPLE WAYS TO ENJOY

BÉCHAMEL SAUCE

Boil 300ml (10fl oz) milk with a slice of onion, a bay leaf, and peppercorns in a pan. Cool, and strain. Melt a knob of butter in a pan. Stir in 2 tbsp flour. Cook for 1 minute, stirring. Remove from heat. Blend in milk. Bring to the boil and simmer for 2 minutes, whisking. Season. Flavour with cheese, herbs, or watercress.

ALL-BUTTER SHORTBREAD

Sift 140g (5oz) plain flour with 30g (1oz) semolina and a pinch of salt. Add 4 tbsp sugar and work in ½ block softened butter. Knead to a dough. Press into a buttered sandwich tin. Prick all over. Bake in the oven at 160°C (325°F/Gas 3) until a pale straw colour. Cool, then cut into wedges.

REAL DRINKING CHOCOLATE

Put ¾ mug Jersey or Guernsey milk in a pan. Add 4 squares high-cocoa-solids chocolate. Whisk to melt. Sweeten to taste. Heat until almost boiling. Return to the mug. Top with whipped cream; dust with ground cinnamon.

QUICK BUTTERMILK OR YOGURT ROLLS

Mix a large mugful plain flour with 2 tsp baking powder and ½ tsp salt. Stir in 5 tbsp plain yogurt or buttermilk and enough milk to form a soft, not sticky, dough. Knead gently. Shape into 6 balls. Put on a greased baking sheet. Bake in the oven at 230°C (450°F/Gas 8) until golden and the bases sound hollow when tapped. Serve warm with butter.

SYLLABUB

Mix the grated zest and juice of ½ lemon with ½ glass white wine and sugar to taste. Whisk in 300ml (10fl oz) double cream to soft peaks. Put into glasses. Chill.

MILK POSSET

Bring some milk just to the boil. Sweeten with honey and add a good slug of brandy. Pour into mugs or glasses. Dust with grated nutmeg.

REAL VANILLA RICE PUDDING

Sprinkle enough pudding rice to cover the base of a 1.2-litre (2-pint) ovenproof dish. Split a vanilla pod and scrape the contents into 600ml (1 pint) milk in a pan; add the pod too. Bring to the boil. Pour over the rice. Remove the pod. Sweeten to taste. Add a few flakes of butter. Bake in the oven at 180°C (350°F/Gas 4) until golden and the rice is tender.

YOUR OWN YOGURT

Warm 600ml (1 pint) UHT milk until hand-hot. Blend 1 tbsp dried milk powder with 5 tbsp live plain yogurt. Gradually whisk in the milk. Pour into a wide-necked vacuum flask. Leave undisturbed until set, about 6 hours. Store in an airtight container in the fridge for up to 3 days.

LEMON YOGURT ICE

Whisk 4 egg yolks with 200g (7oz) sugar and the finely grated zest of 3 lemons in a bowl over a pan of hot water until thick and pale. Remove from pan. Stir in the juice of the lemons. Fold in 600ml (1 pint) thick Greek-style yogurt and the whisked egg whites. Freeze in an ice-cream maker; or in a shallow, freezer-proof container, whisking every 2 hours for 6 hours to break up the ice crystals.

JUNKET

Warm 600ml (1 pint) milk to blood temperature. Sweeten to taste and stir in 2 tsp essence of rennet. Pour into glass dishes, and dust with grated nutmeg. Leave to set. Serve topped with fresh or dried berries and a drizzle of cream.

BREAD AND BUTTER PUDDING

Butter 4–6 slices of bread and cut into triangles. Lay some in an ovenproof dish. Sprinkle with sugar and dried fruit. Repeat the layers. Beat 2 eggs with 600ml (1 pint) milk and strain over. Leave to soak for 30 minutes. Dust with grated nutmeg. Bake in the oven at 180°C (350°F/Gas 4) until golden and set.

CREAM CROWDIE WITH RASPBERRIES

Toast a few spoonfuls of coarse oatmeal until golden. Whip some double cream and flavour to taste with caster sugar and sweet sherry or whisky. Fold in nearly all the oatmeal. Layer in glasses with fresh or thawed frozen raspberries. Decorate with the remaining oatmeal.

HEREFORDSHIRE ORGANIC EGGS

BRIDIE WHITTLE, THE GOOD EGG COMPANY

Bridie comes from a farming background (her parents were Producers of the Year in the Soil Association's 2002 Organic Food Awards) and her brother Adam now runs September Organic Dairy Ltd – the family's organic ice-cream business. Bridie was working with the Soil Association in organic poultry certification and realized she could help her family's businesses by supplying the eggs. Her parents already had 200 hens at their north-west Herefordshire farm, but Bridie increased the flock to 600. The Good Egg Company was formed.

"The farm was already organic, so I had a head start." Bridie has three hen houses, each with 200 birds. She buys organic pullets (young hens) at different times of the year, so they're of varying ages. Her favourite breed is the Silver Link, a robust modern hybrid that's well suited to free-range organic production. "They range far and wide, and of my current three flocks they are always the last to bed!" The organic standard of egg production allows the birds to express their natural instincts: to scratch, range, dustbathe, and forage. Foraging gives the hens a veritable feast of worms and insects, grass, and clover, resulting in bright orange yolks and a wonderful flavour.

The hens are let out at 7am to range and forage. The previous day's eggs are then sorted, graded, and stamped ready for delivery. The eggs are collected mid-afternoon and then, at dusk, once the hens have roosted, they're shut in for the night.

Bridie employs someone to help her grade and box the eggs. All those that don't make the grade, she processes into 5kg (11lb) quantities of liquid egg and sells to her brother for the ice cream. Graded eggs are sold through local box-schemes, delicatessens and wholefood shops, as well as the farm shop, where her parents sell their own organic beef and lamb, and other local farmers' produce. The family bond is strong. Bridie, her husband Ben and baby son Charlie live on the farm, with her parents next door. Although Ben and her parents are fully employed outside of The Good Egg Company, they will happily pitch in and help when needed.

Bridie's hens have a much longer life than they would in a bigger commercial operation: "Modern breeds of hen lay about 300 eggs in their first year, after which they're slaughtered." At The Good Egg Company, Bridie keeps her hens for a year or two then advertises them in the local paper. "They are sold on to have a long and (hopefully) happy retirement as backyard hens."

See p332 for Bridie and Ben's *Spicy Vegetable Frittata*.

OPPOSITE, ABOVE LEFT Bridie with one of her precious hens.

ABOVE RIGHT A bowl of Bridie's freshest eggs, ready for sorting, grading, and stamping.

BELOW The hens are let out during the day to range and forage.

BREEDS

There are numerous hen breeds, many of them hybrids developed to be good layers. We've included an old breed, a popular traditional hybrid, and a modern breed, to show their diversity, plus examples of other feathered, egg-laying friends.

LIGHT SUSSEX HEN
A heavy bird good for meat as well as eggs. Excellent at rearing young and a good layer. Active, hardy, and very adaptable. One of the oldest breeds of chicken.

CALDER RANGER HEN
A cross between Rhode Island Red and Light Sussex, so some have black tails and some white. Good outdoor bird; hardy, disease-resistant, and easy to manage. Lays brown eggs with strong shells.

OLD COTSWOLD LEGBAR HEN
A modern breed from Gloucestershire that produces eggs in different shades of blue, green, and pink. It's a cross between several breeds, including the Araucana, which was brought over from Patagonia in the 1920s and produces blue eggs.

BANTAM HEN
The name describes any small or miniature hen, so there are numerous breeds. They are usually kept as pets but are also good layers. Their eggs are, naturally, smaller than standard hens' and can be in a range of colours.

KHAKI CAMPBELL DUCK
A native breed, developed in Gloucester over 100 years ago, that lays plenty of big, white eggs. It was originally grey and just called Campbell; the khaki colour developed over time as the breed was perfected. It is a hardy and good forager.

GOOSE
The females lay only from February to August, producing around 30 eggs each season. They're great at keeping grass down and are relatively low-maintenance.

QUAIL
Unlike their meat, free-range and organic quail's eggs are available all year round. The birds are small and friendly, enjoy human contact, and love foraging.

EGGS

Eggs are nutritious, quick and easy to cook, and vital for many dishes. However, our insatiable demand for them has made hens, in particular, the horrifying victims of factory farming. We're all aware of their miserable existence — but things are changing. Research in 2007 shows that sales of free-range and organic eggs are outstripping those from caged birds for the first time. So, it is hoped, battery hens will become a thing of the past. Here we look at duck, goose, and little quail's eggs, too, and suggest some great ways of using them. The Soil Association recommends organically reared birds to be kept in flocks of fewer than 500; or a maximum of 2000 with special permission and extra management measures in place. (This compares to a maximum of 16,000 under government free-range regulations.) They must have daytime access outside all their life, in an area of at least 10 square metres per bird. They are allowed to express their natural behaviour, and must be fed on at least 80 per cent GM-free organic feed. There should be no artificial additives in the feed — these can colour eggs, which is why sometimes organic yolks may be paler than non-organic ones.

HOW TO CHOOSE AND STORE

If a use-by date is stamped on them, choose the longest one available. If buying from a farmers' market, ask when the eggs were laid and buy as fresh as possible. Avoid if cracked or dirty. If you are using them quickly, they can be stored at room temperature before cooking. The lion mark on commercial free-range (and caged-bird) eggs shows they have been inoculated against salmonella.

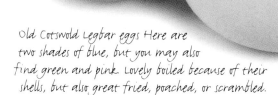

Bantam eggs Like the hens,
they're little. As a guide,
use three bantam eggs to
one hen's egg.

Old Cotswold Legbar eggs Here are
two shades of blue, but you may also
find green and pink. Lovely boiled because of their
shells, but also great fried, poached, or scrambled.

Goose eggs Bigger and stronger-flavoured
than the others; one is equivalent to
about three hen's eggs, so it makes a big
omelette! Great for scrambled eggs,
Yorkshire pudding, and cakes, too.

Hen's eggs Many people prefer
brown eggs, but they're nutritionally
no better than white. Different breeds produce
different shades of white – through cream to brown. Use
in any recipe that calls for eggs.

Quail's eggs Tiny, speckled
eggs, delicious soft or hard-
boiled and pickled. Can be
fried, or poached, and served
on tiny discs of fried bread
for a delicate little treat.

Duck eggs The yolk
is richer than in hen's
eggs, so is good for enriching
cakes and pastries. The whites have more
protein, providing great volume for
meringues and mousses.

PERFECT PAIRINGS

BACON or **HAM** for breakfast, in sandwiches, quiches, or omelettes; **CURRY SPICES** in a sauce or to flavour hard-boiled yolks; **LEMON** as a savoury sauce or soup, in sweet curd, mousse or soufflé, or with olive oil for a dressing; **SPINACH** as a snack, with cheese sauce or on pizza; **HARD** and **BLUE CHEESES** in sauces, to stuff hard-boiled, in soufflés, mousses, or quiches.

SIMPLE WAYS TO ENJOY

TO PREPARE

TO SEPARATE
Break on a plate. Put an egg cup (or, for goose egg, a coffee cup) over the yolk. Hold firmly and drain the white into a bowl.

TO BOIL
Hen's: Put in a pan of cold water. Cover and bring to boil – 3½ minutes for soft; 5–7 minutes for hard.
Duck: Best to coddle. Put in a pan of cold water. Cover, bring to the boil, remove from the heat and leave to stand for 12 minutes. If you boil these eggs, the whites toughen.
Goose: Cook as for hen's, but 11 minutes for hard.
Quail's: Cook as hen's, but 1 minute for soft; 3 minutes for hard.

TO SCRAMBLE
Melt a knob of butter in a heavy pan. Whisk in the eggs. Season. Add a splash of milk. Cook, stirring, until scrambled but creamy.

TO POACH
Cook in a pan of simmering water with 1 tbsp vinegar or lemon juice until cooked to your liking. Remove with a slotted spoon.

TO FRY
Heat oil or butter in a frying pan. Break in the egg. Fry quickly until cooked. Spoon the fat over the yolk. Remove with a fish slice.

QUICK HOLLANDAISE SAUCE
Whisk 2 eggs with 2 tbsp lemon juice in a small pan. Gradually whisk in ½ block melted butter. Cook over a very gentle heat, whisking all the time, until thick. Do not boil. Remove from the heat. Season. Add a pinch of cayenne.

MAYONNAISE
Blend or whisk an egg, an egg white, 2 tbsp lemon juice, 1 tbsp white wine vinegar, and ½ tsp mustard powder. Gradually add 360ml (12fl oz) olive or sunflower oil, a drop at a time (or a thin trickle in a blender). Season.

PÂTÉ-STUFFED EGGS
Halve hard-boiled hen's or quail's eggs. Scoop the yolks into a bowl. Mash. Beat in smooth liver pâté, and a dash of Dijon mustard and lemon juice to taste. Pile back into the whites. Sprinkle with paprika.

ITALIAN-STYLE TOMATO EGGS
Chop large, ripe tomatoes, and stew gently in a little olive oil in a small frying pan, stirring, until pulpy. Season. Break some eggs over the surface. Stir the whites gently, so as not to break the yolks. Season. Cook until the whites are set. Sprinkle with torn basil.

GOOSE EGG CHEESE SOUFFLÉ
Make a roux with a large knob of butter, 2 tbsp flour and 1 tsp mustard. Blend in a teacup of milk. Cook until thick, stirring. Beat in a goose egg yolk (or 3 large hen's egg yolks), some seasoning, and a large handful of grated mature Cheddar cheese. Whisk the egg white (or whites) until stiff. Beat a little into the sauce to slacken. Fold in the rest with a metal spoon. Spoon into a greased soufflé dish. Bake in the oven at 180°C (350°F/Gas 4) until risen, golden, and just firm.

Eggs are sold in four sizes:
Very large: 73g and over
Large: 63–73g
Medium: 53–63g
Small: 53g and under
Medium is usually used for baking. If necessary, if using large (or duck) eggs, reduce other liquid by about 1 tbsp per egg. If using small, increase liquid by up to 1 tbsp per egg.

THE FRESH TEST

If you aren't sure if an egg is still fresh, put it in a glass of water. If it sinks, it is fresh; if suspended in the water, it's still okay; if it floats, it's off.

EGGS BENEDICT WITH SPINACH

Toast crumpets. Spread with butter. Put on flameproof plates. Top each with a slice of ham, chopped and drained cooked spinach, then a poached egg. Spoon Hollandaise sauce over (see opposite). Grill until glazed.

BAKED EGGS WITH HAM

Put a little chopped ham in ramekin dishes. Break an egg into each. Season. Add a spoonful of single cream. Put in a roasting tin; pour 1cm (½in) boiling water around the dishes. Bake in the oven at 180°C (350°F/Gas 4) until cooked to your liking.

PICKLED QUAIL'S EGGS

Hard-boil quail's eggs for 3 minutes. Drain. Rinse with cold water. Put in a bowl, and cover with white vinegar. Leave for 12 hours. Stir twice. The shells go soft. Peel. Put in a pickle jar. Boil the vinegar with an equal quantity of water, a few pickling spices, a dried chilli, and a little sugar. Cool. Pour over the eggs. Cover, and store in the fridge.

OMELETTE WITH FRESH HERBS

Beat 2 eggs. Add a splash of water. Season. Beat in 1 tbsp chopped mixed herbs. Melt a knob of butter in an omelette pan. Pour in the eggs. Lift and stir until set underneath but creamy on top. Carefully tilt the pan over a plate. Fold a third of the omelette over the centre, then the other third over top. Slide on to a plate.

ALCOHOLIC ZABAGLIONE

Whisk 2 duck or hen's eggs, 2 tbsp sugar, and 4 tbsp of your favourite liqueur or sherry in a bowl over simmering water until thick and fluffy. Spoon into glasses. Serve.

VANILLA CUSTARD

Bring to the boil 250ml (8fl oz) milk with ½ split vanilla pod. Cool for 10 minutes. Remove the vanilla. Whisk 3 egg yolks and 1 tbsp sugar until thick. Whisk in the milk. Pour back into the pan. Cook very gently, stirring with a wooden spoon, until thick. Don't boil.

DUCK OR HEN'S EGG MERINGUES

Whisk 2 egg whites until really stiff. Whisk in 4 tbsp caster sugar until stiff and glossy. Fold in a further 4 tbsp sugar. Use 2 spoons to shape the meringues and put on baking parchment on a baking sheet. Bake in the oven at 110°C (225°F/Gas ¼) until crisp and dry, about 2 hours. Cool. Sandwich with whipped cream.

SPICY VEGETABLE FRITTATA

BRIDIE AT THE GOOD EGG COMPANY

The Good Egg Company is run by Bridie Whittle, on her parents' organic farm in rural Herefordshire. See pp326–7.

SERVES 3–4 **PREPARATION TIME** 15 minutes **COOKING TIME** 25–35 minutes.
This is a really simple dish – not very glamorous, but pretty tasty!

1 Heat 3 tbsp of the oil in a large frying pan, add the potatoes and fry for approximately 5–8 minutes or until they start to brown. Add the onion and cook for 2–3 minutes or until they begin to soften, then add the garlic.

2 Grind the chilli and spices together until broken down, add them to the pan, and fry for 2 minutes, stirring frequently.

3 When the seeds begin to pop, add a pinch of salt, the tomatoes, and 1 tbsp water. Reduce the heat and simmer for 10 minutes or until the potatoes are cooked through and tender.

4 Add the spinach and cook for 1–2 minutes until wilted. Remove from the heat and leave to cool for 5 minutes.

5 In a bowl, mix together the eggs and parsley, then stir in the potato and tomato mixture. Wipe the frying pan with kitchen paper. Heat the remaining oil in the pan and pour in the mixture. Cook on a high heat for approximately 5–8 minutes or until it begins to set. When it's all set, carefully turn it over and cook for 2–3 minutes longer to allow the bottom to turn golden. Serve cut into wedges.

INGREDIENTS
4 tbsp vegetable oil
450g (1lb) potatoes, finely diced
1 large onion, finely chopped
3 garlic cloves, finely chopped or crushed
1 dried red chilli, roughly broken
1 tsp black mustard seeds
½ tsp cumin seeds
½ tsp coriander seeds
Salt
200g canned tomatoes with their juice
A good handful of baby spinach
6 large eggs, beaten
4 tbsp chopped fresh parsley

Walnut
&
Honey

£2.50

£2.50

GRAIN

AN ORGANIC GRAIN FARM IN SUFFOLK

ANITA WIGAN, RUSHBROOKE FARM

Anita Wigan has been running Rushbrooke farm, near Bury St Edmunds, Suffolk, since 1996. She and her farm manager, Dominic Watts, made the decision to go organic. "My daughter had allergies, so I'd always been keen on natural cooking and avoiding additives and colours. So it was an easy and logical step to take."

They spent two years researching organic methods, and in 2000 turned the dream into reality. They divided large fields into smaller workable areas, surrounding them with 7km (4⅓ miles) of hedges and grassy margins to provide natural habitat for wildlife. "The birdlife is just incredible now. We see lots of species that we haven't seen in years – even little lapwings." Peewits, as they're also called, once regular visitors to farms throughout the country, have been in decline for the last 25 years, largely due to modern farming methods. "We've also planted 7 acres [2.8 hectares] of indigenous hardwood trees, and plan to plant seven more this winter."

Rushbrooke was one of the first large farms in Britain to convert, producing over 405 hectares (1000 acres) of organic crops. They mainly produce oats, wheat, and barley, but also farm pigs and sheep. The grain is sown from September to March, with organic red clover under-sown in

May. In August, once the crops are harvested, the clover grows through for the organic sheep flock to graze on. What's left is chopped and worked back in to return nitrogen to the soil. Anita is convinced that going organic was the right move. "Seeing the difference in the land, knowing you're not putting loads of chemicals in – properly – is very satisfying."

Anita in the grain store.

Organic farming can raise different problems from traditional methods, but there are people on hand to offer support and advice. For Anita, much of this came from the Soil Association: "They've been a great help – a mine of information. Through them, we've been on trips to see all aspects of organic farming." As a result, Dominic is now committed to showing others how to go about it, too. He was a member of the East of England Steering Group for the Soil Association, and as such he organized trips to Rushbrooke to help potential organic farmers learn more about organic production methods.

See p342 for Anita's *Oaty Blackberry and Apple Crumble*.

See p342 for Anita's *Oaty Blackberry and Apple Crumble*.

OPPOSITE, ABOVE LEFT All harvested grains are cleaned, dried, and stored on the farm.

ABOVE RIGHT Organic seed is used whenever it is available.

BELOW A ripe spring wheat field, ready for harvest.

GRAIN

Main crops grown in Britain for food are wheat (our staple crop), oats, barley, rye, and spelt. Stone milling is the traditional method of making flour: the grains are ground slowly, retaining all the natural oils and goodness, and nothing is added or removed. Modern methods overheat the grain, destroying some nutrients and flavour. Grain used in our food is rarely 100 per cent British; it is often mixed with imported grain to reach the desired standards. In organic flour production, the grain must be organic and the Soil Association monitors and certifies the entire process.

WHEAT

SPELT

OATS

RYE

BARLEY

WHAT WHEN AND HOW

WHAT TYPES

Wheat: Winter and spring crops. Spring is excellent for milling but produces less grain. Available as whole grains or ground into flour. Wholemeal flour is the complete ground grain; brown has some of the husk (bran) and germ removed, and white is processed to remove all the bran and germ. Some varieties are strong, containing high quantities of protein (gluten); others are softer, with less protein. Most commercial white flours are bleached to give them a pure white colour. It's best to choose organic unbleached. There are also speciality flours, like granary or malthouse, mixed with other whole grains and malt (and see barleycorn, below). Wheat germ and bran are also sold separately.

Spelt: An ancient relative of wheat, enjoying a rebirth. It has a different structure from wheat, and is higher in protein and other nutrients.

Oats: A hardy crop that grows well on less fertile soil, so is popular in Scotland, where the soil won't support wheat crops. Available in pinhead, medium, or coarse oatmeal, rolled oats and bran.

Rye: Another hardy crop that grows in all conditions. Ground into flour, it has less protein (gluten) than wheat. Also available as flakes and whole grains.

Barley: Grows in all different climatic conditions. Low in protein, it's sold as flour, both plain and barleycorn, a speciality flour, mixed with wheat, linseed, and malt; as flakes, whole grains (pot barley), and pearl barley. Around 20 per cent of barley produced in the UK is used in the brewing industry to make beer.

HOW TO CHOOSE AND STORE

If you do a lot of baking, buy your flour in bulk to save money. All flours and grains should be stored in sealed containers in a cool, dark place and used within six months. Choose flours suitable for your culinary needs.

Pearl barley When cooked it retains its nutty texture, so it can be cooked for a long time in soups and stews. It can be boiled and served instead of rice and also makes a great, creamy "risotto" (see p115).

Rye flour Low in gluten, rye makes a lovely, nutty, dense loaf. Use instead of, or mixed with, wheat flour for baking.

Rolled oats The most popular form of this grain. Use for porridge, muesli, cakes, crumbles, biscuits, and breads.

Wholemeal flour Strong is good for nutty-flavoured breads; plain and self-raising for biscuits, cakes, pastries, and general cooking.

Spelt flour Lovely, nutty flavour. Can be used in place of wholemeal flour in cooking.

Barleycorn flour Makes a tasty nutritious loaf. Plain barley flour is best mixed with wheat for baking, but is good for coating foods for frying, for binding stuffings and minced mixtures, and for thickening soups and sauces.

Rye grains soak and boil, then add to soups, salads, breads, or breakfast cereals, or dress with olive oil, lemon juice, and plenty of freshly ground black pepper and serve as a side dish.

Wheat grains Can be soaked, then boiled and eaten instead of rice, or used in salads, soups, or added to breakfast cereals. (A non-culinary use is when the raw grains are mixed with dried lavender in wheat bags that can be heated to soothe pain.)

PERFECT PAIRINGS

STRONG WHEAT or **SPELT** with **YEAST**, or mixed with **RYE** or **BARLEY** flour to make bread;

BUTTER spread on bread, rubbed into flour for pastry or biscuits, or to thicken sauces;

HONEY and **DRIED FRUITS**, mixed with **OATS** for breakfast, or in biscuits or cereal bars;

as a coating for **OILY FISH**; **LAMB** and **ROOT VEGETABLES** with **PEARL BARLEY** for traditional Scotch broth; with **VEGETABLES**, **MUSHROOMS**, **CHICKEN**, **HAM**, or **CHEESE** for "risotto";

BEETROOT and **CABBAGE** dishes with **RYE** bread.

SIMPLE WAYS TO ENJOY

TO PREPARE

For best results, sift refined flour with other dry ingredients before making bread, cakes, or biscuits. If using wholemeal flour, just mix thoroughly – no other preparation is necessary.

SCONES

Mix 225g (8oz) plain flour, 4 tsp baking powder, and a pinch of salt. Rub in 60g (2oz) butter. Mix with milk to a soft dough. Knead. Pat out; cut into rounds. Put on a greased baking sheet. Brush with milk. Bake in the oven at 230°C (450°F/Gas 8) until risen, golden, and they sound hollow when tapped.

OAT CAKES

Mix 85g (3oz) medium oatmeal with a good pinch each of salt and bicarbonate of soda. Rub in a knob of butter. Mix with hot water to form a firm dough. Roll out thinly. Cut into rounds. Cook in a hot, lightly oiled pan for a few minutes until firm. Flip over, and cook on the other sides. Cool.

RYE DROP SCONES

Mix 60g (2oz) rye flour with a pinch of salt, 1 tbsp sugar and an egg yolk. Stir in 150ml (5fl oz) milk. Fold in a whisked egg white. Fry spoonfuls in a pan until bubbles pop. Flip over. Brown the other sides. Serve with butter.

SPELT SODA BREAD

Mix 350g (12oz) spelt flour with 115g (4oz) oatmeal, 2 tsp each bicarbonate of soda and cream of tartar, 1 tsp salt and honey. Mix with 300ml (10fl oz) butter-milk. Knead gently. Put rounds on a greased baking sheet. Brush with milk. Slash a cross in the top. Bake in the oven at 220°C (425°F/Gas 7). Test as scones.

PERFECT PORRIDGE

Mix 1 part rolled oats with 3 parts milk and water mixed. Add a good pinch of salt. Cook, stirring, until thick, or cook in the microwave, stirring every minute. Serve with cream or milk, and honey or brown sugar.

WALNUT BREAD

SHEHERAZADE GOLDSMITH

An environmentalist, Sheherazade is also a magazine columnist and author of *A Slice of Organic Life*.

MAKES 2 ring loaves **PREPARATION TIME** 12–15 minutes, plus rising **COOKING TIME** 20–25 minutes. **To help the bread cook well, mist the inside of the oven with a water spray just before baking the dough. The loaf is cooked if it sounds hollow when tapped on the base. It will keep in the bread bin for up to 4 days, and it freezes well.**

1 Mix the flours together, then add the yeast and salt. Add a little of the water and combine the ingredients. Gradually add more water until the mixture becomes a sticky dough.

2 Add the nuts to the dough, and knead for 5–8 minutes until pliable. Place in a lightly oiled bowl, cover with a damp tea towel, and leave to rest until it doubles in size.

3 Turn the rested dough out on to a clean, lightly floured surface and divide it into two equal amounts. Knead each half of the dough into a tight ball. Shape each ball into a ring with a hole the size of a fist. Place on a lightly floured baking sheet, cover with a damp tea towel, and leave again until they double in size.

4 Preheat the oven to 230°C (450°F/Gas 8). Bake the bread in the oven for 20–25 minutes until golden, and the loaves sound hollow when tapped.

INGREDIENTS
400g (14oz) plain, white organic
  strong bread flour
100g (3½oz) dark organic
  rye flour
1½ tsp dried yeast
2 tsp salt
320ml (12fl oz) tepid water
200g (7oz) walnuts, crushed

OATY BLACKBERRY AND APPLE CRUMBLE

ANITA AT RUSHBROOKE FARM

Anita Wigan converted Rushbrooke, a 405-hectare (1000-acre) mixed farm in Suffolk, to organic in 2000. See pp336-7.

SERVES 6–8 **PREPARATION TIME** 15–20 minutes **COOKING TIME** 45 minutes.
You don't have to use cooking apples; a mixture of eaters and cookers is great. The quantity of blackberries can vary – the more the merrier, really, but it depends how you got on picking them without eating too many. Try not to pick the berries after rain; it seems to weaken their flavour and texture.

1 Preheat the oven to 180°C (350°F/Gas 4). Put the apples in a wide, shallow, 2.25-litre (4-pint) ovenproof dish. Add the blackberries. Sprinkle about 3 tbsp of the sugar amongst the fruit. Cover with foil and pop in the oven for 15 minutes just to get the fruit to start to soften.

2 Make the crumble by rubbing together the butter and flour until it resembles breadcrumbs. Add the remaining sugar, then the oats (you could do this in a blender, but add the oats last so they don't get chopped too fine).

3 Remove the fruit from the oven, give it a quick stir, and spread the yummy crumble all over. Cook in the oven for a further 30 minutes or until the fruit is oozing out from beneath the golden crumble. Serve with organic double cream or, better still, custard.

INGREDIENTS
1 kg (2¼lb) apples, peeled, cored and thickly sliced
350g (12oz) blackberries
200g (7oz) dark muscovado sugar
125g (4½oz) butter, diced
125g (4½oz) plain flour
125g (4½oz) coarse oatmeal or porridge oats

RESOURCES

 Soil Association

The Soil Association is a membership charity campaigning for planet-friendly food and farming and believes that soil, food, the health of people, and the health of the planet are all dependent on each other. We were founded in 1946 and drafted the world's first organic standards 30 years ago.

We are perhaps best known for certifying goods as organic. Look for our symbol when you shop – on food, textiles, or health and beauty products – and you can be sure that what you're buying has been produced and processed to the highest organic and animal welfare standards in the world.

By joining the Soil Association you can support the transformation of the UK's food culture, give your beliefs a voice, and become part of the solution to our industrialized diets.

To find out more, visit the following websites:
www.soilassociation.org
www.sascotland.org
www.soilassociation.org/certification
www.soilassociation.org/joinus

ALLOTMENTS UK
The UK's largest allotment community. Advice, tips, and forums on finding and looking after your allotment.
www.allotments-uk.com

ASSOCIATION FOR ORGANICS RECYCLING
Formerly the *Composting Association*. Promotes sustainable management of biodegradable resources, and provides news and information on composting and other recycling methods.
www.organics-recycling.org.uk

BIODYNAMIC AGRICULTURAL ASSOCIATION
Supports, promotes, and develops the biodynamic approach to farming, food, gardening, and forestry.
www.biodynamic.org.uk

BRITISH SUMMER FRUITS
A UK body dedicated to the promotion of British-grown soft and stone fruits. Website features facts and seasonal information.
www.britishsummerfruits.co.uk

BRITISH TOMATO GROWERS' ASSOCIATION
Represents British commercial tomato growers, and provides information on varieties, nutritional facts, growing methods, and recipes.
www.britishtomatoes.co.uk

CERTIFIED FARMERS' MARKETS
Directory, produced by the National Farmers' Retail and Markets Association, of farmers' markets and "pick your own" farms.
www.farmersmarkets.net

CHOOSE BRITISH
Articles on the pleasures and environmental and economic benefits of buying British produce.
www.choosebritish.co.uk

COMPASSION IN WORLD FARMING
Organization campaigning against factory farming, with information on animal welfare and a compassionate shopping guide.
www.ciwf.org.uk

EAT THE SEASONS
Promotes an understanding of food seasons in the UK. Each week they focus on one food in season, and share tips, facts, and recipes.
www.eattheseasons.co.uk

ENGLISH APPLES AND PEARS
A trade association to promote British apples and pears, and safeguard the interests of its members.
www.englishapplesandpears.co.uk

ENGLISH WINE PRODUCERS
The English wine industry's representative body, supporting commercial vineyards.
www.englishwineproducers.com

FAIRTRADE FOUNDATION
The independent certification body in the UK that licenses use of the Fairtrade mark for products that meet international standards, set by Fairtrade Labelling Organization International (FLO).
www.fairtrade.org.uk

FARM RETAIL ASSOCIATION
Represents farmers who sell direct to the public through "pick your own" schemes, farm shops, farmers' markets, and home delivery.
www.farmshopping.com

FOOD COMMISSION
An independent, not-for-profit organization that campaigns for safer, healthier food in the UK.
www.foodcomm.org.uk

FOOD FOR LIFE PARTNERSHIP
A network of schools and communities across England committed to transforming food culture, and reconnecting young people with farms, inspiring families to cook and grown their own food.
www.foodforlife.org.uk

FOOD LOVERS' BRITAIN
Directory of approved local and regional food businesses.
www.foodloversbritain.com

FOOD STANDARDS AGENCY
The home of the Government's food safety watchdog that protects public health and consumer interests in relation to food.
www.foodstandards.gov.uk

GARDEN ORGANIC
The UK's leading organic growing charity, promoting organic gardening, farming, and food. Runs educational and research programmes nationwide, and provides online organic gardening advice.
www.gardenorganic.org.uk

HOLISTIC COOKING AND NUTRITION SCHOOL

Classes on vegetarian, organic, wholefood, and seasonal cooking.

www.holistic-cooking.co.uk

THE HONEY ASSOCIATION

The British honey industry's official website, providing honey news and seasonal recipes.

www.honeyassociation.com

MARINE CONSERVATION SOCIETY

Purchasing and identification guide, developed by the MCS, enabling the consumer to buy fish and seafood that has been sustainably and sensitively harvested.

www.fishonline.org

MARINE STEWARDSHIP COUNCIL

The world's leading certification and eco-labelling programme for sustainable seafood.

www.msc.org

NATIONAL SOCIETY OF ALLOTMENT AND LEISURE GARDENERS LTD

Provides advice and information about registering and looking after an allotment.

www.nsalg.org.uk

ORGANIC CENTRE WALES

Information on organic food and farming in Wales, including a directory of suppliers and markets.

www.organic.aber.ac.uk

ORGANIC MILK SUPPLIERS' COOPERATIVE

A cooperative of around 300 British organic dairy farmers. Features information on organic dairy farming, and a recipe database.

www.omsco.co.uk

THE ORGANIC RESEARCH CENTRE

The UK's leading research, development, and advisory institution for organic agriculture.

www.efrc.com

ORGANIC WALES

Online resource for organic living in Wales, with news, events, reviews, recipes, and a directory of organic suppliers in Wales.

www.organicwales.com

THE POTATO COUNCIL

Promotes and supports British potato growers and trade purchasers.

www.britishpotatoes.co.uk

SEA FISH INDUSTRY AUTHORITY

Works across all sectors of the UK seafood industry to promote good-quality, sustainable seafood. Website provides consumer facts and information on buying seafood, and recipes.

www.seafish.org

SLOW FOOD

An international movement that promotes the consumption of locally produced food products. Promotes local networks of small farmers and artisan food producers.

www.slowfood.org.uk

SUSTAIN

Campaigning organization for better food and farming. The website contains information on its food projects.

www.sustainweb.org

TRUE FOOD NETWORK

Greenpeace's campaign for the clear labelling of genetic engineering in food.

www.truefoodnow.org

VEG BOX RECIPES

Recipes for veg box users and anyone interested in local, seasonal, organic food.

www.vegbox-recipes.co.uk

WOMEN'S INSTITUTE COUNTRY MARKETS

A directory of local markets run by Women's Institutes around the country.

www.wimarkets.co.uk

WORLDWIDE OPPORTUNITIES ON ORGANIC FARMS

A worldwide network that links volunteers to organic farms that provide food and accommodation in return for help on the farm.

www.wwoof.org

ORGANIC HERO WEBSITES:

Pink Pig Organics

www.pinkpigorganics.co.uk

Tolhurst Organic Produce

www.tolhurstorganic.co.uk

Caws Cenarth Cheese

www.cawscenarth.co.uk

Growing with Grace

www.growingwithgrace.co.uk

VISIT OUR CONTRIBUTORS' RESTAURANTS:

Sally Clarke

Clarke's

124 Kensington Church Street, London W8 4BH

www.sallyclarke.com

Arthur Potts Dawson

Acorn House Restaurant

60 Swinton Street, London WC1X 9NT

Tel: 020 7812 1842

www.acornhouserestaurant.com

Oliver Rowe

Konstam

2 Acton Street, London WC1X 9NA

Tel: 020 7833 5040

www.konstam.co.uk

Atul Kochhar

Benares

12a Berkeley Square House, Berkeley Square, London W1J 6BS

Tel: 020 7629 8886

www.benaresrestaurant.com

Skye Gyngell

Petersham Nurseries Café

Petersham Nurseries, off Petersham Road, Richmond, Surrey TW10 7AG

Tel: 020 8604 3627

www.petershamnurseries.com

INDEX

Recipes in **bold**

Produce profiles, including Perfect Pairings and Simple Ways to Enjoy, in *italics*

A

almonds: plum and marzipan clafoutis **185**
  trout with almonds and herbs **215**
apples *164–8, 194*
  apple and lemon marmalade **313**
  apple cut-and-come-again cake **170**
  apple, raisin, and pumpkin seed breakfast bars **169**
  oaty blackberry and apple crumble **342**
  roast pork belly with caramelized apple **267**
  winter cabbage salad **75**
apricots *180–82*
  apricot toffee brioche pudding **184**
Arbroath smokies *238–41*
artichokes *see* globe artichokes; Jerusalem artichokes
Asian greens *76–8*
asparagus *50–3*
  asparagus cream cheese quiche **52**
aubergines *54–8*
  griddled aubergine and bean salad **56**

B

bacon *270–2*
  celeriac and smoked bacon soufflé pie **67**
baked beans: Pink Pig cowboy casserole **273**
barley *338–40*
  all-year mushroom barley risotto **115**
basil *158–61*
bay leaves *158–61*
beans *90–92*
beef *256–8*
  braised brisket **261**
  fillet steaks on pâté croûtes **259**
beetroot *64–6*
  carrot and beetroot salad **63**
  pot-roasted pheasant with shallots and **297**

berries *172–5*
bilberries *172–5*
bistro salad with frisée lettuce **153**
black pudding *270–2*
blackberries *172–5*
  damson "soup" with **186**
  oaty blackberry and apple crumble **342**
blackcurrants *188–9*
  fragrant blackcurrant and rosemary cheesecake **191**
bloaters *238–41*
blueberries *172–5*
  warm duck breast salad with **292**
borage *158–61*
bread, walnut **341**
breakfast bars, apple, raisin, and pumpkin seed **169**
bream *see* red bream; sea bream
brill *226–8*
brioche pudding, apricot toffee **184**
broad beans *90–2*
broccoli, purple sprouting *82–4*
Brussels sprouts *70–2*
Brussels tops *70–2*
buckling *238–41*
butter *322–5*
buttermilk *322–5*

C

cabbage *70–2*
cakes: apple cut-and-come-again cake **170**
  carrot cake with soft cheese frosting **61**
calabrese *82–4*
  creamy calabrese and blue cheese puffs **87**
carrots *58–60*
  carrot and beetroot salad **63**
  carrot cake with soft cheese frosting **61**
cauliflower *82–4*
  pickled cauliflower and baby onion salad **86**
cavolo nero *76–8*
celeriac *64–6*
  celeriac and smoked bacon soufflé pie **67**
celery *88–9*

cheese *310–20*
  blue cheeses *318–20*
  creamy calabrese and blue cheese puffs **87**
  deep-fried Caerphilly with apple and lemon marmalade **313**
  hard cheeses *310–12*
  mustard-, cheese-, and ham-topped turkey steaks **291**
  soft cheeses *314–16*
  spinach, fresh tomato, and blue cheese pizza **81**
  stuffed chicken under a brick **287**
cheesecake, fragrant blackcurrant and rosemary **191**
cherries *180–3*
chervil *158–61*
chestnuts *204–5*
chicken *282–4*
  slow-roast chicken **285**
  stir-fried chicken with noodles **286**
  stuffed chicken under a brick **287**
chickpeas: roasted garlic and pumpkin hummus **106**
  roasted red pepper and chickpea soup **132**
chicory *148–52*
chillies *134–6*
  fiery peanut and pepper noodles **137**
Chinese leaf *148–52*
chives *158–61*
chocolate strawberry shortcake **176**
chowder, salmon with whisky **216**
clafoutis, plum and marzipan **185**
clams *248–51*
cobnuts *204–5*
  leaf, chanterelle, and cobnut salad **154**
cockles *248–51*
cod *220–2*
  Thai green fish curry with mangetout **223**
coley *220–2*
coriander *158–61*
courgette flowers *102–4*
courgettes *102–4*
crab *242–5*
  crab and leek bisque **246**
crayfish *242–5*
cream *322–5*
crème brûlée, raspberry and hazelnut **179**

crumble: crunchy vegetable **74**
  oaty blackberry and apple **342**
crustaceans *242–5*
cucumber *156–7*
cured meats and sausages *270–72*
currants *188–9*
curry, Thai green fish **223**

D

dab *226–8*
dairy produce *322–5*
damsons *180–3*
  damson "soup" with blackberries **186**
dandelion leaves *148–52*
dill *158–61*
Dover sole *226–8*
duck *288–90*
  warm duck breast salad with blueberries **292**
  wild duck *294–6*
duck eggs *328–31*

E

eggs *328–31*
  French bean, garlic, and tomato omelette **94**
  plaice fillets with egg sauce on bruschetta **231**
  spicy vegetable frittata **332**
  wild nettles and scrambled egg **79**
elderberries *172–5*
elderflowers *172–5*

F

fennel *88–9*
fennel, wild *158–61*
figs *192–3*
finnan haddies *238–41*
fish *212–41*
fish and pumpkin chips **225**
flageolet beans: griddled aubergine and bean salad **56**
flat fish *226–8*
flat (helda) beans *90–92*
flounder *226*
flour *338–40*
flowering greens *82–84*
Ford Barton Farm *274–5*

French beans *90–92*
  French bean, garlic, and tomato omelette **94**
frittata, spicy vegetable **332**
fruit *164–202*

G

game birds *294–6*
gammon *270–2*
garlic *158–61*
  roasted garlic and pumpkin hummus **106**
globe artichokes *48–9*
Glyneithinog Dairy Farm *308–9*
goat *276–8*
goat's cheese *314–6*
goat's milk *322–5*
Good Egg Company *326–7*
goose *288–90*
goose, wild *294–6*
goose eggs *328–31*
gooseberries *172–5*
grains *338–40*
grapes *192–3*
green beans *90–92*
  chunky bean soup **93**
greengages *180–3*
grey mullet *232–4*
grouse *294–6*
Growing with Grace *100–101*
guinea fowl *294–6*
gurnard *232–4*

H

haddock *220–22*
  fish and pumpkin chips **225**
haggis *270–72*
halibut *226–8*
  halibut in rosemary and garlic crust **230**
ham *270–72*
  mustard-, cheese-, and ham-topped turkey steaks **291**
hare *300–301*
haslet *270–72*
hazelnuts *204–5*
  raspberry and hazelnut crème brûlée **179**
hearts, lamb *276–8*
herbs *158–61*
herring *212–14*

honey *206–7*
horseradish *158–61*
hummus, roasted garlic and pumpkin **106**

I

ice cream, rhubarb and custard **202**

J

Jerusalem artichokes *128–9*
John Dory *232–4*
juniper and pepper sauce, fillet of venison with **302**

K

kale *76–8*
kidneys *276–8*
kippers *238–41*
kohl rabi *70–2*
  partridge with roasted pears, walnuts and **299**

L

lamb *276–8*
  lamb casserole with cider **279**
  pot-roasted leg of lamb with gooseberry, mint, and sage jelly **280**
lamb's lettuce *148–51*
langoustines *242–5*
leaf, chanterelle, and cobnut salad **154**
leafy greens *76–8*
leeks *108–10*
  crab and leek bisque **246**
  leek and potato soup **127**
lemon: apple and lemon marmalade **313**
lemon sole *226–8*
lettuce *148–51*
  bistro salad with frisée lettuce **153**
liver: calve's liver *256–8*
  chicken livers *282–4*
  coarse liver pâté with watercress and mushrooms **265**
  lamb's liver *276–8*
  pig's liver *262–4*
lobster *242–5*
loganberries *172–5*
lollo rosso *148–51*
lovage *158–61*

M

mackerel *212–14*
  with rhubarb sauce **218**
mangetout *96–7*
  Thai green fish curry with **223**
marjoram *158–61*
marmalade, apple and lemon **313**
marrow *102–4*
marsh samphire *138–9*
marzipan: plum and marzipan clafoutis **185**
meat *256–78*
  beef and veal *256–8*
  cured meats and sausages *270–72*
  lamb *276–8*
  pork *262–4*
medlars *196–8*
milk *322–5*
mint *158–61*
mizuna *148–52*
molluscs *248–51*
monkfish *232–4*
  filo-topped monkfish blush **235**
mushrooms *112–14*
  all-year mushroom barley risotto **115**
  coarse liver pâté with watercress and **265**
  leaf, chanterelle, and cobnut salad **154**
mussels *248–51*
  with fennel, garlic, and tomatoes **252**
mustard cress *148–52*
mustard greens *148–52*
mutton *276–8*

N

nettles *76–8*
  wild nettles and scrambled egg **79**
noodles: fiery peanut and pepper noodles **137**
  stir-fried chicken with **286**
nuts *204–5*

O

Oakwood Farm *194–5*
oats *338–40*
  apple, raisin, and pumpkin seed breakfast bars **169**
  oaty blackberry and apple crumble **342**
offal *256–8*, *262–4*, *276–8*, *282–4*

oily fish *212–14*
omelette, French bean, garlic, and tomato **94**
onions *108–10*
  pickled cauliflower and baby onion salad **86**
  tomato and onion tart **147**
oregano *158–61*
oxtail *256–8*
oysters *248–51*

P

pak choi *76–8*
parsley *158–61*
parsnips *64–6*
partridge *294–6*
  with roasted pears, kohl rabi, and walnuts **299**
pâté, coarse liver with watercress and mushrooms **265**
pea shoots *96–7*
peanut butter: fiery peanut and pepper noodles **137**
pears *196–8*
  partridge with roasted pears, kohl rabi, and walnuts **299**
  pear and cream pie **199**
peas *96–7*
  summer pea soup with mint gremolata **98**
peppers *130–36*
  fiery peanut and pepper noodles **137**
  roasted red pepper and chickpea soup **132**
pheasant *294–6*
  pot-roasted pheasant with beetroot and shallots **297**
pies: celeriac and smoked bacon soufflé pie **67**
  creamy calabrese and blue cheese puffs **87**
  pear and cream pie **199**
  rabbit and sweetcorn pie **305**
pilchards *212–4*
Pink Pig cowboy casserole **273**
Pink Pig Organics *268–9*
pizza: spinach, fresh tomato, and blue cheese **81**

plaice *226–8*
  plaice fillets with egg sauce on bruschetta **231**
plums *180–83*
  plum and marzipan clafoutis **185**
pollack *220–22*
pork *262–4*
  roast pork belly with caramelized apple **267**
potatoes *116–25*
  leek and potato soup **127**
  spicy vegetable frittata **332**
poultry *282–90*
prawns *242–5*
pumpkin *102–4*
  fish and pumpkin chips **225**
  roasted garlic and pumpkin hummus **106**
purple beans *90–92*

Q

quail's eggs *328–31*
quiche, asparagus cream cheese **52**
quinces *196–8*

R

rabbit *300–301*
  rabbit and sweetcorn pie **305**
radicchio *148–52*
radishes *156–7*
raisins: apple, raisin, and pumpkin seed breakfast bars **169**
raspberries *172–5*
  raspberry and hazelnut crème brûlée **179**
razor clams *248–51*
red bream with spice rub **236**
red cabbage *70–72*
  winter cabbage salad **75**
red mullet *232–4*
redcurrants *188–9*
Rendall, Robbie *210–11*
rhubarb *200–201*
  mackerel with rhubarb sauce **218**
  rhubarb and custard ice cream **202**
risotto: all-year mushroom barley risotto **115**
  traffic light risotto **107**
rocket *148–52*
romanesco *82–4*